Recommended

COUNTRY INNS

New England

"Recommended Country Inns" series

"The guidebooks in this new series of recommended country inns are sure winners. Personal visits have ensured accurate and scene-setting descriptions. These beckon the discriminating traveler to a variety of interesting lodgings."
—*Norman Strasma, publisher of* Inn Review *newsletter*

The "Recommended Country Inns" series is designed for the discriminating traveler who seeks the best in unique accommodations away from home.

From hundreds of inns personally visited and evaluated by the author, only the finest are described here. The inclusion of an inn is purely a personal decision on the part of the author; no one can pay or be paid to be in a Globe Pequot inn guide.

Organized for easy reference, these guides point you to just the kind of accommodations you are looking for: Comprehensive indexes by category provide listings of inns for romantic getaways, inns for the sports-minded, inns that serve gourmet meals . . . and more. State maps help you pinpoint the location of each inn, and detailed driving directions tell you how to get there.

Use these guidebooks with confidence. Allow each author to share his or her selections with you and then discover for yourself the country inn experience.

Editions available:
Recommended Country Inns
New England • Mid-Atlantic and Chesapeake Region
The South • The Midwest • West Coast
Rocky Mountain Region • The Southwest

Recommended
COUNTRY INNS™
New England

Twelfth Edition

by Elizabeth Squier
illustrated by Olive Metcalf

A Voyager Book

The Globe Pequot Press

Chester, Connecticut

Library of Congress Catalog Card Number: 73–83255

ISBN: 0-87106-308-5

Manufactured in the United States of America
Twelfth Edition/First Printing

For Suzy Chapin
We started this together in 1973.
What a navigator you were,
lovey; where did the years go?
Love, Elizabeth.

Contents

Indexes

About This Inn Guide

This inn guide contains descriptions of country inns in the six New England states. You'll find them in alphabetical order by state—Connecticut, Maine, Massachusetts, New Hampshire, Rhode Island, and Vermont—and alphabetically by town within each state. Preceding each state listing are a map and a numbered legend of the towns with inns in that state. The map is marked with corresponding numbers to show where the towns are located.

I have personally visited every inn in this book. *There is no charge of any kind for an inn to be included in this or any other Globe Pequot country inn guide.*

Indexes: At the back of the book are various special-category indexes to help you find inns on a lake, inns that serve Sunday brunch, inns that have cross-country skiing on the property, and much more. There is also an alphabetical index of all the inns in the book.

Rates: With prices fluctuating so widely in today's economy, I quote an inn's current low and high rates only. This will give you a good indication, though not exact, of the price ranges you can expect. Please realize that rates are subject to change. I have not included the tax rate, service charge, or tipping suggestions for any of the inns. Be sure to inquire about these additional charges when you make your reservations. The following abbreviations are used throughout the book to let you know exactly what, if any, meals are included in the room price.

EP: European Plan. Room without meals.

EPB: Room with full breakfast. (No abbreviation is used when continental breakfast is included.)

MAP: Modified American Plan. Room with breakfast and dinner.

Credit cards: MasterCard and Visa are accepted unless the description says "No credit cards." Many inns also accept additional cards.

Personal checks: Inns usually accept personal checks unless the description says "No personal checks."

Reservations and deposits: Be prepared to pay a deposit when you make your reservation at most of the inns. Be sure to inquire about refund policies.

Meals: Meals included in the cost of the room are indicated with the rates; other meals available at the inn will be in the "Facilities and activities" section of an inn's description. I list some of my favorite foods served at an inn to give you a general idea of the type of meals you can expect, but please realize that menus are likely to change.

Children: Many inns are ideal for children, but you know your child best; an inn's description will help you decide if it's a place where your child will be happy. I do not list children's rates, but many inns have them for children who stay in the same room or suite as their parents.

Pets: Pets are not permitted at the inns unless otherwise stated in the description. If you need to find a place to leave your pet, call the inn before you go. They may be able to make arrangements for you.

Wheelchair accessibility: Some descriptions mention wheelchair accessibility to rooms or dining rooms, but other inns may have accommodations for the handicapped. Therefore, if you're interested in an inn, call to check if there is a room suitable for a handicapped person.

Air conditioning: The description will indicate if an inn has rooms with air conditioning. Keep in mind, however, that there are areas of New England where air conditioning is totally unnecessary.

Alcoholic beverages: Some inns permit their guests to bring their own bottle (BYOB), especially if there is no bar service. If this fact is of interest to you, look in the inn's description for a mention of a bar, liquor license, or BYOB.

Smoking: If you see the comment, "No smoking inn" in an inn's description, you will know that no smoking is permitted anywhere in the inn. An index is devoted to these inns at the back of the book. In addition to these inns, there are other inns that may restrict smoking to certain designated areas indoors. Call an inn directly to find out about its exact smoking policies.

☛ While I have not rated the inns, when I found something particularly outstanding or different about an inn, I inserted a pointing finger ☛ into the description as a special note.

E: Stands for Elizabeth. This was my chance to add a note to some inns on a special, personal delight. It is not intended as a rating.

A Few Words about Visiting New England Inns

When I first started writing *Recommended Country Inns—New England* back in 1973, country inns were relatively scarce. Since that time, however, the number of country inns has been rapidly growing as more and more people have tired of the monotony of motels and thruway hotels and have begun searching for the infinitely more warming pleasure of a good country inn.

New England is full of good country inns. Its four seasons are ideal for inngoers to discover all the joys of the region—the glorious fall foliage colors and crisp, cool days; the brisk days of winter as crowds converge on the multitude of downhill ski slopes or cross-country ski areas; spring with its dogwoods, daffodils, and tulips in bright array wherever you look; and the warm, blue-skyed days of summer, when the myriad of lakes and rivers and the miles of seashore offer so much opportunity for excitement or relaxation. I love the way so many old New England houses have been turned into gracious country inns, offering guests the opportunity to thrive on history, interesting architecture, and a unique ambience. When you're a guest in New England, you find a myriad of things to do—visiting a historical site, climbing a mountain, sailing on a lake, biking on a country road past farms and pastures, walking in a national forest, picking apples in an orchard, browsing in antique shops, and much more. And finally, New England is a small region, so it doesn't take very long to travel from one area to another, offering travelers the opportunity to discover all its joys even on a short vacation.

With the constantly growing number of New England inns, it has become more and more difficult for me to wade through the volumes of mail from new country inns. I have had to be increasingly selective in choosing the best inns in each state. Do not be distressed if an inn you like is not in this guide. Please understand that my definition of a country inn is that it must have lodging as well as good food, and it must have a certain ambience that appeals to me. I prefer that the inns I select serve at least two meals a day and be open most of the year, but I have made exceptions when an inn seems just too special to leave out of this guide.

By my descriptions and comments I have tried to indicate the type of atmosphere you can expect to find in an inn, whether it would be a fun place to bring your children to, or whether it would be more appropriate to leave the children at home. Do not forget that the very reason you are passing up a motel or a hotel is for the bit of adventure and surprise you will find sitting in a weathered farmhouse, eating country cooking, chatting with a discovered friend, and finding new delight in a very old tradition.

So, enjoy! This *Recommended Country Inns—New England* was compiled for you, fellow lovers of New England country inns.

Elizabeth

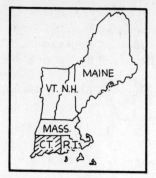

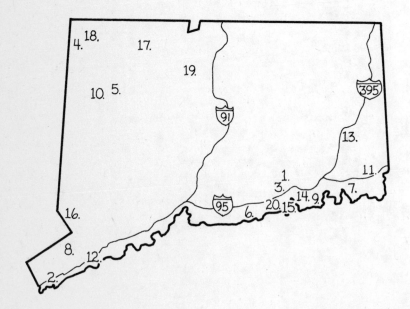

Connecticut

Numbers on map refer to towns numbered below.

Griswold Inn
Essex, Connecticut
06426

Innkeepers: Bill and Victoria Winterer
Address/Telephone: 36 Main Street; (203) 767–1812
Rooms: 23, including 9 suites; all with private bath and phone, some with fireplace.
Rates: $85 to $95, double occupancy; $125 to $165, suites; continental breakfast.
Open: All year except Christmas Eve and Christmas Day.
Facilities and activities: Lunch, dinner, Sunday brunch, children's menu, bar.

Essex is a very special town right on the Connecticut River. Although it was settled long before the Revolution, Essex is still a living, breathing, working place, not a re-created museum of a town. The first warship of the Continental Navy, the *Oliver Cromwell*, was built and commissioned here in 1776.

"The Gris," as the inn is fondly called by everyone, is the highlight of anyone's trip to Essex. When you come in from the cold to the welcome of ☞ crackling fireplaces, you are doing what others have done before you for 200 years. You can lunch or dine in the cool dimness of the Library or the Gun Room. A special spot is the Steamboat Room, where the mural on the far wall floats gently, making you feel that you are really on the river. Their collection of ☞ Currier & Ives is museum-size and quality. ☞ There is music almost every night—old time banjos, sea chanteys, Dixieland jazz, or just good piano—but never rock 'n' roll.

In the bar is a great, old-fashioned popcorn machine. Bill Winterer gives popcorn to all the children who come in. Do ask for some. It's one of many personal touches that make this nice kind of inn such a special place.

The Hunt Breakfast is the renowned Sunday brunch at the inn. This bountiful fare is worth a trip from anywhere. The selection is extensive, with enough good food to satisfy anyone's palate. Dinner just gets better every time I visit. I've enjoyed Osso Bucco and fettucine with two-mushroom sauce. The chicken stew with dumplings almost got me. The awful awful New York strip sirloin steak is awful big and awful good.

The guest rooms are old, but nice. The Oliver Cromwell Suite is in the main building, with a woodburning fireplace, comfortable couches, a four-poster bed, and a lovely bar for your very own. There is a very nice view of Middle Cove from here. The Garden Suite, located across the street, has a fireplace, wet bar and refrigerator, and two double beds. Very nice.

How to get there: Take the Connecticut Turnpike to Exit 69, and follow Route 9 north to Exit 3. Turn left at the bottom of ramp to a traffic light, turn right, and follow this street right through town to the river. The inn is on your right, about 100 yards before you get to the river.

∽✖∾

E: *My favorite thing about The Gris? Love that popcorn machine in the bar. I also like Marmalade, the inn cat.*

The Homestead Inn
Greenwich, Connecticut
06830

Innkeepers: Lessie Davison and Nancy Smith
Address/Telephone: Field Point Road; (203) 869–7500
Rooms: 17, plus 6 suites; all with private bath, color TV, clock radio, phone.
Rates: $90, single; $135 to $175, double; $160 to $175, suites; continental breakfast.
Open: All year.
Facilities and activities: Full breakfast, lunch Monday through Friday, dinner seven days a week. Dining room closed Christmas Day, New Year's Day, and Labor Day. Bar, small conference center.

There are very good reasons why this lovely 1799 inn has been chosen as the ☛ best country inn in the country. Jacques Thiebeult is the French chef who oversees the superb food served here. The entire staff makes you feel like royalty. I think we all need this kind of treatment once in a while.

The dining room is elegant in a rustic fashion; hand-hewn chestnut beams, brick walls, fireplaces, skylights, and well-spaced tables with comfortable chairs. A simple bunch of flowers is on each table.

The inn's rooms are beautifully refurbished and each has a

name. William Inge wrote *Picnic* while staying at the inn in the 1950s, and the name of the room he stayed in is the Picnic Room. I stayed in this one, too. The Poppy Room is a single with the smallest bathtub I believe was ever made. The Tassel Room has his and her desks, the Sleigh Room has old sleigh beds, and the Robin Room has delicate stencils on the walls. They were found under six layers of wallpaper dating back to 1860. The Bride's Room has a queen-sized canopy bed.

The Independent House is the ☛ newest addition to the inn. There are eight glorious rooms out here. The bathrooms are large and have tub, shower, and bidet. All the rooms have porches, and the furnishings are wonderful. The cottage has a lovely suite and two other bedrooms, all very nice and quiet.

La Grange is the dining room and the food is fabulous. Besides the extensive menus, there are many specials. One that I had was ☛ poached fresh Dover sole, the best I have ever eaten. The inn is noted for its fresh fish and wonderful, tender veal prepared many interesting ways. Another dinner offering is "Black Angus" sirloin béarnaise. A real winner is *mélange de fruits de mer au safran*—lobster, shrimp, scallops, and mussels in a creamy saffron sauce. The presentation of the food is so picture perfect, you could almost eat the plate. The ironstone place settings in Wedgwood's Chinese Bird pattern and the beautiful stemware are exquisite.

One of the luncheon dishes is escallops of veal, served with chestnuts, cream, and cognac. Some of the hors d'oeuvres are fresh poached Arctic salmon or a pot of snails with cream, Pernod, and herbs. The desserts, needless to say, are spectacular.

Do I like it here! I just wish I lived a bit closer.

How to get there: From New York take I–95 north to Exit 3. Turn left at the bottom of the ramp, then left again at the second light onto Horseneck Lane. Turn left at the end of the lane onto Field Point Road. The inn is in ¼ mile on the right.

From Boston take I–95 south to Exit 3. Turn right at the bottom of the ramp. Turn left at the first light onto Horseneck Lane and proceed as described above.

❀

E: The very well-known interior designers John and Virginia Saladino are responsible for the renovation of this lovely inn.

Copper Beech Inn
Ivoryton, Town of Essex, Connecticut
06442

Innkeepers: Eldon and Sally Senner
Address/Telephone: 46 Main Street; (203) 767–0330
Rooms: 4 in inn, 9 in carriage house; all with private bath.
Rates: $95 to $155, double occupancy, continental breakfast.
Open: All year.
Facilities and activities: Restaurant closed on Mondays, Christmas Eve, Christmas Day, and New Year's Day. Dinner, full license. Greenhouse cocktail lounge open on Friday and Saturday in summer and Saturday rest of year.

One of the most beautiful copper beech trees in Connecticut shades the lawn of this lovely old inn and is the reason for the inn's name.

The grounds are beautiful. Eldon, who really is a gardener, has done wonders with the property. There is an ☛ authentic English garden, many bulbs are in bloom at different times of the year, and everything is just breathtaking.

Sally is an interior designer, and her expertise really shows in this inn. The Senners' seven-year-old son, William, shows promise of being a good innkeeper. When asked who he is, he states that he is the innkeeper, with two assistants, his mother and father.

Accommodations at the Copper Beech are wonderful. There are four rooms in the inn itself, and they have unbelievable ☛ old-fashioned bathrooms. The towels are soft and fluffy. Nine more guest rooms are in the carriage house, and each one has a Jacuzzi tub, so wonderful after a day of exploring the lovely town of Essex, Mystic, and other area attractions. The carriage house has an elegant country atmosphere. The halls have very nice early nineteenth-century botanical prints. In fact, there is nineteenth-century art all over the inn and a wonderful collection of fine oriental porcelain. The facilities are not well suited for children under eight years of age.

The four dining rooms have comfortable Chippendale and Queen Anne chairs. The Garden Porch, which is a favorite place for me, features white wicker and nice Audubon prints on the walls. The spacious tables are set far apart for gracious dining. Fresh flowers are everywhere and the waiters are friendly and courteous.

The hors d'oeuvres menu is a beauty. When I come here I love to have their ☛ beef filet with a curry sauce. Do try it. The lobster bisque is always superb, and there are about twelve more soups to choose from. Good fresh fish is used for entrees. The lobster is always easy to eat; no struggling with it here. My friend Lucy Goodale and I ordered different veal dishes. The veal was so tender we didn't need to use a knife. Beef Wellington and roast rack of lamb are always winners here. Desserts are super. I love chocolate and raspberries, so I had some in the form of a cake and mousse and berries. No matter what you order, it is good at the Copper Beech.

How to get there: The inn is located 1 mile west of Connecticut Route 9, from Exit 3 or 4. Follow the signs to Ivoryton. The inn is on Ivoryton's Main Street, on the left side.

Olive Metcalf

Wake Robin Inn
Lakeville, Connecticut
06039

Innkeeper: Henri J. P. Manassero
Address/Telephone: Route 41; (203) 435–2515
Rooms: 24, including 2 suites; all with private bath, TV, phone, air conditioning, and 3 with balcony.
Rates: $85 to $140, double occupancy; $200, suites; EP.
Open: All year.
Facilities and activities: Breakfast, dinner, Sunday brunch. Bar, lounge, meeting room, swimming pool. Nearby: golf, tennis, boating, river rafting, horseback riding, skiing, playhouses, hayrides, sleigh rides, carriage rides.

Built in 1896 as the exclusive Taconic School for Girls, this building became the Wake Robin Inn in 1913. Perched on a hillside on seventy-five acres, it's a beauty. Henri earned his reputation as a first-class hotelier in major cities around the world. The Paris Plaza and New York's Pierre are just a couple of his former hotels. His experience surely does show here.

Moya Manassero, a renowned interior designer, decorated all of the rooms. There's a country French flavor in some and a Nantucket feeling in another. The views from the rooms are breathtaking.

The library, which has a nice fireplace, is ideal for small seminars. A fireplace is also in the common room, and the bar is small and intimate.

Savarin, the inn's restaurant, is elegant. The fireplace is white brick and the walls are covered with a deep rose wallpaper. The china is Wedgwood "Potpourri" and beautiful. ☛ The well-spaced tables are a plus, and brass candelabra and fresh flower bouquets complete the scene. I love beginning a dinner with an appetizer like burgundy snails or shrimp salad with citrus fruit. Creamy mussel soup and fresh asparagus soup garnished with crisp pieces of asparagus are both superb. Try the veal medallions with shiitake mushrooms and tarragon sauce. ☛ Coquilles St. Jacques is served on a bed of fresh spinach—a different approach to this dish. The swordfish is excellent. For dessert, try a bowl of raspberries with cream or a fruit tart; there are many more possibilities.

The young French chef and culinary consultant, Patrice Boely, was chef at a five-star restaurant in Paris for seven years. He is a master chef of France, one of only 200 in the world. With all of this behind Henri, I ask you, how could he miss?

❋

How to get there: From Hartford take Route 44 west to Lakeville and then Route 41 south to the inn.

> *Man has tendencies of many temperatures,*
> *the warmest of which is hospitality.*

The Litchfield Inn
Litchfield, Connecticut
06759

Innkeeper: Dana Thomas
Address/Telephone: 432 Bantam Road; (203) 567–4503
Rooms: 30; all with private bath, air conditioning, TV, phone, smoke
   alarm, and some with wheelchair accessibility.
Rates: $70 to $95, double occupancy, continental breakfast.
Open: All year.
Facilities and activities: Breakfast, lunch, dinner, Sunday brunch. Dining
   room closed Christmas Day. Bar, lounge, gift shop.

The first thing that greets you as you enter the inn is the 🖝
9-foot chandelier over the delicately carved main staircase. How
nice to be a bride and make your royal descent here. Breathtaking,
I'm sure.

There are singles, doubles, and suites, all beautifully furnished
in early American style. They all have air conditioning, smoke
alarm, television, and telephone. Some even have their own bar.
There also are 🖝 rooms for the handicapped.

The Tapping Reeve Room is the inn's main lounge and bar,
offering choice beverages and a luncheon menu that features
soups and overstuffed sandwiches. There is live entertainment
here Thursday through Sunday all year long. On Wednesdays a

wonderful man plays the beautiful baby grand piano. The Terrace Room with greenery and sunlight is another place for lunch. What a menu! I found a favorite dish of mine here: ☞ chilled beef tenderloin, served with horseradish–sour cream dressing and red potato salad. The crepes and egg dishes are spectacular.

And now to dinner. The main dining room is lovely with its wide-planked floors and well-spaced tables. It's such a wonderful setting in which to savor the food. The menu varies and has many specialties. I love clams casino, and they have good ones here. Cajun shrimp is another appetizer of merit. Some of the inn's favorites are glorious beef like prime ribs (weekends only) and tournedos au poivre, veal piccata, Boston scrod, sole, and swordfish. There also is a great fettucine Alfredo. Delicious! Of course there are many other selections. Be sure to cap off your meal with a cup of Royal Kona Hawaiian coffee. It is very interesting. Enjoy a glass of fine wine with your dinner.

Sunday brunch (reservations are a must) is beautifully done. From Steamship Round and four or five other hot dishes to assorted salads and a dessert table. Oh my!

How to get there: From I–84 in Danbury, take Route 7 north to Route 202 to Litchfield. The inn is on the left.

✳

E: *The four lovely fireplaces in the inn keep you warm on a cold winter's day.*

Madison Beach Hotel
Madison, Connecticut
06443

Innkeepers: Betty and Henry Cooney, Sr., Kathleen and
    Roben Bagdasarian
Address/Telephone: 94 West Wharf Road; (203) 245–1404
Rooms: 35, plus 4 suites; all with private bath, air conditioning, cable TV.
Rates: In-season, $95 to $130; suites, $150 to $195; double occupancy,
    continental breakfast. Off-season, $50 to $115; suites, $125 to $175;
    double occupancy, continental breakfast. $10 less for single.
Open: March through December.
Facilities and activities: Lunch, dinner. Bar, lounge, conference room,
    private beach on Long Island Sound.

If you are fortunate enough to own a boat, do come to
Madison, drop your anchor, and row right in to the Madison
Beach Hotel. If you don't own a boat, you don't need to hesitate
to come here. The hotel is very easy to reach and should not be
missed.

This Victorian beauty dates back to the 1800s. It has had
many uses and a lot of names, but it has never been better than it
is today. The whole inn has been refurbished with an abundance
of tender love and care.

Each of its rooms and magnificent suites has its own entrance and 🖝 balcony overlooking the Long Island Sound and beach. The rooms are large and airy and furnished with antique oak bureaus and wicker and rattan furniture. Soft puffs cover the wicker, so you just sink into comfort. The four suites are absolutely breathtaking; each has its own kitchen, and the views from all of them are just wonderful.

There is a distinct nautical flavor to the wharf dining room and the lovely crow's-nest dining room on the upper level. The luncheon menu is extensive. The lobster salad roll is huge, and even I could not quite finish it. Several cold salad plates are offered. These are so nice on a hot day. For dinner they have queen- or king-sized cuts of 🖝 roast prime ribs of beef served with horseradish sauce. This is such a nice way to serve beef. The stuffed veal chop is different and very good. From the sea there are sixteen entrees, each one sounding more enticing than the next. And on Friday and Saturday nights, there is good entertainment by a trio.

The beach is private, 75 feet of it. The water is clear with no undertow, so the children are safe. There is good fishing off the inn's pier. Or sit on the porch in one of the many wicker rockers and just enjoy where you are.

How to get there: From I–95, turn right onto Route 79 if coming from New York and left if coming from Rhode Island. Go right at the third traffic light onto Route 1. Turn left at the Madison Country Club. The inn is at the end of the road on the water.

olive Metcalf

Stevens Inn at Cafe Lafayette
Madison, Connecticut
06443

Innkeeper: Ellen Belmont
Address/Telephone: 725 Boston Post Road; (203) 245–2380
Rooms: 5 share 2 baths.
Rates: $60 to $75, double occupancy, continental breakfast.
Open: All year.
Facilities and activities: Lunch, dinner, Sunday brunch, bar. Nearby: sailing, swimming, fishing.

In 1837 the inn was built as the Madison Methodist Church, made of local timber and all hand-fitted by local craftsmen. In the early 1920s it was converted into an inn.

There are four dining rooms. One that I like in particular is the Greenhouse. My favorite lunch here is always delicious. Ellen had eggs Benedict one day I was here and they looked very good. A good many selections are on the menu. Champagne brunch on Sunday includes a split of champagne. Very nice indeed.

The dinner menu is extensive. Hors d'oeuvres include pâté, fondue, and smoked salmon, to name a few. Soups are excellent. Lobster bisque is a winner. Beef stroganoff, Wiener schnitzel, and veal sauté are just three examples of the delicious entrees. Rack of lamb is always good and on weekends they have leg of lamb. I have had their fillet of sole, which is very fresh. And then there are the French regional specials, such as bouillabaisse and duckling with bing cherry sauce. No matter what you order, the food here is delectable. In summer come and dine outside on the lawn. On Friday nights you'll find music and dancing.

The rooms are nice with attractive wallpapers. The shared baths are a good size. You can relax in a common room where there is a television, and continental breakfast is set up in another room.

This is an in-town inn, so you'll find it's busy at lunchtime. The pub is fun; it is a good meeting place for friends.

How to get there: From I–95 take Exit 61. Turn onto Route 79, going toward Route 1 and Madison center. Go left on Route 1, and at the next corner, at Wall Street, turn left. The inn's driveway is just beyond the post office.

꙳

E: *The infamous Reverend Hayden of this church was tried for the murder of a young lady parishioner in 1879, but he was acquitted. Rumor has it that his ghost still hangs around the attic.*

The Inn at Mystic
Mystic, Connecticut
06335

Innkeeper: Jody Dyer
Address/Telephone: Routes 1 and 27; (203) 536–9604; restaurant, (203) 536–8140
Rooms: 5 in 2 houses; all with private bath.
Rates: $155 to $195, double occupancy, EP.
Open: All year.
Facilities and activities: Breakfast, lunch, Sunday brunch, dinner every night except on Christmas Eve, Christmas Day, and Sundays from December 1 to April 1. Bar, lounge, room service, swimming pool, tennis, canoes, sailboats, walking trails. Nearby: museums, Mystic Seaport, Mystic Marinelife Aquarium, charter boats and tours.

Every time I think about this beautiful spot, I want to go back there. The views from the inn extend from Mystic Harbor all the way to Fishers Island; they are absolutely breathtaking.

The inn and gatehouse are situated on eight acres of land amid pear, nut, and peach trees and ☞ English flower gardens. From the Victorian veranda—furnished, of course, with beautiful old wicker—the view of the natural rock formations and ponds (I watched birds have their baths) and beyond to the harbor is worth a trip from anywhere.

Built in 1904, the inn is elegant. The large living room has walls covered with magnificent pin pine imported from England and contains lovely antiques and comfortable places to sit. The rooms in both the inn and the gatehouse are beautifully done. Some have fireplaces. My room had a canopy bed, and was it ever comfortable! They all have interesting baths with ☛ whirlpool soaking tubs or Thermacuzzi spas. One has a view across the room to the harbor. Now that's a nice way to relax. Look south out the windows and you'll see Mason Island; on a clear day you can see Long Island and Montauk.

The Flood Tide restaurant has a wonderful executive chef, Bob Tripp, who orchestrates the Tableside Classics prepared or carved at your table. Never have I seen a whole roast chicken for two on any menu except here. What a nice idea. I had baked stuffed two-tail Maine lobster—two claws and two tails and very good. Pork tenderloin with lingonberries almost got me. On my most recent visit, my friend Arneta Dow and I had chateaubriand for two, which was exquisite. All the food is memorable. The ☛ luncheon buffet is lavish, or ask for a picnic basket to take out sightseeing. They have thought of everything to make your stay pleasant. Sunday brunch, as you can imagine, is a bountiful affair.

The lounge is pleasant for lighter fare and is right at the swimming pool. A piano player provides music on a parlor grand piano every night and Sunday brunch. A wedding up here would be ambrosia.

How to get there: Take Exit 90 from I–95. Go 2 miles south through Mystic on Route 27 to Route 1. The inn is here. Drive up through the motor inn to the inn at the top of the driveway.

Olive Metcalf

Roger Sherman Inn
New Canaan, Connecticut
06840

Innkeeper: Henry Priegor
Address/Telephone: 195 Oenoke Ridge; (203) 966-4541
Rooms: 7; all with private bath, air conditioning, TV, phone.
Rates: $60 to $85, single; $90 to $110, double; continental breakfast.
Open: All year except Christmas Day.
Facilities and activities: Lunch, dinner, Sunday brunch, bar. Nearby: golf,
 tennis, nature center.

It is so nice to have Henry back in this guide. He was the innkeeper of another inn sometime ago. The Roger Sherman, which was built in the mid-1700s, had fallen into disrepair, but Henry gutted the old building and wow, what a job he has done. It is within walking distance of New Canaan's town center. This is a wonderful area in Connecticut's esteemed Fairfield County in which to spend a few days.

The rooms are large and nicely furnished with comfortable chairs and couches and good beds. There are five lovely dining rooms. One is a pretty private one for up to ten people. It's on the main floor along with three other dining rooms and a neat pub and lounge. The porches wrap around the inn, and in warm weather food and cocktails are served here overlooking the lush green lawns.

Downstairs is the ☛ wine cellar–dining room that seats up to twenty-six people. There is a wonderful collection of wines along some of the walls. Wherever you eat, you will find the food sumptuous. There are daily specials for lunch and dinner. At lunch on Monday, for example, there's cold poached fresh Norwegian salmon, and on Thursday prime ribs of beef are served. Of course there are other things to order. Dinner has items like ☛ cold cucumber and tomato soup, wonderful salads, rack of lamb (a longtime favorite of mine), desserts (I just adore their crepes Suzette—oh, are they good). The chef has been with Henry for twenty-five years, and that means you can count on memorable meals.

How to get there: The inn is located on Route 124 North in New Canaan.

❧

E: *Black tie on New Year's Eve. Tableside service seven days a week.*
Orchids in the bay window. Oh, what a nice place to be.

> *The dog nuzzled my leg. The fire sent out a glow.*
> *The drink was good. Only at an inn.*

olive Metcalf

Lighthouse Inn
New London, Connecticut
06320

Innkeeper: Don Tillett
Address/Telephone: 6 Guthrie Place; (203) 443–8411
Rooms: 27 in main building, 24 in carriage house; all with private bath,
    phone, TV.
Rates: $105 to $210, double occupancy, continental breakfast.
Open: All year.
Facilities and activities: Breakfast, lunch, dinner, Sunday brunch. Elevator,
    private beach. Nearby: U.S. Coast Guard Academy, U.S. Naval
    Submarine Base, Mystic.

    The mansion, known as "Meadow Court," was completed in
1902. In 1928 it became the Lighthouse Inn. And what an inn it
is!
    The accommodations are sumptuous. There are ☛ no two
rooms alike. Many of the antiques were found in flea markets and
auctions in Connecticut and surrounding states. Numerous quality
reproductions are also featured in the rooms. You will find
armoires with television sets concealed in them, canopy and
four-poster beds, wicker pieces, Victorian wing chairs, quilt racks,
and more. The fireplaces are nonfunctional, but they are filled with
☛ glorious baskets of silk flowers. Many of the rooms have the

most beautiful wreaths I have ever seen. Twenty-six of the rooms in the main building have whirlpool tubs. The staircase that goes to the upper floors is truly a masterpiece. This is an inn not to be missed.

☛ Saturday night dancing is here. Why, oh why, isn't there more of it everywhere? Music in the lovely Meadow Court Lounge is also fun, and all of the people are so nice. The inn provides a fine setting for seminars and any type of corporate gathering. Wherever you are, it's all just glorious.

The dining rooms are spacious. Waiters and waitresses know their business, and food presentation is done so well. I had clams casino, which were served in a beautiful way. My friend Arneta had the inn's famous clam bisque. I tasted it, and oh my, I can see why it's famous. We both enjoyed the excellent tenderloin of beef special.

On a nice day, guests can wander down to a private beach. And at all times of the year, inn guests enjoy the inn's proximity to the Mystic Seaport Museum and the Mystic Marinelife Aquarium, the U.S. Coast Guard Academy, U.S. Naval Submarine Base, and much more.

I get good reports all the time about this inn. Don't miss this one.

How to get there: Take I–95 north to Exit 82. Turn right, and at the second stoplight turn right onto Colman Street. At the end of the street, turn left onto Bank Street. Take the second right onto Montauk Avenue. At the end of the street, turn right onto Pequot Avenue. At the first stop sign, turn right onto Lower Boulevard. The inn is in a half block, on the right.

❧

E: *After forty-some years, they still have the chef who prepares their famous Delmonico potatoes.*

olive Metcalf

Boulders Inn
New Preston, Connecticut
06777

Innkeepers: Kees and Ulla Adema
Address/Telephone: Route 45; (203) 868–7918
Rooms: 17, including 2 suites and 8 guest houses; all with private bath.
Rates: $110 to $150, single; $145 to $225, double; MAP. EP rates available in the off-season.
Open: All year except Tuesdays.
Facilities and activities: Breakfast, dinner. Sunday brunch from Labor Day to Memorial Day. Bar, tennis court. Nearby: swimming, boating, bicycling, hiking, cross-country skiing.

The stone boulders from which the inn was made jut right into the inn, and so the name, Boulders Inn.

If you have the energy, take a hike up Pinnacle Mountain behind the inn. From the top of the mountain, you'll be rewarded with a 🖙 panorama that includes New York State to the west and Massachusetts to the north. Nice to enjoy the woods without having to go very far.

If you're not a hiker, you can enjoy the marvelous countryside right from the inn. There is an outside terrace where, in summer, you may enjoy cocktails, dinner, and spectacular sunsets. The spacious living room has large windows, and its comfortable chairs and couches make it a nice place for tea or cocktails. The dining room is octagonal in shape and provides a wonderful view of the lake. Some very good food is served here. There are some different appetizers like artichoke hearts with smoked trout mousse, sweetbreads with watercress sauce, and squid or leeks vinaigrette. And the entrees—oh my. Native roast leg of lamb au jus with shiitake mushrooms. Venison with lingonberries and chestnut puree. Quail. The list goes on and on. ☞ Kees serves very interesting wines by the glass.

All the guest accommodations have a view either of the lake or of the woods and are tastefully furnished. ☞ There are eight cozy guest houses, all with fireplaces. Say hello to Mouse and Fred, the inn cats.

How to get there: From New York take I–84 to Route 7 in Danbury; follow it north to New Milford. Take a right onto Route 202 to New Preston. Take a left onto Route 45, and you will find the inn as you round onto the lake.

❀

E: *Kees and Ulla have done nice things to the inn. They have interesting paintings, Quimper pottery made in France is on display, and the cut and pierced lampshades were all made by Ulla.*

The Hopkins Inn
on Lake Waramaug
New Preston, Connecticut
06777

Innkeepers: Franz and Beth Schober
Address/Telephone: 22 Hopkins Road; (203) 868–7295
Rooms: 10, plus 1 apartment; 8 with private bath.
Rates: $50 to $60, double occupancy, EP. No credit cards.
Open: April to December.
Facilities and activities: Breakfast for house guests only, lunch, dinner. Bar, lounge, private beach on lake. Nearby: golf, tennis, and horseback riding.

Surrounded by majestic trees on particularly beautiful grounds, this inn overlooks lovely Lake Waramaug. The inn has glorious, unmatched views of the lake.

In season there is 🐟 dining under the magnificent maple and horse chestnut trees, and dine you will. The inn has a 🐟 trout pond where you can pick the fish you fancy, and next you have trout meunière; fresher fish would be hard to find.

Franz is the chef, and a few of his specials include lamb curry, veal piccata or milanaise, and boeuf bourguignon. Those are for lunch. For dinner how about bay scallops in a special garlic sauce, and backhendl with lingonberries. And there is always a special or two. On Sundays, instead of brunch, they have Sunday dinner all day with wonderful lamb and pork roasts. ☛ Many Austrian dishes are served here.

The dining rooms are cheerful. The fireplace has ceramic square tiles across the mantel, and the decorations are wine racks full of wines from all over the world. Naturally their wine list is quite impressive and pleasantly, fairly priced.

There is a private beach down at the lake for use by inn guests. Bicycling, hiking, horseback riding, golf, and tennis are available nearby.

The rooms are very clean, neat, and country-inn comfortable. Almost all of the rooms have a view of the lake.

How to get there: Take I–84 to Route 202 East to Route 45 in New Preston. Turn left on Route 45 and follow it 2 miles past the lake. Take your first left after the lake. Then take the second right onto Hopkins Road.

❧

E: Strawberries romanoff, meringue glacé, coupe aux marrons, and homemade cheesecake. Need I say more?

*"The best landscape in the world
is improved by a good inn in the foreground."*
—Dr. Samuel Johnson

The Inn on Lake Waramaug
New Preston, Connecticut
06777

Innkeepers: Kevin and Barbara Kirshner
Address/Telephone: 107 North Shore Road; (203) 868–0563; (800) LAKE–INN
Rooms: 23; all with private bath, air conditioning, TV, phone.
Rates: $85 to $105, per person, double occupancy, MAP. Package plans available.
Open: All year.
Facilities and activities: Lunch May through October. Bar, indoor pool, sauna, exercise room, game room, meeting house, cross-country skiing, ice skating, boating, lake swimming. Nearby: tennis, golf, horseback riding, downhill skiing.

The second largest natural lake in Connecticut fills part of the view you have from this old Colonial inn that dates back to 1795. There are enormous 100-year-old sugar maples and a magnificent hawthorn tree.

There is so much to do here both inside and outside the inn. Winter is a fairyland. The innkeepers keep an ⬛ area on the lake cleared for skating. Cross-country skiing starts just outside the door. Downhill skiing is but twenty minutes away. Summer brings boating and swimming or just enjoying the shaded lawns and sandy beach. The inn has a showboat that takes you around the lake. A nice way to see it all. Bicycles are also available. Nearby are golf, tennis, and horseback riding.

Inside the inn is year-round fun. Try the heated swimming pool with a whirlpool lagoon and a sauna. Memorabilia from long ago decorate the walls of the game room that has pool, Ping-Pong, electronic and other games, and even a jukebox. The newest addition to the inn is the ☛ exercise room. Good thing they have it with the abundant food served here.

A meeting house is available for conferences and weddings. It even has a fireplace.

The dining rooms are large and well appointed, serving good food year round. There is a jalousied dining room that has a hand-painted rug on the floor. This was a first for me. The food is good, with such appetizers as sauté of oysters and leeks in sauce mornay with a roasted garlic crouton, and linguini Provençale with capers, garlic, anchovies, and tomatoes. One delicious entree is sauté of jumbo shrimp in tomato concassée and tarragon cream sauce. They also have roast rack of lamb and wonderful freshly baked bread.

For antique lovers there is a gracious old fireplace made from the bricks that once were ballast on English sailing ships.

This is a wonderful place for the whole family or just one tired "inn creeper" like me. I arrived at a long day's end and spent about an hour in the pool. What a way to relax.

How to get there: From New York take I–84 to Route 7 in Danbury; follow it north to New Milford. Take a right onto Route 202 to New Preston. Take Route 45 west and follow signs to the inn. From Boston take the Massachusetts Turnpike to I–86. Follow it to I–84. Exit from I–84 onto Route 4 in Farmington. Continue on Route 4 to Route 118, and in Litchfield, pick up Route 202 and follow it to Route 45 West.

❧

E: *Christmas is a fabulous festival, with lighted Christmas trees, and a ☛ handbell choir concert to usher in the hundreds of little lights. It's enjoyed by all, including Jake, the inn's golden retriever.*

Olive Metcalf

Randall's Ordinary
North Stonington, Connecticut
06359

Innkeepers: Bill and Cindy Clark
Address/Telephone: P.O. Box 243; (203) 599–4540
Rooms: 12; all with private bath, some with air conditioning.
Rates: $85 to $140, double occupancy, continental breakfast.
Open: All year except Christmas Eve, Christmas Day, and New Year's Day.
Facilities and activities: Lunch, dinner, bar. Hiking, cross-country skiing, hay rides.

When you walk into the rustic dining rooms of Randall's Ordinary, the aroma of wood is most appealing. The wide boards in the floors creak, and you might wonder what century you are in. Honest, it's this one. This inn dates back to 1685 and had additions in 1720 and 1790. The Underground Railroad hid slaves here in 1830; there's a trapdoor to prove it. Indian shutters are here, too.

The Randall family built it all and cooked their meals over an open hearth. Today the Clarks still do it the Randall way. They are ☛ self-taught in the art of hearth cooking, and they wear the colonial dress of that era.

The food is glorious. The wood gives the food a special taste. My friend Lucy Goodale and I watched our lunch being prepared on one of the three open hearths. Quite a sight. I had 🖝 lamb chops that were the best I've ever had. Lucy had delicious scallops done the Clarks' way. Rhubarb chutney was served with both. It was exquisite. Roast goose with wild rice stuffing was another lunch special.

There is one seating for dinner at seven o'clock. Reservations are a must. All three fireplaces are used in the evening. Popcorn and cheddar and crackers are offered first. Soup such as corn chowder and breads (the spider cornbread is superb) come next, and then an unhurried dinner. The Clarks try to do one poultry, one roast, and one seafood main dish. One vegetable is mashed potatoes and turnips. The desserts are Colonial, such as Indian pudding. You really ought to go.

The barn, circa 1819 and hand hewn, came from New York. It has been re-erected on this property and now houses wonderful rooms. Some have lofts. Two have 🖝 spiral staircases. There are skylights and whirlpool baths and air conditioning and a tremendous and fun cattle scale, so it's the best of both worlds. The inn itself has three guest rooms with working fireplaces.

There are twenty-seven acres for wandering on, cross-country skiing, or hiking. An African gray parrot named Ashes lives on the second floor. What a ham. I really think you should check this one out.

How to get there: Take Exit 92 from I–95 onto Route 2 North. The inn is in ⅓ mile.

❧

E: *One fireplace has an old round oven with a clock on top. Put the bird or roast in, hang it up, and wind the clock. The oven turns and browns the food perfectly.*

Olive Metcalf

Silvermine Tavern
Norwalk, Connecticut
06850

Innkeeper: Francis C. Whitman, Jr.
Address/Telephone: 194 Perry Avenue; (203) 847–4558
Rooms: 10; all with private bath.
Rates: $60 to $65, single; $80 to $90, double; continental breakfast.
Open: All year.
Facilities and activities: Lunch, dinner, Sunday brunch. Restaurant closed
    Tuesdays from September to May. Bar, TV in parlor.

Although the Colonial crossroads village known as Silvermine has been swallowed up by the surrounding Fairfield County towns of Norwalk, Wilton, and New Canaan, the Silvermine Tavern still lies at the heart of a community of great Old World beauty. It has a remarkable way of sweeping you worlds back in time.

This is one of the most popular dining places in the area, known for delicious New England traditional food. Thursday night is set aside for a fantastic buffet supper featuring steaks, fried chicken, and many salads, all of which you top off with a great array of desserts. Sunday buffet brunch features twenty different dishes. Some of the inn specialties are oysters country gentlemen, scallops Nantucket, mussels steamed in wine, and roast duckling with an apple cider sauce. The food may be savored in one of the six dining rooms or ☛ on the riverside deck, which is open from June through September. On the old millpond below, the ducks and swans wait, hoping for some leftovers.

Silvermine Tavern is furnished with old oriental rugs, antiques, old portraits, and great comfortable chairs and sofas surrounding the six huge fireplaces. The main dining room is decorated with over 1,000 antiques, primarily old farm tools and household artifacts. Also in here is an 1887 Regina music box. The drop of a coin will turn a huge disk and the music will begin. This is a really fun antique. In the front parlor, in front of a cheery fire, you can enjoy sherry and petit-fours at the end of your day. This is the life.

The guest rooms are comfortably furnished, many of them with old-fashioned tester beds. One of my favorite rooms has its ☛ own deck overlooking the lovely millpond.

If you wish, you can stroll by the waterfall and feed the ducks and swans on the millpond. Across the road from the Tavern you will find the Country Store, run by Frank's wife. It has a back room that is a museum of antique tools and gadgets. It also has a fine collection of Currier & Ives prints. Do take a leisurely drive around the back roads near the inn, too. They are a delight. Also in this area you have the well-known Silvermine Guild of Artists.

How to get there: From the Merritt Parkway take Exit 39 onto Route 7 south. Go south to the second traffic light and turn right onto Perry Avenue. Follow it to a stop sign and turn left. The inn is on the right.

31

Olive Metcalf

Norwich Inn
Norwich, Connecticut
06360

Innkeeper: Edward Safdie
Address/Telephone: Route 32; (203) 886–2401
Rooms: 65, including suites; all with private bath.
Rates: $125 to $185, per room, EP.
Open: All year.
Facilities and activities: Breakfast, lunch, dinner, Sunday brunch. Bar, lounge, meeting rooms, croquet, badminton, tennis court, spa. Cross-country skiing and 18-hole golf course adjacent to inn.

The Norwich Inn began as a hotel in 1929 and has a colorful past. For the present it has been totally refurbished, and it is truly elegant. The inn is a lovely red brick building on a hill, surrounded by huge elms, maples, and oaks. The grounds are beautifully manicured.

Everything you could possibly want is here. The magnificent restaurants are beautifully decorated. The Prince of Wales Bar has a log-burning fireplace, and the Windsor Room is set up for games. The Hunt Room, a meeting room, is done in English decor. There are other conference rooms on the lower floor. The Grand Ballroom is so nice for weddings, banquets, and meetings. The Sunroom is a tranquil place to have a cocktail, and the 🖝 deck is so lovely. It overlooks the Norwich Golf Course. Lunch, dinner, and Sunday brunch are served here in warm weather. For a special party, there is a pit for a clambake. Lobster, clams, mussels, corn, and potatoes cook all day and are so good.

Best of all is the ☛ fabulous spa, which features the best exercise equipment. There are life-cycle bikes, herbal wraps, whirlpool and sauna, hydrotherapy equipment, and massages. Aerobics, aquacise, and dancing are fun. The spa food is delicious; you would never know that it's low in calories. The owners are experienced in spas, as they own ☛ The Greenhouse Spa in Dallas, the California Terrace, and Spa Monte Carlo in Monaco.

I love chintz, and the huge lobby has chintz upholstered armchairs and sofas. An enormous bird cage in which a few Zebra Finches live is the focal point of the room.

The rooms and suites are just so lovely. Many have raised four-poster beds, all new, of course, and very comfortable. You'll need to use the stepstool that is thoughtfully placed here to climb up into bed. What luxury.

This is a different type of inn, business and pleasure together.

How to get there: From the Boston area, take I–95 south. Take Exit 83 onto Route 32 north. The inn is within 1¼ miles, on the left side. From New York, take I–95 north to Exit 76 onto I–395. Take Exit 79A onto Route 32 north. The inn is 1½ miles north, on the left side.

Olive Metcalf

Bee and Thistle Inn
Old Lyme, Connecticut
06371

Innkeepers: Bob and Penny Nelson
Address/Telephone: 100 Lyme Street; (203) 434–1667
Rooms: 11, plus 1 cottage; 10 with private bath.
Rates: $64 to $110, double occupancy; $165 to $185, cottage; EP.
Open: All year except Christmas Eve, Christmas Day, and first two weeks of January.
Facilities and activities: Breakfast. Lunch and dinner every day except Tuesday. Sunday brunch. Bar, lounge, library.

This lovely old inn, built in 1756, sits on five and one-half acres bordering the Lieutenant River in historic Old Lyme, Connecticut. During summer the abundant flower gardens keep the inn filled to overflowing with color.

The guest rooms are all tastefully decorated. Your bed, maybe a four-poster or canopy, is covered with lovely old quilts or afghans. The bath towels are big and thirsty. How I love them. The cottage is air-conditioned and has a reading room, bedroom with queen-sized bed, kitchen, bath, and a large TV room. A deck goes around the outside.

There are six fireplaces in the inn. The one in the parlor is most inviting—a nice place for a cocktail or just good conversation. On Saturdays there is ☞ a harp player in here, and she is excellent.

☞ Breakfast in bed is an especially nice feature of the inn. Freshly squeezed orange juice is a refreshing way to start any day. Muffins made fresh each day, buttery crepes folded with strawberry or raspberry preserves, and much more. Lunch is interesting and inventive. One item is cold sliced duck served with a basil and tomato mayonnaise and melon. Sunday brunch is really gourmet. ☞ Stir-fried duck and pheasant are glorious. I could eat the menu. And, of course, dinners here are magnificent. Candlelit dining rooms, ten appetizers, and entrees such as fresh tuna baked with shrimp and artichoke hearts and served with a sauce made of white wine, lemon, tarragon, and shallots. The list goes on and on. The menu changes seasonally, each time bringing new delights.

This is a fine inn in a most interesting part of New England. You are in the heart of art, antiques, gourmet restaurants, and endless activities. Plan to spend a few days when you come.

How to get there: Traveling north on I–95, take Exit 70 immediately on the east side of the Baldwin Bridge. At the bottom of the ramp, turn left. Take the first right at the traffic light, and turn left at the next light. The inn is the third house on your left. Traveling south on I–95, take Exit 70; turn right at the bottom of the ramp. The inn is the third house on your left.

olive Metcalf

Old Lyme Inn
Old Lyme, Connecticut
06371

Innkeeper: Diana Field Atwood
Address/Telephone: 85 Lyme Street (mailing address: P.O. Box 787); (203) 434–2600
Rooms: 13; all with private bath, phone, clock radio.
Rates: $75 to $125, continental breakfast.
Open: All year except January 1 to 14.
Facilities and activities: Lunch, dinner, bar. Dining room closed Mondays.

Sassafras is the inn cat who has a neat lounge named after her. Here you'll find television, games, books, and a lovely fireplace for your enjoyment, along with comfortable chairs and couch. The Victorian bar room has a back bar that is over one hundred years old, which was found by the innkeeper in Philadelphia. There is a ☛ beveled mirror over it that most museums would covet. A ☛ raw bar is offered in here for light suppers. A very cozy and comfortable room.

The rooms here at the inn are grand. The new wing has eight rooms. The beds are all four-posters. All rooms have telephones and clock radios, Victorian couches and/or delightful wing chairs. You will find mints on your pillow at night.

There are four separate dining areas and the food is superb.

The menu, of course, changes with the seasons, but I'd like to give you just a few ideas. At lunch one appetizer that appealed to me was oysters Toscanini, oysters poached in white wine with prosciutto, mushrooms, and shallots, glazed with Gruyère and cream. There also are nice salads and sandwiches. Try Two Bird Sandwich—chicken and duck salad with herbs and walnuts served on pumpernickel. Delicious.

Dinner is spectacular. Their ☞ Old Lyme Inn Pasta is so divine I won't even describe it. You must come and try it. Veal of the day, loin of lamb in puff pastry, it just goes on. The desserts have been written up in food magazines and have won awards. That's how good they are. Continental breakfast is served to guests every day except weekends, when a breakfast buffet is offered.

The inn can handle small conferences, weddings, parties, reunions, and such. It would be a lovely place to have a wedding, and is easy to find just off Interstate 95. There is much to do and see in this pretty town and area.

How to get there: Traveling north on I–95, take Exit 70 immediately on the east side of the bridge. At the bottom of the ramp, turn left. Take the first right at the traffic light, and turn left at the next light. The inn is on the right. Traveling south on I–95, take Exit 70. At the bottom of the ramp, turn right. The inn is on the right.

❦

E: *Do look around the inn. It is full of fascinating things.*

Saybrook Point Inn
Old Saybrook, Connecticut
06475

Innkeeper: Stephen Tagliatela

Address/Telephone: 2 Bridge Street; (203) 395–2000, (800) 243–0212 from outside Connecticut

Rooms: 65, including 6 suites; all with private bath, phone, TV, air conditioning, refrigerator, and 40 with working fireplace.

Rates: $99 to $220, double occupancy; $275 to $495, suites; EP. Package plans available.

Open: All year.

Facilities and activities: Breakfast, lunch, dinner. Banquet and meeting facilities; health club with whirlpool, sauna, and steam; spa; indoor and outdoor pools; marina with 120 slips and floating docks. Nearby: charter boats, theater.

"Experience the magic at Saybrook Point Inn." These are the inn's words, and they're so true. The panoramic views of the Connecticut River and Long Island Sound are magnificent. From the moment you walk into the lobby, the Italian-marble floors, beautiful furniture, and glorious fabrics let you know this is a special inn. Even the carpet is hand loomed.

All the guest rooms and suites have a water view, and most have a balcony. They are lavishly decorated with eighteenth-century–style furniture, and ☛ imported Italian marble is used in the bathrooms with whirlpool baths. Also in the rooms are a miniature wet bar and refrigerator; an unbelievable ☛ telephone that turns on lights; double, queen-, or king-sized beds; and more. The suites feature VCRs and data ports for personal computers and fax machines. Secretarial services are also available.

Planning a wedding or business conference? No problem. The inn has banquet facilities for all occasions. The ballroom seats 240 people. Smaller meetings would be ideal in the library, which holds up to sixteen people, or the executive suites.

Breakfast, lunch, and dinner are served in an exquisite room that overlooks the inn's marina, the river, and the Long Island Sound. There was a full moon the evening I dined here. What a beautiful sight to enhance the memorable food. Appetizers like smoked Norwegian salmon, escargots, smoked pheasant, and Beluga caviar are an elegant way to begin your dinner. Pastas are canneloni, linguine, or wild mushroom. I had one of the best racks of lamb I have ever had. There is always a fresh seafood special. My friend had shrimp Provençale—shrimp sautéed with garlic, shallots, and scallions. A flower may be a garnish on your plate; you can eat it. Do try to save room for dessert. I had ☛ chocolate–chocolate chip cake, which was dark and beautiful and delicious. The service is superb.

How to get there: From I–95 northbound take Exit 67 (southbound, take Exit 68) and follow Route 154 and signs to Saybrook Point.

✹

I have enjoyed the hospitality of a good inn
and am ready for the day ahead.

The Elms
Ridgefield, Connecticut
06877

Innkeepers: Robert and Violet Scala
Address/Telephone: 500 Main Street; (203) 438–2541
Rooms: 20; all with private bath, TV, phone.
Rates: $85, single; $95 to $125, double occupancy; continental breakfast.
Open: All year except Wednesdays and Christmas Day.
Facilities and activities: Lunch, dinner, Sunday brunch, bar. Piano entertainment on Fridays, Saturdays, and at Sunday brunch.

In 1760 a master cabinetmaker built this charming Colonial house that is now known as The Elms. It is on a historical site, for it was here that the Battle of Ridgefield was fought during the Revolution. Since 1799, when the house became an inn, the same loving care and artistry that marked its beginning has been applied to every phase of its operation.

Peter, the maitre d', is very informative. It is always nice to have such a person in a country inn. He has been with this family-owned inn since 1978. The dining rooms are all on the first floor of the original inn. The brochure says, ☞ "To partake of a meal is no mundane experience in eating, but rather an adventure in dining." Very well stated, for the food and wines are stupendous. The lunch menu features good soups, salads, pastas, omelettes, curries, and on and on. Then for dinner there are about sixteen appetizers alone, plus soups, salads, and pastas. For entrees there are always specials. I had veal Francesca, and it was delightfully served by courteous waiters. There is something for everyone. The desserts are sinfully good, but the topper for me (because I am allergic to caffeine) was ☞ decaffeinated espresso. A great ending to a perfect evening.

☞ Noel Regney plays music from the forties and fifties. It's delightful background music, for he does not play too loud. Noel also wrote a song. Do ask him for it. More inns would be wise to find a good piano and player. It really adds to the charm and warmth of the inn.

The newly refurbished guest rooms have all the modern conveniences, but still are rich in the mellow mood of yesteryear. Four-posters, canopies, and brass beds are the order here.

How to get there: The inn is located at 500 Main Street in Ridgefield. From Route 7 take Route 35 right into town.

✸

E: *Nice to have family-owned and -run inns and a staff that stays for years.*

Olive Metcalf

Stonehenge
Ridgefield, Connecticut
06877

Innkeepers: David Davis and Douglas Seville
Address/Telephone: P.O. Box 667; (203) 438–6511
Rooms: 14, plus 2 suites; all with private bath, color TV, phone.
Rates: $75 to $90, single; $90 to $120, double occupancy; $200, suite;
    continental breakfast.
Open: All year. Closed New Year's Day.
Facilities and activities: Breakfast, dinner, bar, lounge. Swimming pool.

The setting for Stonehenge is serenely beautiful. Outside the inn is a lovely pond, which is bedecked with swans and aflutter with Canada geese and ducks stopping in on their migratory journeys. When I visited here in the spring, the red and yellow tulips were at their best.

In June of 1988 the lovely old farmhouse that was the main building of the inn was destroyed in a terrible fire. But now a new Stonehenge has risen. The rooms, all different, are beautiful. No matter whether you're in the guest house or cottage or inn, the accommodations are elegant, color coordinated, and comfortable. The suite has facilities for light cooking. Most of the rooms have queen- and king-sized beds. All overlook the lake and wooded hillside.

A lovely continental breakfast is brought to you in your room, along with a 🖝 copy of the morning newspaper. The breakfast consists of freshly squeezed juice, delicious muffin or Danish pastry, and coffee.

The common room has a fireplace flanked by bookcases. The large dining room has picture windows overlooking the pond and terraces. It has always been justifiably famous for its gourmet dinners. The original Stonehenge shrimp in crisp beer batter with a pungent sauce is still here and glorious. Some of the appetizers are a crepe of wild mushrooms with Gruyère cheese, and fresh hearts of palm wrapped in prosciutto. There are good salads to choose from, followed by entrees like crisply roasted duckling with wild rice and black currant sauce, or breast of chicken filled with fresh spinach and Gruyère cheese, wrapped in puff pastry, and served with a champagne sauce. You could even have 🖝 roast baby suckling pig (five days notice for this one). The desserts are stupendous. Do come and try some. Decaffeinated espresso gets my vote.

This is a beautiful place for a wedding or any special function.

How to get there: From the Merritt Parkway, take Exit 40. Go north on Route 7. The inn's sign is in 13 miles, on the left. From I–84, go south on Route 7. The inn's sign is in 4 ½ miles on the right.

✳

If all inns were alike,
they simply would not be inns.

olive Metcalf

West Lane Inn
and
The Inn at Ridgefield
Ridgefield, Connecticut
06877

Innkeepers: Maureen Mayer and Ray Kuhnt; chef, Johannes Brugger
Address/Telephone: 22 West Lane; (203) 438–7323; Ridgefield, (203)
   438–8282
Rooms: 20; all with private bath, air conditioning, TV, and some with
   fireplace.
Rates: $90, single; $125, double; EPB.
Open: All year.
Facilities and activities: Lunch, dinner, Sunday brunch, bar, lounge, piano
   nightly.

We have a first here, two separate inns next door to each
other. West Lane Inn has the rooms and serves breakfast and a
light menu from the pantry. The Inn at Ridgefield serves delicious
lunch and dinner.
   Rich oak paneling and lush carpeting along with a crackling
fire greet you as you enter West Lane. The bedrooms are luxurious,
with individual climate control, color television, radio, and tele-

44

phone. Each room has either one king- or two queen-sized beds. Some have ☞ working fireplaces. These are really nice on a cold night.

The breakfast room is bright and cheerful, serving freshly squeezed orange juice. A West Lane breakfast special is yogurt with bananas, honey, and nuts. Cold cereals in the summer, and hot cereals in the winter; Danish, muffins, or toast; or a poached egg are offered. Everything is done very nicely. The pantry selections are available from noon until late in the evening. There are tuna fish salad plates, several sandwiches like grilled cheese—even peanut butter and jelly—and more. There also are desserts.

The ends of the old wooden wine and whiskey crates that line the porch of The Inn at Ridgefield let you know there are good things inside. Dinner features hors d'oeuvres like pâté of pistachio and truffles with sauce Cumberland, onion soup calvados gratinée, or cold vichysoisse. Then entrees such as ☞ frogs legs (they are really good), fresh Dover sole, chateaubriand, and roast rack of spring lamb follow. There are wonderful salads and desserts. Crepes Suzettes for two is an old favorite. And believe me, there are more, plus good coffees.

Both inns are just around the corner from the famous Cannon Ball House, which was struck by a British fieldpiece during the Revolution. There are quite a few stores to browse in, as well as antique stores. The Aldrich and Hammond museums are in town, and you are close to several fine summer theaters. Ridgefield is such a pretty town to visit.

How to get there: Coming north from New York on Route 684, or Route 7 from the Merritt Parkway, get off on Route 35 and follow it to Ridgefield. The inns are on Route 35 at the south end of town.

Old Riverton Inn
Riverton, Connecticut
06065

Innkeepers: Pauline and Mark Telford
Address/Telephone: P.O. Box 6; (203) 379–8678
Rooms: 12; all with private bath.
Rates: $60 to $150, double occupancy, EPB.
Open: All year except first week of January and first two weeks of March.
Facilities and activities: Lunch, dinner every day but Mondays and Tuesdays. Dining room has wheelchair accessibility. Bar.

The Old Riverton Inn was originally opened in 1796 by Jesse Ives. It was on the post road between Hartford and Albany and was known as Ives Tavern. It has passed through many hands since then, and the hands that now have it are very capable.

The Grindstone Terrace was enclosed to make it useful all year. The floor of this room is made of grindstones, which, according to 100-year-old records, were quarried in Nova Scotia, sent by ship to Long Island Sound, and then up the Connecticut River to Hartford. From there they were hauled by oxen to Collinsville, where they were used in the making of axes and machetes. A lot of history is here. Once Riverton was known as "Hitchcocksville," because the famous Hitchcock factory is here. It is open each day except Sunday until 5 P.M.

46

The colonial dining room has, of course, Hitchcock chairs and a ☛ lovely bow window chock-full of plants. I sat here for luncheon one day and had delicious broiled scrod. The menu offers a lot of choices. Chicken salad plate looked really enticing. Dinner appetizers, such as the homemade soups, also are good. I had the onion soup, and it was delicious. There are several seafood entrees, each one looking better than the next. Other specialties of the inn include boneless breast of chicken marengo, veal Français, and veal maison. Chef Leo Roy really has a way with food.

A stained-glass window is in the bar. In charge of this charming room is a ☛ bartender from the Philippines who, like most of the help, has been here for years.

There is a ☛ working fireplace in one bedroom. It's a large room with a sitting area and queen-sized bed. A few rooms have canopy beds. Mints on the pillows at night is a very special touch I love. A comfortable lounge and library is on this floor, providing you with games, tons of books, and lots of quiet.

Antiques, galleries, a general store, the Hitchcock Museum, the Seth Thomas factory outlet, the Tartan Shop, Kitchen Shop, not to mention the Cat Nip Mouse Tearoom, are all here.

How to get there: The inn is 3½ miles from Winsted. Take Route 8 or Route 44 to Winsted. Turn east on Route 20, and it is approximately 1½ miles to the inn.

❋

E: *One room has a ''new'' old tub that's a pip. Go and see.*

Under Mountain Inn
Salisbury, Connecticut
06068

Innkeepers: Marget and Peter Higginson
Address/Telephone: Route 41; (203) 435–0242
Rooms: 7; all with private bath.
Rates: $75 to $85, per person, double occupancy, MAP.
Open: All year except mid-March to mid-April and two weeks in mid-December.
Facilities and activities: For the public, dinner Thursday through Monday during summer and fall, and Friday and Saturday during winter. Nearby: swimming, canoeing, skiing, fishing, golf.

Under Mountain Inn was built in the early 1700s. Wood found in the attic was known as "king's wood" because of its special width. It now is the paneling on the front of the bar.

The house is Colonial in style and has been 🖛 lovingly restored. Each of the seven guest rooms has Posturepedic mattresses. There are queens, doubles, and twins, so take your choice. Marget has a wonderful collection of stuffed animals, and you will find one or two on your bed. What a homey feeling this added touch provides. You also will find sherry and mints in your room for your enjoyment.

There are three acres of grounds, so in the summer you can

wander out under the trees and enjoy their beauty. Shading the inn and terrace is a tree that is rumored to be the oldest thorned locust in Connecticut. Coco and Sugar are the two inn dogs. They surely are a handsome pair. Sneakers is the inn cat.

The dining rooms are charming. There are three plus one private one. Peter is the chef. You may start with Scottish salmon or one of Peter's good soups. Go on to entrees such as roast goose with chestnut stuffing, crabmeat au gratin in a pastry shell, beef steak and kidney pie . . . I could go on and on. Desserts are homemade and scrumptious. The menu, of course, changes seasonally. In the morning you are served a full English breakfast.

There is much to do in this area of Connecticut. The inn has ☞ brochures to help you plan your day. You will find canoeing, fishing, swimming, horseback riding, tennis, skiing, and more. There also are many good private schools in this area.

How to get there: Take Route 41 north for 4 miles from Salisbury. The inn is on the left. From New York State, take I–684 to Route 22, then Route 44 to Route 41.

✣

Well cooked, well served, and well eaten,
a meal at a good country inn.

Simsbury House
Simsbury, Connecticut
06070

Innkeeper: Kelly Hohengarten
Address/Telephone: 731 Hopmeadow Street; (203) 658–7658
Rooms: 30, plus 3 suites, in 2 buildings; all with private bath, phone, TV,
   and 2 with wheelchair accessibility.
Rates: $85 to $140, double occupancy, continental breakfast.
Open: All year.
Facilities and activities: Lunch, dinner, Sunday brunch. Lounge, conference
   rooms. Nearby: shopping; antiquing.

Built in 1820, Simsbury House recently stood vacant for
twenty-four years while vandals, time, and weather took their toll.
But today, after a lot of hard work, frustration, and expense, it has
been beautifully transformed into a fine inn and restaurant.

Relatives of the former owners provided old photographs of
the house that were a good reference as it was restored. Two local
craftswomen made leaded-glass windows to match the originals.
The oak parquet flooring in the inn *is* the original. The furniture
consists of antiques and fine handmade reproductions from England. For example, the four-poster mahogany beds were carved
by English cabinetmakers, and they are beauties. Most of them are
king-sized and oh, so comfortable.

Twelve hundred rolls of wallpaper and five thousand yards of fabric were used in restoring the inn and carriage house. The color schemes—blue, green, rose, and burgundy—recur among the rooms. The suites in the carriage house are sumptuous. One has a whirlpool tub. This is the life! All the rooms are different, and each one has an outside terrace.

The inn has a ☛ sprinkler system throughout, as well as smoke detectors. There are two rooms for the handicapped.

The dining room, divided into three sections, has an emerald green cotton print, a matching colored linen, and an English wool plaid on the walls. It is a wonderful place to savor the food prepared by the chef, a graduate of the Culinary Institute. Breakfast, lunch, Sunday brunch, and dinner are quite an undertaking, but he does it all so well. The menus are grand, with something for everyone. The chef insists on the freshest ingredients and emphasizes light sauces for his seasonal menus of game, seafood, lamb, and veal. One time for brunch I had crabmeat in phyllo, and it was so good. Fisherman's stew at dinner is also excellent. Desserts, well, one I had here was ☛ chocolate and raspberries. I would drive hours just for it.

How to get there: From I–84 take Exit 39 onto Route 10 and go to Simsbury. The inn is on the left.

olive Metcalf

Water's Edge Inn
Westbrook, Connecticut
06498

Innkeeper: Paul Cullen
Address/Telephone: 1535 Boston Post Road; (203) 399–5901, (800) 222–5901 outside Connecticut
Rooms: 64 rooms and suites; all with private bath, cable TV, phone.
Rates: $140 to $250, double occupancy, EP.
Open: All year.
Facilities and activities: Breakfast, lunch, dinner, Sunday brunch. Bar, lounge, room service, entertainment on holidays and special occasions, spa, indoor and outdoor pools, executive retreat and conference center, banquet rooms, tennis, private beach on Long Island Sound.

There is a song that says, "This one's for me." Well, here it is, and what a gem! Sitting up high, overlooking 🖝 Long Island Sound, the inn is a turn-of-the-century resort. With its own sparkling private beach, it offers swimming, plus boating on the inn's fleet of catamarans, sailfish, and paddle boats.

The dining room is decorated in soft shades of peach, rose, and gray. The food is magnificent. One appetizer that offers a little of everything is the coastal seafood sampler. It's wonderful. The seafood and lobster bisque with crab is excellent. There is a choice of several salads. I had the scrod entree one night and duckling another. Both were very good. I love the way the food is arranged so prettily on the plates.

☛ Sunday brunch is a delight. It is so popular that reservations are a must. Chefs make Belgian waffles to order, as well as ☛ omelettes with almost anything inside. Roast beef, roast turkey, fish, fruit, and vegetables are also offered. The pastries will really finish you. I know they did my friend Arneta and me. Wow, were they good!

There's an outdoor patio for cocktails and dining in summer called Le Grille. It is just fabulous with its view of the Sound. The lounge is warm in feeling, and has a nice fireplace besides. The bar has comfortable chairs and has the style of a pub.

The rooms and suites are sumptuous. Most of them have a king- or a queen-sized bed. All have comfortable chairs and views of something pretty. Some have a balcony, and there are wet bars in the suites.

The health club has platform tennis, day and night tennis courts, indoor and outdoor swimming, and sauna. There are banquet and conference rooms for ten to 200 persons. The inn's grounds are very nice for a walk. And there is much to do in this lovely area—marinas, state parks, the lovely town of Essex nearby, and much more.

How to get there: From I–95, take Exit 65 at Westbrook. Go south to Route 1, then go east approximately ¼ mile and look for the inn's sign.

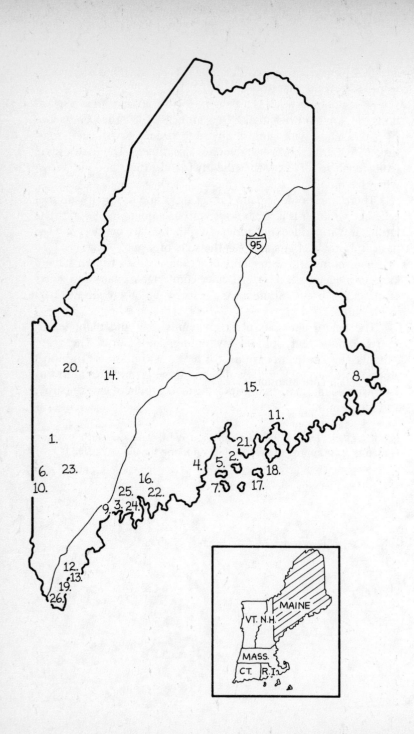

20.   14.

15.   8.

11.

1.   21.
                  2.
23.   4. 5.   18.
6.   16.   7.   17.
10.   25. 22.
         9. 3. 24.

12.
13.
19.
26.

MAINE

VT. N.H.

MASS.
CT. R.I.

Maine

Numbers on map refer to towns numbered below.

The Bethel Inn
Bethel, Maine
04217

Innkeepers: Dick Rasor; manager, Ray Moran
Address/Telephone: P.O. Box 49; (207) 824–2175
Rooms: 150; all with private bath and phone, 56 with fireplace.
Rates: $65 to $120, per person, double occupancy, MAP. Package rates
   available.
Open: All year.
Facilities and activities: Lunch, bar, lounge. Gift shop. Golf, tennis, swim-
   ming pool, lake house with sailfish and canoes, cross-country skiing,
   saunas, exercise room, indoor games, supervised activities for chil-
   dren. Own walking tour guide. Nearby: downhill skiing.

   The Bethel Inn faces the village common of Bethel, Maine,
which is a National Historic District complete with beautifully
restored churches, public buildings, and private homes. The rear of
the inn overlooks its own 200 acres and 18-hole championship
golf course.
   Guest rooms have private baths and direct-dial telephones.
They are well done and very comfortable. A number of rooms
have been recently redecorated with country-print wallpaper,
thick carpeting, and fresh paint.
   The huge living room, music room, and library are beautifully

furnished for the utter comfort of the guests. The piano, by the way, is a Steinway.

Dining is a pleasure, either in the charming main dining room or on ☛ the year-round dining veranda overlooking the golf course. You'll find such entrees as prime ribs, roast duck, and lobster and crabmeat casserole on their extensive menu. Just before sunset, look out over the golf course. You'll see literally hundreds of swallows diving into the chimney of the utility building next to the course.

Downstairs is the Mill Brook Tavern. Jim Stoner, a blind jazz pianist, plays the piano here, five nights a week, year round. Mill Brook cuts through the golf course and was the site of ☛ Twitchell's mill erected in the early 1700s in Sudbury, Canada, which is now Bethel, Maine.

Down here in the bar and lounge is a light supper menu, which is nice for the late hiker or skier. In the winter you can have hot cider, hot buttered rum, and glögg. Lunch is nice in the screened-in terrace lounge, but the drinks are even better. They're called the Kool Krazy Bouncy and Hot drinks. I managed to taste three of them. Oh boy.

The lake house, 3 miles away on Lake Songo, features clambakes and barbecues and all water sports.

Skiing is super up here with Sunday River (I love that name) and Mount Abram right at hand. The inn has special ski packages. Do check them. And as ☛ a special special, they have over 42 kilometers of groomed cross-country trails for your pleasure.

The new recreation center has a heated swimming pool for use all year, saunas, exercise room, lounge, and game room. You'll never be at a loss for something to do at The Bethel Inn.

How to get there: Bethel is located at the intersection of U.S. Route 2 and Maine Routes 5 and 26. From the south take Exit 11 off the Maine Turnpike at Gray and follow Route 26 to Bethel. The inn is on the green.

∽

E: *Afternoon teas, punch parties, and lobster bakes are nice to find in an inn.*

The Sudbury Inn
Bethel, Maine
04217

Innkeepers: Cheri and David (Fuzzy) Thurston
Address/Telephone: P.O. Box 369; (207) 824–2174
Rooms: 14, plus 3 suites; all with private bath.
Rates: $60 to $80, double occupancy, EPB.
Open: All year.
Facilities and activities: Dinner, bar, lounge. Nearby: skiing, ice skating, canoeing, tennis, golfing, hiking.

This inn is located in the very pretty village of Bethel in the mountains of western Maine. The town is home to Gould Academy, one of Maine's foremost prep schools, which was founded in 1836. Near the inn are miles of maintained cross-country ski trails, downhill skiing, ice skating, canoeing (flat and white-water), tennis, golfing, and hiking the Appalachian Trail. The inn provides easy access to the White Mountain National Forest. The fall foliage around this area is breathtakingly beautiful.

The whole inn has been refurbished and renovated, quite a task. The bar is made of 🖝 bird's-eye maple and is a one-of-a-kind beauty. A fireplace is in here, and on cold nights this is the place to be.

The food served here is good and plentiful Yankee cooking.

Everything from soups and breads to desserts is homemade. The inn is famous for its ☛ chowder. I like inventive cooking, and sole Roujolet (sole wrapped around scallop and shrimp mousse in phyllo dough and topped with a white wine sauce) is a good invention. So is chicken chardonnay—boneless chicken breast in a chardonnay sauce topped with julienne carrots, small braised onions, and mushrooms. Fuzzy's favorite is ☛ barbecue country-cut spareribs, and I love them too.

The guest rooms are clean, neat, and comfortable. There is a gallery off the lobby where local craftspeople display their work for sale. This is a very nice touch. Rockers are on the front porch. You can sit and watch the world go by.

How to get there: Take Exit 11 off the Maine Turnpike and follow Route 26 to Bethel. The inn is on lower Main Street.

*

A day by the fire, a hot ale in hand,
and the idiot cares of the world are as nothing.

olive Metcalf

Blue Hill Inn
Blue Hill, Maine
04614

Innkeepers: Don and Mary Hartley
Address/Telephone: Route 177; (207) 374–2844
Rooms: 11; all with private bath. No smoking inn.
Rates: In-season, $120 to $160, double occupancy, MAP. Lower rates in
   off-season.
Open: All year.
Facilities and activities: Restaurant closed Mondays. Full license. Nearby:
   cross-country skiing, swimming, boating, golf, tennis, concerts.

Blue Hill Inn is another ☞ no smoking inn. This is really
nice.

The inn was built in 1830 as the home of Varnum Stevens. It
has been an inn since 1840. It is located just up the hill from the
head of the bay. There are tall beautiful elms all around the
property. The garden area is lovely, and during the summer
cocktails are so nice out here.

There are two common rooms to relax in. You can feel free to
curl up in a chair and read, or you can play with their puzzles.
Fireplaces are so nice up here on a cold night. A variety of
accommodations is available. All the rooms are comfortable, and
all have their own private bath. You'll find some queen- and

60

king-sized beds and some fireplaces in the rooms. The inn's facilities are not well suited to children under thirteen.

Every evening before dinner guests are invited to the ☞ innkeepers' reception, where hors d'oeuvres are served and cocktails are available. The inn guests enjoy meeting each other and making new friends. Dinner is a six-course affair served by candlelight. The first course is soup, and the second is a good salad. The third course is an appetizer, which might be a fish pâté or smoked salmon with avocado and dill sauce. A sorbet to cleanse your palate is the fourth course. The entree could be ☞ steamed lobster, Maine scallops, or veal Marsala. Fresh fish is special here. All this is followed by a grand dessert: fruit tarts, cheesecake with rhubarb sauce, chocolate mousse torte, among others, and a cup of hot coffee or tea. The inn has a fine wine list to accompany your meal. And in the morning your breakfast is a hearty and filling one.

How to get there: From Belfast, follow Route 3 through Searsport to Bucksport. Bear right after crossing the Bucksport Bridge. After a few miles, turn right onto Route 15 to Blue Hill. Turn right on Main Street, then bear right again onto Route 177. The inn is the first building on your left at the top of the hill.

Olive Metcalf

The Captain Daniel Stone Inn
Brunswick, Maine
04011

Innkeeper: Bill Bennett
Address/Telephone: 10 Water Street; (207) 725–9898
Rooms: 21, plus 4 suites; all with private bath, wheelchair accessibility, and some with phone, TV, VCR, Jacuzzi.
Rates: $99 to $165, double occupancy, continental breakfast.
Open: All year.
Facilities and activities: Lunch, dinner, Sunday brunch. Bar, lounge, function rooms, elevator. Canoeing, boating, fishing, tennis.

This Federal-style home overlooking the lovely Androscoggin River was built in 1819 for Captain Daniel Stone and his family. His daughter, Narcissa Stone, inherited the house and improved the land around it. Today it is known as Narcissa's Hill, and the restaurant is the Narcissa Stone Restaurant.

You enter into an open and airy lobby with a beautiful staircase. A lovely fireplace divides the lounge and restaurant. In the summer there is a beauty of a veranda for your use. Lunch features good soups and salads, grilled hamburgers, and different sandwiches, as well as daily specials like quiche and seafood.

Begin your dinner with appetizers such as escargots with garlic and tomatoes, or maybe you'd prefer one of their excellent soups. Go on to entrees like the seafood Nicoise, veal *champignons,* or veal a la *crevettes,* which is veal with shrimp, scallions, lemon, and white sauce. Or perhaps you'd like chicken marsala or prime rib? The desserts, of course, are wonderful.

On the second floor are a parlor with a fireplace and a breakfast room. It has a refrigerator and toaster oven. Breakfast is a self-serve buffet with fresh fruit, yogurt, coffee, and more, and the daily newspaper is on hand. The rooms and suites are individually decorated, with Federal-style furnishings and plush carpets. Several rooms have whirlpool tubs, color cable television, full-length mirrors, tables or desks to work on, and telephones (even in the bathroom!). There are extra pillows and blankets. The inn has a ☛ complete sprinkler system with alarm equipment for your safety.

You can even come to the inn for a meeting, business conference, or family reunion. Two function rooms offer complete services. The Captain's Room holds up to sixty people, and the Bowdoin Room is for forty people. There also are smaller meeting rooms for up to twelve people.

How to get there: Take Exit 22 from I–95 North into Brunswick. Follow Route 1 northbound until you see a sign for Route 24/South Maine Street. Turn right, then turn left onto Mason Street at traffic light. In 1 block turn left onto Water Street.

✸

E: *Books on tape and videotapes are available at the desk.*

Camden Harbour Inn
Camden, Maine
04843

Innkeepers: Sal Vella and Patti Babij
Address/Telephone: 83 Bay View Street; (207) 236–4200
Rooms: 22; all with private bath, 8 with fireplace, and 8 with balcony or deck.
Rates: $145 to $185, double occupancy, EPB.
Open: All year.
Facilities and activities: Dinner served May to October. Bar, television in lounge, entertainment. Nearby: golfing, skiing, sailing.

Camden Harbour is one of the best-known ports in Maine, and it's one of the prettiest, too. In the late nineteenth century when Camden was bustling with cargo and fishing schooners, the inn was built to accommodate passengers who traveled from Boston to Bangor by steamship. Today, boats of yesteryear, both sail and power, as well as beautiful yachts of today, moor here by the rolling mountains that come right down to the rocky shores. The inn sits up high above all this and provides a ☞ panoramic view all around. The new porch is terrific, and guests enjoy it from early morning coffee to evening nightcaps.

All of the guest rooms are different in character. They are furnished with period antiques, Victorian pieces, and wicker. Two overlook the harbor and bay and have outside decks. Another is a suite with a foyer, wet bar, sitting room adjacent to a large deck, and a comfortably furnished bedroom with a working fireplace. Another room has a large sitting area and a brick patio that overlooks the outer harbor. Other rooms have fireplaces, and some have private outside entrances with reserved parking. The inn is equipped with sprinklers and heat and smoke detectors.

The Thirsty Whale Tavern serves simple suppers. The menu is posted on the chalkboard each evening. The new dining room, which has beautiful views, has its own menu. The appetizers are interesting. ☞ Shrimp Tsukeyaki, skewered shrimp marinated in a Japanese sauce and grilled, is outstanding. Oysters and mussels are prepared in some very different ways. Some entrees are crab Dijon; three deliciously different lobster dishes, including lobster grapefruit salad; and duck with raspberry cassis, a new way with duck. Shrimp fettucine alla Romano is great; add mushrooms and prosciutto and it's a plus. There are good beef and veal selections on the menu.

There are walking tours, bicycle trips, and nature walks in and around Camden. ☞ There is hardly a spot in this whole lovely Maine town that is not worth a visit. In July the Penobscot Folk Festival draws crowds to the Rockport Opera House.

This is a wonderful town to muddle about in for days.

How to get there: From Route 1, which runs through the center of town, turn up Bay View Street to number 83.

The Pentagöet Inn
Castine, Maine
04421

Innkeepers: Virginia and Lindsey Miller

Address/Telephone: P.O. Box 4; (207) 326–8616

Rooms: 16, plus 1 suite; all with private bath, suite with fireplace. No smoking inn.

Rates: $159 to $179, double occupancy, MAP.

Open: April through November.

Facilities and activities: Bar, extensive wine list. Nearby: fishing, sailing, golf.

The Pentagöet is a lovely inn located on the unspoiled coast of beautiful Penobscot Bay. Built in 1894, this Victorian inn offers the traveler warmth and a very friendly atmosphere.

Part of the inn is Ten Perkins Street, the building next door, which is more than 200 years old. The suite is here. I stayed in it and it's a gem. It has a working fireplace, and wood is supplied so you can light yourself a fire some cold evening. All the rest of the rooms in both buildings are lovely, too. Some have little alcoves with views of the town and harbor. Some are small and have odd shapes, but this goes well with a country inn. Seven rooms have queen-sized beds.

There is a library to the right as you come in the door of the main inn. Lots of books, a piano, nice and soft stereo music, and very restful couches give this room the perfect relaxed atmosphere. The sitting room is to the left with a woodburning stove and a beautiful picture window.

The wraparound porch is a delight. Good food is served in the new dining room. Breakfast when I was here included ☛ Maine strawberries, which arrived early in the morning, freshly picked at a local farm. Homemade granola, sourdough blueberry pancakes, and homemade jellies add up to a good breakfast. All baking is done right here. Good dinner appetizers include shrimp piccata— prepared with little Maine shrimp—lobster crepes, and Maine crabmeat crepes. Pork tenderloin, peppered ribeye steak, and lobster thermador are some of the entrees. I had ☛ lobster pie, a lazy and delicious way to have lobster.

The Maine Maritime Academy is located here, and its training ship, the State of Maine, is docked at the town wharf. The local professional theater group, ☛ Cold Comfort Productions, performs four nights a week. The Downeast Chamber Music School also summers in Castine. Sometimes on a Sunday afternoon you will find them performing on the inn's porch. The innkeepers and Bilbo Baggins, the inn cat, will really make your stay here a pleasant one.

How to get there: Take I–95 from Portland to the "Coastal Region— Brunswick, Bath, Route 1" Exit. Follow Route 1 to Bucksport, and 2 miles beyond turn right onto Route 175. Take Route 175 to Route 166, which takes you into Castine.

✳

Trifles make an inn, but an inn is no trifle.

Clive Metcalf

Westways Country Inn
Center Lovell, Maine
04016

Innkeeper: Nancy Tripp
Address/Telephone: Route 5, Box 175; (207) 928–2663
Rooms: 7, plus 6 houses; 3 rooms and all houses with private bath.
Rates: $135 to $195, double occupancy, MAP. Package plans available.
Open: All year except April and November.
Facilities and activities: Full liquor license. Recreation building with bowl-
ing, Ping-Pong, pool, card room, lending library. Private beach and
marina on Kezar Lake, swimming, boating, sailing, tennis. Nearby:
canoeing, cross-country and downhill skiing, golf.

Westways was built in the 1920s as the executive retreat of
the Diamond Match Company. It is a look into the past that is a
pure delight.

The living room overlooking Kezar Lake is large, with a huge
stone fireplace and comfortable couches and chairs. On cool nights
in winter your dinner is served in here on glorious ☛ Spode
china. The appetizers might be quiche or stuffed mushrooms. The
soup may be stracciatella. Your salad is served with homemade
dressings, and the entrees consist of two nightly choices. One day
I was there one of the choices was lobster. But your choice may be
veal Cordon Bleu or fresh red snapper, prime ribs, or steak. Great,

creative desserts and coffees come next. This is indeed the way to live.

All of the rooms are gracious, most overlook the lake, and all have ☛ libraries. The president of Diamond Match was quite a reader, and his collection is here for you to enjoy. By the way, all of the rooms are different; some have wicker headboards and some have four-poster beds. There is a body shower in the bath on the first floor that is unbelievable. It is certainly one of a kind.

The houses are scattered over 120 acres of property. Some have a view of the lake. During the summer they are rented on a weekly basis, but in off-season they can be rented for a minimum of two nights. They range in size from three bedrooms up to a seven-bedroom, three-bathroom house. Families like to come here for reunions. I can see why.

The boathouse overlooks the lake and is comfortable for reading or just idle meditation. ☛ The view of the White Mountains from here is fantastic. There are over one hundred acres in all that go with the inn, plus a sandy beach and a picnic area where a seaplane once was kept.

How to get there: Coming either way on Route 302 turn north at Fryeburg, Maine, onto Route 5. Fourteen miles north the lake will appear on your left, and the inn's entrance (marked with a sign) is on your left about 6 miles up the lake.

The Pilgrim's Inn
Deer Isle, Maine
04627

Innkeepers: Jean and Dud Hendrick
Address/Telephone: Main Street; (207) 348–6615
Rooms: 13, plus 1 cottage; 9 with private bath.
Rates: $65 to $75, per person, double occupancy, MAP. Cottage $120, EP;
$180, MAP. No credit cards.
Open: Mid-May through October.
Facilities and activities: Bar, lounge. Nearby: bicycles, sailboats for charter,
swimming. Golf or tennis at the island country club as their guest.

In 1793 Ignatius Haskell built this lovely house, following the
specifications of his wife who demanded the luxuries of city living
on their country estate. He had his own sawmill nearby and built
the house out of northern pine. Today you are welcomed to this
rambling inn by the glowing hearths of its many fireplaces.

The inn is heated by wood stoves, and each room has one.
The beds are very comfortable. All of the rooms are different and
have a view of the pond or Northwest Harbor. The third floor has
marvelous views and a great room. Actually, there are five rooms
on the third floor, but one is huge.

The inn has all the right touches, such as tons of 🐦 books, a
huge fireplace, and soft well-worn wood floors and walls in the

common rooms and taproom. There is a small service bar and the
☛ honor system is in effect. If it's before the six o'clock cocktail
hour, you know to leave your tab on the bar.

Crisp linens and flowers are on the tables of the candlelit
dining room, which once was a barn. It just glows. Dinner may be
poached salmon or tenderloin of beef, done many ways. One night
is lobster night. There is a different special every night of the week.
Soups are interesting—Billi-bi, cream of celery, and more, accompanied by a different bread each night. All the baking is done right
here. A full breakfast is served. It is a ☛ sumptuous buffet, with
baskets of muffins, homemade granola, meats and cheeses, mel-
ons, and fruit. You are also offered eggs. You may never want to
leave.

The inn dog is Mr. Beaudandy, and he sure is a dandy.

How to get there: From Route 1 turn right after Bucksport onto Route 15,
which goes directly to Deer Isle. In the village turn right on Main Street.
The inn is on your left.

✱

A well-run inn and a man on a diet
go together about as well as
an arsonist and a bale of hay.

olive Metcalf

Lincoln House Country Inn
Dennysville, Maine
04628

Innkeepers: Mary Carol and Gerald Haggerty
Address/Telephone: Dennysville; (207) 726–3953
Rooms: 10, in 2 buildings; 4 with private bath, 2 with wood stove, 2 with fireplace.
Open: All year.
Rates: $60 to $70, per person, double occupancy, MAP.
Facilities and activities: Dinner by reservation. Full license. Swimming, fishing, boating on river. Nearby: skiing.

When you walk in the side door of the inn, you are in what once was the summer kitchen and now is a library full of books with a huge fireplace hung with old cooking equipment and one Japanese wok. On through Mary Carol's kitchen you find two delightful dining rooms. Beyond is a large living room with a baby grand piano. This is an inn where you can feel totally at home.

Mary Carol's kitchen really turns out exceptional food, including the best 🐑 lamb I have ever had. It was prepared quite differently, and only Mary Carol can tell you how. Her breakfast muffins almost outdo her lamb.

The inn is a handsome, yellow, foursquare Georgian Colonial perched above the Denny River, one of the few rivers where you can find the Atlantic salmon. John Audubon once stayed here and was so impressed he named the "Lincoln Sparrow" for his hosts. The inn was built by an ancestor of President Lincoln in 1787.

Jerry is a master restorer and perfectionist. It shows all over the inn. The woodshed, a village pub, has 🖛 a bar that Jerry carved from a 4,000-pound elm trunk with a bear's head carved at one end. The woodshed has fun on Thursday nights in the winter. It is "open mike" time and local amateurs come and do their thing. On Sundays it is international dart shoots with neighboring Canada. The U.S. seems to always win; whether this is their ability or Jerry's liberal beers, we do not know.

You will love this inn, but it is a long way off, so do make reservations ahead.

How to get there: Route 1 goes right by Dennysville. Driving up take the second sign into Dennysville, just after you have crossed the Denny River. Turn left and you will find the inn almost immediately on your right.

⊂ৡৡ

E: *Bald eagles and osprey are seen here, and families of seals swim in the river. It is a long way up here but worth every mile.*

Harraseeket Inn
Freeport, Maine
04032

Innkeepers: Nancy and Paul Gray
Address/Telephone: 162 Main Street; (207) 865–9377, (800) 342–6423
Rooms: 47, plus 7 suites; all with private bath, TV, phone, wheelchair
  accessibility, and some with Jacuzzi, fireplace, wood stove, wet bar.
Rates: $85 to $225, double occupancy, EPB. Special packages available.
Open: All year.
Facilities and activities: Lunch, high tea, dinner. Tavern, full liquor license,
  function rooms. No smoking in the dining room. Nearby: shopping,
  nature walks, fishing, boating.

The inn is named for the Harraseeket River, which runs
through the town and into Casco Bay. It was built in 1850 and is
Greek Revival in style. Everything about it is elegant, which is not
a surprise, as its sister inn is the very elegant Inn at Mystic in
Mystic, Connecticut.

Freeport has long been known for L.L. Bean and a ton of
other famous outlet stores, all of which are just a 🐾 short walk
from the inn. Oh my. If shopping is not your thing, however,
Casco Bay and South Freeport Harbor are nearby, where you can
rent a boat and go sailing or fishing. Nature lovers will be in
heaven at the Audubon Sanctuary and Wolfneck Park.

The rooms and suites are grand. There are canopied beds, antiques, telephones, cable televisions, and even ☞ modems for personal computers. Twenty-four rooms have a Jacuzzi, two have a steam bath, sixteen have a fireplace, and one has a wood stove. Whatever you're looking for, it's all here. You can even arrange a meeting or business conference at the inn, as there are function rooms that overlook the terrace.

Your day begins with a superlative breakfast buffet. Early birds can have coffee at six o'clock. It's nice to find inns that serve lunch. I had crepes filled with lobster Madeira and my friend had the chicken stir-fry. The lunch menu is extensive, but the dinner menu is even more so. There are appetizers, soups, salads, and lots of entrees. Like The Inn at Mystic, they have Tableside Classics, which are prepared and carved at your table. You can have a whole chicken, roast rack of baby lamb, chateaubriand, and various fruits of the sea. ☞ They even have two-tailed lobster, honest. The maple syrup–braised loin of pork is just one of the feasts from the land. Desserts—well, by now you can imagine. Each one is better than the last. The chocolate fondue is an orgy. The Broad Arrow Tavern has its own lighter menu of burgers, pastas, lobster salad, sandwiches, and even a bucket of steamed clams. I could go on and on.

How to get there: Take I–95 north to Exit 20 to Freeport. The inn is on Main Street.

🌿

E: *This whole inn is just grand. The innkeepers are native to Maine, and though this is a large inn, it has not lost its charm.*

olive Metcalf

The Oxford House Inn
Fryeburg, Maine
04037

Innkeepers: John and Phyllis Morris
Address/Telephone: Route 302; (207) 935–3442
Rooms: 5; 3 with private bath.
Rates: $65 to $85, double occupancy, EPB.
Open: All year.
Facilities and activities: Lunch summer and fall, dinner, Sunday brunch, lounge with a full license. Nearby: canoeing, swimming, fishing, antiquing.

John and Phyllis have a lot of innkeeping experience and know just how to make an inn inviting and comfortable. There's one thing for sure: They have put together a ☛ marvelous brochure. It says this is the way The Oxford House might have appeared back in 1923, looking through the windows of a spanking new Jordan motor car.

The rooms are charming and very restful. All of them are named after the names of rooms on the original blueprints. Perhaps you'll sleep in the Sewing Room. The tub in one shared bathroom is the largest I've ever seen. Care for a swim?

At dinnertime you'll delight as I did in the outstanding and creative dishes offered on the menu. For example, Turkey Waldorf is an entree you'll not find many places. It is medallions of turkey breast sautéed with apples and walnuts, then splashed with applejack and cream. Pork, pears, and port is another entree done in a rich port and ginger sauce. How about ☞ Canadian steak pie? This is an individual pie made of pieces of choice sirloin and mushrooms in a rich wine sauce. Very nice indeed. Three innovative steaks are also offered. House pâté of the day might be how you'd like to begin your meal. I think it's nice to find variations in pâtés. Or maybe ☞ Maine crab chowder will catch your eye. It's good and different. Needless to say, the desserts are all homemade.

On those cold Maine nights, the tavern is very inviting. It has a television, books, and a wood stove.

In warm weather the screened porch is used for dining. I really like porches, and this one is a beauty. You can sit here and look out at the beautiful surrounding mountains or the lovely gardens. Peace and quiet are at hand.

How to get there: The inn is on Route 302 in Fryeburg, 8 miles east of North Conway.

✒

*To eat merely to live
is a crime against man
for which the gibbet is
inadequate punishment.*

Olive Metcalf

The Domaine
Hancock, Maine
04640

Innkeeper: Nicole L. Purslow
Address/Telephone: Route 1; (207) 422-3395
Rooms: 7; all with private bath.
Rates: $160, double occupancy, MAP.
Open: May to end of November.
Facilities and activities: Bar, lounge. Nearby: boating, swimming, fishing.

How nice to find an *auberge Provençale* this far up in Maine. On
the first floor are the bar and lounge, and a grouping of wicker
furniture is around the wood stove. Nicole has one of the wine
coolers and servers that are so handy, and someday I'm going to
have a small one like it in my home. The French provincial dining
room has crisp linens, gleaming copper, and fresh flowers.

Now for the best part, and that is the food. Nicole, a graduate
of the Cordon Bleu school of cooking in Paris, runs one of the
finest French restaurants in the East. It was started in 1946 by her
mother, who died in 1976. Over the years, the inn has received
accolades from many publications. The most important accolade of
all comes from the many returning guests.

Nicole's 🖙 exquisite entrees and appetizers change with the
seasons. Pâté de foie maison or *saumon fumé d'ecosse* are just two of

the appetizers. Move on to coquilles St. Jacques Provençale, veal a la crème, or steak bordelaise. There is no way I can say enough about her food. It is divine. The full breakfast can be had in the dining room, at your ☞ own table in your room, or on the decks overlooking the pines and gardens. The inn's honey from its own hives or homemade jams go on croissants, muffins, or scones. They come with ☞ French cafe au lait or pots of tea, making you feel you are in a true European auberge.

Each room has its own character. They are named for herbs. They all have a library and several have private porches.

There are many things to do in this area, including roaming about on the inn's fifty-five acres, and Nicole will be glad to help you plan your day.

How to get there: The inn is about 9 miles above Ellsworth on Route 1.

✱

E: *In the huge fireplace in the dining room are a rotisserie and a grill Nicole had made in France. On cool evenings she cooks here. Very nice touch!*

Olive Metcalf

The Kennebunk Inn
Kennebunk, Maine
04043

Innkeepers: Arthur and Angela LeBlanc
Address/Telephone: 45 Main Street; (207) 985–3351
Rooms: 34, plus 2 suites; 29 with private bath, all with air conditioning.
Rates: Off-season, $45 to $125; in-season, $65 to $125; double occupancy,
    EP.
Open: All year except Christmas Day.
Facilities and activities: Full breakfast June to October; continental breakfast
    off-season. Lunch and dinner every day except Sunday. Sunday
    brunch October through June, and Sunday dinner in off-season. Bar,
    lounge. Nearby: fishing, swimming.

The inn is located right smack on Route 1 in the heart of town,
convenient to everything. Even the beaches are very close at hand.

Built in 1799, the inn was in total disrepair when the
LeBlancs bought it. With a tremendous amount of work and
attention to detail, they have restored the inn to its current state of
being a proper in-town country inn.

All of the beds have new mattresses and all bedrooms are
air-conditioned. A modern touch like air conditioning in an old
inn is great. There are some brass headboards, and if I know
Angela, there will be more. Now Angela has put ☞ hair dryers in

80

all the bathrooms. Throughout the inn the wallpapers are French imports, and they are beautiful.

The upstairs foyer is a nice spot to gather. There are couches and chairs, television, puzzles, games, and books. Family photographs hang on the walls here, and it is quite a family. When you are at the inn, do read the back of the menu. It tells you all about the family.

The dining room has colorful tablecloths, and the food served here is impeccable. For breakfast, among many dishes, is Omar Pacha, baked eggs on sautéed onions and topped with cheese. Another dish is King Neptune's Delight, two fresh eggs enthroned on crab meat on English muffins and crowned with hollandaise sauce. There are also croissants and scones baked daily. Luncheon is equally interesting, with burgers, soups, salads, and some hot specials.

It's really nice of this inn to prepare some dinner dishes that are ☞ low in calories and cholesterol; they are marked with a red heart on the menu. Of course, if you're able to eat whatever you want, there are lots of choices for you, too. Angela's veal is sautéed veal with prosciutto, crowned with Reggiano cheese. King Arthur's tournedos are topped with lobster, shrimp, scallops, and shiitake mushrooms in a light brandy cream. Alyse's lobster in Drambuie cream is heavenly, as is the inn's seafood pie. There are good beef and chicken selections and great pastas. Be sure to order a piece of ☞ Angela's apple-cranberry pie, the grand prize winner in *Yankee* magazine's apple pie competition. Taste it and you'll know why it won. Arthur and Angela also have a wonderful restaurant on the water called Seascape's. It is at Cape Porpoise in Kennebunkport.

How to get there: Take Exit 3 from I–95 (the Maine Turnpike) to Kennebunk. The inn is at 45 Main Street.

✸

E: *Angela says they have the best chowder in New England. Period!*

olive Metcalf

The Captain Jefferds Inn
Kennebunkport, Maine
04046

Innkeeper: Warren Fitzsimmons
Address/Telephone: P.O. Box 691; (207) 967–2311
Rooms: 12, plus 3 suites; all with private bath.
Rates: $85 to $110, double occupancy; $125 to $135, suites; EPB. No
    credit cards.
Open: All year except January through March and November.
Facilities and activites: Full breakfast only meal served. BYOB.

The inn was built in 1804. Its style is Federal, complete with
a magnificent Federal fence. It is absolutely fabulous throughout.
To go along with all of this are 🖝 two inn dogs whose names
absolutely convulse me. Jenny Millstone and Isabelle Necessary
were strays; I have never seen anything funnier than the two of
them. There are also a long-haired Maine coon called Tessie
Fitzharris and a white cat, Betty White.

Warren was in the antique business before he became innkeeper, and he furnished the inn from his stock, except for
mattresses and box springs. There's a spectacular 🖝 majolica
collection of more than 1,000 pieces. Cupboards overflow with
antique china and pottery. The mirror in the dining room is most
unusual; a landscape scene with overhanging trees is painted right

on it. An unusual étagère that is made of shells and holds boxes made of shells is a work of art. There is a captain's bridge stairwell, reminiscent of a sea captain's lookout post. It is all just beautiful, but it is not well suited to children under twelve.

The guest rooms are color coordinated. Laura Ashley wallpapers, the ☞ finest sheets that can be obtained, extra pillows, magnificent antique bedspreads, and the furniture is as you would expect, beautiful. White wicker on the porch, a Steinway grand piano in the living room, six fireplaces, a lovely sun porch, and a brick terrace all add to the exceptional ambience of the inn. The plants remind me of home; they are trees.

Breakfast is good and it is fun. It is served at a huge mahogany table. In warm weather it is served on the terrace. Warren cooks. If you stayed a week, your breakfast would be different every day. Blueberry crepes, French toast with Grand Marnier, New England flannel (corned beef hash with dropped eggs), Italian eggs, and it goes on and on.

The inn provides setups for your drinks. There are plenty of restaurants nearby for lunch and dinner.

How to get there: Take Exit 3 from the Maine Turnpike. Turn left on Route 35 south to Kennebunkport. At the traffic light, turn left. Go over the drawbridge. Look for the sign for Ocean Drive. Take it ⅓ mile to Arundel Wharf. The next left is Pearl Street, where the inn is located.

∽

E: *I think you can tell I sure do like it here.*

Captain Lord Mansion
Kennebunkport, Maine
04046

Innkeepers: Beverly Davis and Rick Lichfield
Address/Telephone: Ocean Avenue; (207) 967–3141
Rooms: 22, plus 1 suite; all with private bath, 17 with working fireplace.
Rates: $100 to $225, double occupancy, EPB.
Open: All year.
Facilities and activities: Breakfast only meal served. BYOB. Gift shop.
    Nearby: Perkins Cove and Rachel Carson Wildlife Refuge.

This is a truly grand inn. The mansion was built in 1812 and has had such good care that the front bedroom still has the wallpaper that dates from that year. Another room has wallpaper that dates back to 1880. Some of the original Lord furniture is in the house. For example, the ☛ handsome dining room table with carved feet and chairs belonged to Nathaniel Lord's grandson, Charles Clark, and is dated 1880. Throughout the inn are portraits of past owners in the Lord family.

A three-story suspended elliptical staircase, a hand-pulled fireplace that works, a gold vault, and double Indian shutters are but a few of the wonderful things to be found in the inn. There are fireplaces, oriental rugs, old pine wide-board floors, and claw-footed tables. It's almost a comfortable museum, which is not well suited to children under twelve. The innkeepers give 🖝 conducted tours a couple of times a week. Rick knows the history of the house and loves to tell it.

Eleven of the guest rooms in the inn have working fireplaces. There are fourteen in all throughout the inn. Most of the rooms have padded, deep window seats, a great place to relax and daydream. One of the beds is a four-poster 12 feet high. Rugs and wallpaper, thanks to Beverly's eye for decoration, are well coordinated, thirsty towels are abundant, and extra blankets and pillows help make your stay better than pleasant.

Breakfast is the only meal served in the inn, but what a meal! It is family style. Two long tables in the kitchen are set with Wedgwood blue. There are two stoves in here side by side, a new one and an old coal one about a hundred years old. The breakfast bell is a hundred-year-old music box. You'll start your day with good baked food like rhubarb nut bread, French breakfast puffs, pineapple nut upside-down muffins, oat and jam muffins, or strawberry bread. The recipes are available in the lovely gift shop, so now I can bake some of these yummies at home. In addition you'll have eggs, cereal, and fruit—all this, plus an exquisite mansion, good staff, and great innkeepers.

The Captain's Hideaway is a secluded cottage three houses from the inn. The Garden Room has a private entrance from a brick patio, a working fireplace, a nice sitting area, a queen-sized four-poster bed, cable television, whirlpool tub, and private phone. The Captain's Room, which is really a suite, has a tremendous private bathroom with a 🖝 two-person whirlpool tub, large shower, and a fireplace. A queen-sized canopy bed, fireplace, and sitting area are in the bedroom. A full gourmet breakfast is served to Captain's Hideaway guests in the lovely parlor, by candlelight.

This is a bring-your-own-bottle inn, and from the scenic cupola on its top to the parlors on the first floor, you will find many great places to enjoy a drink.

How to get there: From I–95 take Exit 3 to Kennebunk. Turn left on Route 35 and drive through Kennebunk to Kennebunkport. Turn left at the traffic light at the Sunoco station. Go over drawbridge and take first right onto Ocean Avenue. Go ³⁄₁₀ mile and turn left at the mansion. Park behind the building and take the brick walkway to guest entrance.

The Kennebunkport Inn
Kennebunkport, Maine
04046

Innkeepers: Rick and Martha Griffin
Address/Telephone: Dock Square (mailing address: P.O. Box 111); (207) 967–2621
Rooms: 34; all with private bath and TV, some with air conditioning.
Rates: $69 to $145, double occupancy, EP.
Open: All year.
Facilities and activities: Breakfast buffet, dinner every night in summer and six nights a week rest of year. Bar, lounge, pool. Nearby: beaches, boating, fishing, tennis, golf, shopping.

The Kennebunkport Inn was built in the late 1890s by Burleigh S. Thompson, a wealthy coffee and tea merchant. It was magnificent then, and it still is. It was turned into an inn in 1926, various changes were made, and today it is noted for its charm, warmth, and grace.

☛ Born to shop? Well, you are right in the heart of all the fine shops of Kennebunkport—antiques, arts and crafts, clothing, and lots more. One year I ordered some cut lampshades from one of the shops, and they arrived at my home in fine shape. The town also offers fine beaches, tennis, fishing, boating, golf, theaters, and much more. The inn has a nice swimming pool.

The inn is elegant, a true nineteenth-century mansion. The River House, built in the 1930s as an annex to the inn, is a lovely place to be, but then so are all of the rooms in the inn. Every room has a color television and lots of comfort, and the inn rooms are air-conditioned. Coming back to your room after shopping or sightseeing in busy Kennebunkport is a joy.

The piano bar–lounge is open Wednesday through Sunday in the summer and Friday and Saturday in the spring and fall. It has a neat fireplace and a friendly bartender.

Dinner is elegantly served by candlelight in two dining rooms on tables covered with pink and white napery. It is a meal you will truly enjoy. Ask Rick to recommend some wine to complement your dinner. ☛ He is a connoisseur of fine wines and has developed an excellent wine list. The breakfast buffet has lots of goodies—melon, cereal, muffins, and much more. Martha and Rick are very good innkeepers. They work at it and it shows.

How to get there: Take Exit 3 from the Maine Turnpike. Turn left on Route 35 and go south to Kennebunkport. At the traffic light, turn left, go over the bridge, and the inn is ahead on the left.

❧

The cheers of millions are for politicians,
while the quiet appreciation of a well-cooked
chop is but for a few.

Old Fort Inn
Kennebunkport, Maine
04046

Innkeepers: David and Sheila Aldrich
Address/Telephone: P.O. Box M; (207) 967–5353, (800) 828–3678, FAX
  (207) 967–4547
Rooms: 16, plus 2 suites; all with private bath, TV, wet bar, and 4 with
  Jacuzzi.
Rates: $90 to $225, double occupancy, continental breakfast buffet.
Open: Mid-April to mid-December.
Facilities and activities: Breakfast only meal served. BYOB. Swimming pool,
  tennis, antiques shop. Nearby: bikes for rent, ocean.

  When you enter the Old Fort Inn, you are in an excellent
antique shop. Next you are in a huge living room that overlooks
the swimming pool. The pool has ☞ a solar cover that enables the
inn to stretch its swimming season a bit. I know it works because
I have one on my pool. This is a lovely, comfortable living room
with a fireplace, a super spot to curl up and read a book.
  The rooms are charming. The beds are lovely canopied or
four-poster ones with good, comfortable mattresses. The towels
are color coordinated, which I always love. There is a nice library
in the foyer. One of the suites has a sitting room, two bedrooms,
and two bathrooms. There is a television in each room, and four

rooms have Jacuzzis. To go with these modern touches are the inn cats Bogart and Samantha. And to go with the cats is the great inn child, Shana. She is some innkeeper. You will love her.

The breakfast buffet is super. You can pick and choose from all types of teas and juices, fresh fruit, baked breads, croissants, and ☛ sticky buns, which are fantastic.

The inn provides a ☛ laundry. Until you have been on the road a week or so, you do not know how convenient such a facility is. The inn also provides a place to shower and change if you are checking out and still want to swim in the pool or the ocean that is only one block away.

The Carriage House has very interesting shadow boxes displaying nineteenth-century clothing. The living room over here is so comfortable and quiet. On the other hand, in the main house's living room you must meet Walter, who "plays" the piano.

How to get there: Take I–95 to Exit 3. Turn left on Route 35 for 5½ miles. Go left at the traffic light at the Sunoco station and proceed ⅓ mile to Ocean Avenue. Go ⁹⁄₁₀ mile to Colony Hotel, then turn left and follow the signs to the inn (about ½ mile).

White Barn Inn
Kennebunkport, Maine
04046

Innkeeper: Laurie J. Bongiorno
Address/Telephone: Beach Street (mailing address: RR 3, Box 387); (207) 967–2321
Rooms: 18, plus 7 suites; all with private bath and some with phone, TV, Jacuzzi, kitchen.
Rates: $110 to $235, double occupancy, continental breakfast and tea. Packages available.
Open: All year.
Facilities and activities: Dinner, Sunday brunch, full license. Meeting room, bicycles. Nearby: beach, shops, galleries, golf, tennis.

A pre–Civil War farmhouse and its signature white barn have been transformed into this lovely inn, which is just a short walk from the beach and the charming village of Kennebunkport with its colorful shops, galleries, and boutiques. When you consider the inn's exquisite food and its warmth and graciousness, it comes as no surprise that it is the only Maine member inn of 🖝 *Relais et Châteaux* and one of just twenty in the United States.

A feeling of hospitality is evident throughout the inn. When you enter your room, you find a basket of fruit, flowers, luxurious toiletries, and a robe for you to wear. At night your bed is turned down and a pillow treat is left.

The rooms in the inn itself are attractively decorated with antiques, armoires, and brass and iron beds in a variety of sizes. The Gate House's rooms are large, with cathedral ceilings, ceiling fans, dressing areas, queen-sized beds, and wing chairs. May's Annex has seven suites with fully equipped kitchens, king-sized beds, sleep sofas, and color televisions.

The sun room is the boardroom, seating up to fourteen people; it's a perfect, sunny spot for small meetings, retreats, and reunions. The breakfast room is large and cheerfully decorated with flower arrangements. The main dining room is the barn; a lovely lounge and piano bar are here, too. ☛ Candlelight, linens, and soft music are nice touches. The menu changes seasonally.

When I think about the food, I want to go back for more. The appetizers are divine. Bacon-wrapped sea scallops come in a maple mustard cream. A vegetable terrine is served with a sweet pepper sauce. One of the soups is chilled cream of peach with a blueberry swirl. A sorbet is brought to you before the main course. The Dijon-marinated grilled double lamb chops with a raspberry-mint demi-glace were superb. Maine lobster is served in a variety of ways, and there is always the catch of the day. The desserts are worth going off your diet for.

After dinner, go relax in the living room with a glass of port or brandy, a book from the inn's well-filled bookshelves, or one of the many current magazines. Or you could be ambitious and go for a ride along the beach on one of the inn's bicycles. Just do go and enjoy.

How to get there: From the Maine Turnpike, take Exit 3 to Kennebunk. Follow Route 35 south 6 miles to Kennebunkport, then continue through the traffic light onto Beach Street. The inn is in ¼ mile on the right.

The Inn on Winter's Hill
Kingfield, Maine
04947

Innkeepers: Richard and Diane Winnick and Carolyn Rainaud
Address/Telephone: RR 1, Box 1272; (207) 265–5421, (800) 233–9687
Rooms: 34, in 2 buildings; all with private bath, phone, cable TV.
Rates: $75 to $139, double occupancy, EP.
Open: All year.
Facilities and activities: Full breakfast summer only; pastry and coffee, rest
   of year. Lunch, dinner, Sunday brunch. Dinner for public Thursday
   through Saturday. Bar, lounge, meeting and banquet facilities. Hot
   tub, swimming pool, tennis, cross-country skiing, ice skating. Nearby:
   downhill skiing, hunting, fishing, hiking, golf, white-water rafting,
   canoeing, Stanley Steamer Museum.

   The Inn on Winter's Hill, located in the midst of the western
Maine's Bigelow, Sugarloaf, and Saddleback mountains, sits on
top of a six-acre hill on the edge of town. This Neo-Georgian
manor house was designed by the Stanley (steam car) brothers
and built at the turn of the century for Amos Greene Winter as a
present for his wife, Julia. It is listed on the National Register of
Historic Places. Today it is owned by a brother and sister who are
doing a great job as innkeepers, following a longtime tradition of
casual elegance and warm hospitality.

Accommodations are varied and range from the turn-of-the-century luxury rooms in the inn to the modern rooms in the restored barn. Every one is very comfortable, with nice bathrooms, wonderful views, cable television, and telephone.

Julia's Restaurant is elegant and the food served here is excellent. The night I was here I had crackers and garlic cheese spread and pineapple wrapped in bacon for appetizers. My garden salad with house dressing was followed by a light sorbet and then ☞ Sole Baskets, which were superb. The other entrees were turkey pot pie, chicken cordon bleu, and Wellington. Desserts are grand. Sunday brunch is extensive. Next time I'm here, I'll have spinach pie for brunch, or would I prefer crepes Benedict? Oh, it's all so good, it's hard to choose.

The No-Name Lounge has its own menu and a fifties' vintage jukebox, fish tank, and Richard's old Lionel train on a ledge above the lovely bar. In the more formal lounge area is an old piano, which came by oxcart from Boston for Julia Winter. It took two and a half months to arrive.

Spring, summer, fall, or winter, there is so much to do up here. Winter brings cross-country skiing from the door and ☞ ice skating on the lighted outdoor rink. And remember, downhill skiing at Sugarloaf is minutes away. Hunting, fishing, canoeing, and hiking along the Appalachian Trail welcome outdoors people in the other seasons.

How to get there: Kingfield is halfway between Boston and Quebec City, and the Great Lakes area and the Maritimes. Take the Maine Turnpike to the Belgrade Lakes Exit in Augusta. Follow Highway 27 through Farmington to Kingfield. The inn is on a small hill near the center of town.

One Stanley Avenue
Kingfield, Maine
04947

Innkeeper: Dan Davis
Address/Telephone: Stanley Avenue; (207) 265–5541
Rooms: 6; 3 with private bath.
Rates: $50 to $60, double occupancy, EPB.
Open: All year.
Facilities and activities: Restaurant closed May and November. Dinner, bar.
   Nearby: skiing, ice skating, golfing, mountain climbing, white-water
   rafting.

The house at Three Stanley Avenue is a lovely Queen Anne
Victorian house, circa 1899. It is one of the three Stanley homes in
Kingfield. Here are the guest rooms for the inn, neat, clean, and
comfortable.

One Stanley Avenue, right next door, is the restaurant for the
inn. This house is in the National Register of Historic Places. In the
front hall is a 🖝 beautiful old oak reach-in refrigerator that holds
the inn's wine collection at perfect temperatures. There's a real
beauty of a piano, a Chickering square piano, refurbished and
ready to play. The small bar is also here.

The restaurant rates three stars in the *Mobil Travel Guide.* Dan
is a rather inventive chef, and there are three charming dining

rooms in which to enjoy Dan's food. ☛ Roast duck with rhubarb glaze. I never would have thought of this combination in a hundred years, but it is excellent. Pork is served with port wine and juniper-berry sauce. Another entree is Atlantic salmon with Dan's own sauce McIntire, named after his maternal heritage. Blackberry chicken sounds divine. I do love to cook with fruits.

The desserts are also magnificent. Rhubarb strudel, creme Celeste, Indian pudding a la mode, and many more. Come on up here and enjoy Dan's fine cooking.

Sugarloaf Mountain is close by, providing superb downhill and cross-country skiing. An 18-hole golf course is on the Sugarloaf property. White-water rafting is an exciting spring and summer sport, and many lakes surrounding the area provide other water sports. No matter what season you come, you'll always find an abundance of things to do.

How to get there: Take the Maine Turnpike to the Belgrade Lakes Exit in Augusta. Follow Route 27 through Farmington to Kingfield. In town, turn right on Route 16. Cross a bridge, and turn right to stay on Route 16. Stanley Avenue is the first street on the left.

*One good night in a country inn
can keep the mind in quiet order
for many moons.*

Olive Metcalf

The Lucerne Inn
Lucerne, Maine
04429

Innkeeper: Tom Spaulding
Address/Telephone: Route 1A; (207) 843–5123
Rooms: 25; all with private bath, TV, phone, air conditioning, and working fireplace.
Rates: $78 to $143, double occupancy, EPB.
Open: All year except Christmas Day.
Facilities and activities: Lunch July through October 15, dinner, Sunday brunch, bar and lounge. Swimming pool. Boating, fishing, and ice skating on Phillips Lake.

This is a rare beauty of an inn. You really could be in Europe. It sits on ten acres overlooking Phillips Lake. The lake is nice for boating, fishing (in winter it's ice fishing), or ice skating. The regal mountains make such a beautiful picture that you feel as if you're in Switzerland.

The Lucerne started as a farmhouse and stable. It became an inn in 1814. Today it's such a lovely inn that it has four diamonds from AAA. It deserves them.

All the delightful rooms have a 🖝 wood-burning fireplace, a color television, air conditioning, electric heat, a telephone, nice comfortable furniture, and a beautiful view. They also have private bathrooms in which you'll find a heated towel bar and a whirlpool bathtub. What more, you ask? Well, on every Saturday night of the year from eight o'clock to midnight, there is ☞ dance music from the 1940s played by the house band. And from October 16 through May 31, the inn has an ☞ escape-weekend package. You really should try it. Dinner on Friday and Saturday, dancing, breakfast, and Sunday brunch are part of the package. This is a really great getaway inn for adults, as it is not well suited to children.

The dining rooms are lovely with marvelous views. The food is glorious. There are nine different seafood entrees. One is seafood mornay—shrimp, scallops, and crabmeat served in the inn's special cheese sauce. Three poultry dishes are on the menu, including chicken teriyaki (they use their own special sauce). The beef entrees are spectacular. You'll also find lamb and veal. Veal piccata is a real favorite of mine. Or perhaps you'd like Surf and Turf?

This really is a beautiful part of the world. Bar Harbor and Acadia National Park are close by. The inn is just thirty-five minutes from Bangor International Airport, so what are you waiting for?

How to get there: Take I–95 to Exit 45A, just south of Bangor. At the exit take I–395 to Route 1A east. In about ten minutes you will find the inn on your right. It is located on Route 1A, halfway between Bangor and Ellsworth.

The Newcastle Inn
Newcastle, Maine
04553

Innkeepers: Ted and Chris Sprague
Address/Telephone: River Road; (207) 563–5685
Rooms: 15; all with private bath. No smoking inn.
Rates: $85 to $95, double occupancy, EPB. $120 to $140, double
  occupancy, MAP.
Open: All year.
Facilities and activities: Dinner six nights a week from July to October,
  Friday and Saturday rest of the year. Full license, gift shop. Nearby:
  swimming, cross-country skiing.

This is another no smoking inn. Good for the Spragues.
The inn is in the lovely Boothbay region, only 14 miles from
Boothbay Harbor and 16 miles to Pemaquid with its famous
lighthouse, fort, and sandy beach. This is a very interesting and
distinctive part of Maine.
The lovely porch, full of white wicker furniture, has a view of
the ☛ Damariscotta River. This is a nice place to while away the
time talking to other guests and making friends. The Stenciled
Room has some beauties on the floor. There is a television in here,
and once while I was visiting a lively bridge game was going on.
The living room with a fireplace has a very comfortable couch and

98

some very attractive chairs. The dining room is at the end of this room.

Breakfast is a joy. It's a four-course, gourmet one. Dinner is an elegant five-course affair. Just listen to this dinner menu: Scallops in puff pastry as the appetizer. Red-and-yellow-pepper bisque as the soup. Cream biscuits with garden salad. Rack of lamb with chive cream sauce, wild mushrooms, sautéed cherry tomatoes, and beet greens for the main course. The dessert makes me swoon: frozen white chocolate mousse with chocolate sauce and chocolate leaves. Good? You bet.

The inn dog, Destiny, is a love who is always happy to get a pat on the head. The rooms are clean and comfortable. White curtains, white spreads, extra pillows, and an electric fan if needed. The inn's facilities are not well suited to young children.

How to get there: When going north on Route 1, take the Newcastle exit to the right. Stay to your left; the inn is about 4 blocks down the road on River Road.

✻

E: *Christmas fruit bread, iced winter-cherry soup, individual baked pancakes with lemon juice and lemon zest, and sliced ham for breakfast! Wow!*

> *The glowing carriage lamp beside the door*
> *of a country inn when viewed through a cold rain*
> *erases the rigors of the day*
> *and promises a fine, fine evening.*

Olive Metcalf

The Bradley Inn
New Harbor, Maine
04544

Innkeepers: Louine and Ed Ek
Address/Telephone: HC 62, Box 361; (207) 677–2105
Rooms: 10; 1 with private bath.
Rates: $50 to $90, double occupancy, expanded continental breakfast.
Open: May through October.
Facilities and activities: Dinner daily mid-June to mid-October; rest of year, weekends only. Bar and lounge. Nearby: ocean, tennis, golf, boating trips.

Pemaquid, an Indian word meaning "long finger," is an appropriate name for the point of land that extends farther into the Atlantic Ocean than any other on the rugged Maine coast. This information is from the inn's brochure. What a wonderful ride it is out here; and once you arrive, the terrain is breathtaking. You're just a short walk from the ☞ Pemaquid Lighthouse or the beach with its lovely white sand. In the nearby seaside village of New Harbor, you can watch the working boats. Fort William Henry is close by. I drove around the point, parked my car, and watched the surf beating on the rocks below. It was quite a sight.

There are lovely flowers in front of the inn. Inside is an attractive living room with a fireplace and a baby grand. On weekends a 🖛 piano player is here. The cocktail lounge has a wood-burning stove. The private dining room can accommodate forty people; it's a nice place for a small conference. I really liked the porch off this room. The main dining room has French doors that open to the porch.

The tables in the main dining room have very pretty napery, pink on pink. The menu changes quite often. One of the appetizers is 🖛 carpaccio, which is thinly sliced inn-cured beef with herbed olive oil. You also could try the smoked sampler or the soup. Marinated Black Angus steak, rack of lamb, pork tenderloin, lobster, and salmon are just some of the entrees. Desserts are wonderful. The inn has a good wine list.

From the second- and third-floor rooms, you can see the water. This is Johns Bay. There are terrycloth robes in the rooms. They're so nice for the beach. Bring along your children, who will enjoy the inn and the inn poodles—an apricot one, Meg, and a chocolate one that's full of pepper, Mel.

How to get there: Take the Maine Turnpike to No. 9, Falmouth–Route 1 interchange. Take I–95 to Brunswick, 21 miles. Continue on Route 1 to Damariscotta, 27 miles, and from there follow Route 130, 14 miles to the inn.

olive Metcalf

Asticou Inn
Northeast Harbor, Maine
04662

Innkeeper: Dan Kimball
Address/Telephone: Northeast Harbor; (207) 276–3344, (207) 276–3702
Rooms: 36, plus 3 cottages and 3 suites; 34 with private bath.
Rates: $180 to $240, double occupancy, MAP.
Open: Mid-June to mid-September.
Facilities and activities: Lunch, Sunday brunch, bar, lounge. Nearby: boating, swimming, tennis, golf.

For over one hundred years, the inn has been situated at the head of Northeast Harbor. I do believe I could sit forever on the deck that overlooks the harbor, without ever getting tired of the view.

There are many sitting areas in the inn. All of them are very comfortable. The cocktail lounge has the same ☞ beautiful view that the deck has. It certainly is a nice place to gather and have some cheer. Another cozy area has a television and tables for backgammon or cards and other games.

Dinner is served in a lovely dining room with floral murals, crisp linens, and fresh flowers. The dinner menu changes every day. I love ☞ bacon-wrapped scallops and they were here. Chicken in a lemon cream sauce with mushrooms was different and good. ☛ Roast prime ribs of beef are always nice to find on a menu. Believe me, there is something for everyone on this menu. Chocolate Decadent Cake was scrumptious. And in the morning when you're ready for breakfast, you'll find anything you could possibly want available. There's nothing ho-hum about breakfast here.

Accommodations are varied. Some are large, and some are small, and all are comfortable and clean. The cottages are nice and private. Two of them have four rooms each.

During the day you can take a cruise from the town dock. A real beauty is the *Black Jack*, a friendship sloop. From Bar Harbor there are nature cruises, a cruise to Baker Island, and dinner and clambake cruises. These are a lot of fun.

How to get there: From Augusta follow Route 3 east through Ellsworth to the Trenton Bridge and Mount Desert Island. Continue on Route 3; just before you get to Northeast Harbor, turn left and the inn will be on your right.

✳

E: *A sumptuous roast beef and seafood buffet is offered on Thursday nights, followed by dancing. That's for me!*

Olive Metcalf

Gorges Grant
Ogunquit, Maine
03907

Innkeeper: Diane Hughes
Address/Telephone: Route 1; (207) 646–7003
Rooms: 36; all with private bath, TV, VCR, phone, refrigerator.
Rates: $110, double occupancy, EP.
Open: All year.
Facilities and activities: Full breakfast, dinner, bar and tavern. Conference
    center, heated swimming pool, indoor exercise pool, whirlpool baths,
    croquet. Nearby: ocean.

The brochure for Gorges Grant is really beautiful. It states,
"True luxury knows no season." They are so right. Everything
you could want is here. Each room has a television, telephone,
and a videocassette recorder with movie rentals at the front desk.
Local seasonal information is available on Channel 12 to let you
know what is going on in the area. Babysitting services are
provided. There are an exercise jet pool and hot tub inside,
and outdoors you'll find a heated pool and croquet lawn. What
else do you need? Well, the ocean is really close by, and the
Marginal Way is a beauty of a walk. In-season there are coastal
cruises and deep-sea fishing. Off-season are the sailboarding
competition, Christmas by the Sea, and the Christmas Prelude in
Kennebunkport.

The rooms are beautifully appointed and very complete. The walk-in dressing rooms are a joy.

All the food served in the dining room is just grand. For breakfast you can have any of the usual items, or you can have eggs Benedict, and that's nice. In addition, a breakfast special is offered every day. At dinner, one appetizer is a wonderful seafood cocktail—two large shrimp, a half lobster tail, and two oysters on the half-shell. Baked oysters with crab is another good appetizer. Nice salads come next, and then there are entrees like fresh Maine lobster, roast duckling, Cajun swordfish, and more. For dessert, there's a heavenly ☛ chocolate mousse cake, a fresh fruit tart . . . the list goes on and on. The wine list is impressive, but then the whole inn is.

How to get there: From Boston, take I–95 to the Yorks-Ogunquit exit. At the traffic light turn left, going north on Route 1. In about 15 minutes you will be in the center of Ogunquit. Continue through the center of town on Route 1, and in ³⁄₁₀ mile the inn will be on the left side.

olive Metcalf

The Old Village Inn
Ogunquit, Maine
03907

Innkeeper: Benjamin J. Lawlor
Address/Telephone: 30 Main Street; (207) 646–7088
Rooms: 1, plus 6 suites; all with private bath.
Rates: $65 to $85, double occupancy; $85, suite; continental breakfast.
Open: All year.
Facilities and activities: Dinner, bar, lounge. Dining room closed Sundays
and Mondays in winter. Nearby: fishing, swimming, boating, summer
theater.

Ben Lawlor has a good in-town inn that dates back to 1833.
A picture of the inn, done by John Falter, was on the cover of the
August 2, 1942 *Saturday Evening Post.* One of the beds has a
headboard made from four ladder-back chairs. Several rooms have
views of the Ogunquit River and ocean.

The suites are just great.

The Ogonquit Room is a perfect spot for a private party for up
to twenty persons. It has nice views. The Greenhouse is one of the
dining rooms, and, of course, you eat here surrounded by lovely
greenery. It has a great ocean view. The Bird & Bottle is another
one of the dining rooms. The full breakfast that you can order
includes many of the usual things, plus some extras like the inn's

☛ egg frittata or a fluffy parmesan, crab, or zucchini quiche served with home fries. Texas French toast is served with cream cheese and fruit and topped with brown sugar. Yum.

One dinner appetizer I love is ☛ fresh Maine crab au gratin. Add the special salad—Caesar, which I adore—and entrees like shrimp and scallop kebab or baked haddock with thyme walnut butter, or fresh Maine lobster. The chef's special of the evening always gets rave reviews.

Hard on the rock-bound coast of Maine, this inn has interests for all. The famous Ogunquit Playhouse is here, as is the newer off-Broadway repertory theater. There is plenty of fishing and swimming as well as two unusual walking trails.

The Marginal Way winds you along the spectacular bay and sea, and the Trolley Trail follows an abandoned line through the woods. I have never gone by, or even near, Ogunquit without a stop at this good inn.

How to get there: The inn is at 30 Main Street in the middle of Ogunquit. Main Street is Route 1.

olive Metcalf

The Rangeley Inn
Rangeley, Maine
04970

Innkeepers: Ed and Fay Carpenter
Address/Telephone: P.O. Box 398; (207) 864–3341, (800)–MOMENTS
Rooms: 36; all with private bath.
Rates: $52 to $73, single; $59 to $80, double occupancy; EP. MAP
available.
Open: All year.
Facilities and activities: Breakfast, dinner, bar, lounge, banquet facilities.
Dining room closed Easter to Memorial Day and Thanksgiving to
Christmas. Nearby: fishing, boating, swimming, hiking, tennis, golf-
ing, hunting, skiing, snowmobiling.

As their brochure says, "From out of the past. Try our
old-fashioned comfort and hospitality." The Carpenters really
mean it. The Rangeley Inn is in a lovely part of the world, 1,600
feet above the ocean. Two daughters help run the inn; Susan is the
chef and Janet tends the front desk and is headwaitress. Ed and
Fay are everywhere.

The bar and lounge area is quite large. Here, Ed and I enjoyed
a ☞ few games of pool. A nice wood-burning stove takes the chill
off the air and the bar stools are really comfortable. There also is a
nice television room, furnished with couches and lounge chairs
and decorated with plants that add a lot of charm.

Almost all the rooms are carpeted and all are 🖝 very clean. The baths have wonderful claw-footed tubs; some rooms have showers. A bath in an old bathtub is heavenly. You can be up to your neck in water; you can't do this in a modern tub. Five bathrooms have whirlpool tubs.

Susan is a fine chef. She prepared a chicken dish when I was here that was delicious. I topped it off with a favorite dessert, 🖝 strawberries dipped in chocolate, served with whipped cream flavored with Kahlúa.

Spring brings superb fishing for brook trout and landlocked salmon. Some brooks are open only to fly-fishing. Wildflowers and migrating birds are plentiful, so bring a camera. Summer is ideal for boating, swimming, hiking, tennis, and golf. Fall is spectacular fall foliage and hunting. Winter, of course, brings snow activities. Saddleback is nearby for downhill skiing, and cross-country skiing and snowmobiling are everywhere.

In any season of the year, Angel Falls, 20 miles away, is impressive and worth a visit. It is a 50-to-60-foot fall. Beautiful!

How to get there: From the Maine Turnpike, take Exit 12 at Auburn. Pick up Route 4 and follow it to Rangeley.

✱

E: *There is organ music Memorial Day to Thanksgiving, and a dance band is here in ski season.*

The Claremont
Southwest Harbor, Maine
04679

Innkeeper: John W. Madeira, Jr.
Address/Telephone: P.O. Box 137; (207) 244–5036
Rooms: 30, plus 3 suites and 11 cottages; all with private bath.
Rates: In-season, $130 to $155, double occupancy, MAP. Off-season, $60
   to $85, double occupancy, EP. No credit cards.
Open: May 15 to October 15.
Facilities and activities: Lunch July 15 through Labor Day, service bar, full
   license. Tennis court, dock and moorings, croquet courts, badminton,
   bicycles, rowboats, library. Nearby: three golf courses, sailing, fresh-
   water swimming, summer theater, Acadia National Park.

The Claremont has been a landmark on the shores of Somes
Sound, the famous fjord of beautiful Mount Desert Island, for
more than a century. It was entered in the National Register of
Historic Places in 1978. It has known only three owners in its
lifetime. The current owner is Mrs. Allen McCue.

There is so much to do and see up here. Every year there is a
croquet tournament. The Claremont Croquet Classic has
gained wide recognition as the home of nine-wicket croquet, one
of America's few truly amateur sports. You can sit in a cozy chair
at the bay window in one of the upstairs suites and watch this
event in sheer comfort.

The library–game room has a nice fireplace. There are a lot of places here to sit down and just relax. Most activities center around the waterfront, where a dock, float, and deep-water moorings are available for guests. The boathouse is nice for lunch and pre-dinner cocktails.

The dining room, done in pink and white napery, offers marvelous ☛ views of the mountains of Acadia and Somes Sound. The joy you'll get from the views will be well matched by your pleasure in the excellent food. Iced Maine crabmeat cocktail caught my eye, and so did the seafood crepes—lobster, scallops, crabmeat, and whitefish in an herbed crepe. Baked chicken champagne was another winner. Of course, the king of them all, boiled Maine lobster, is served here.

How to get there: Take the Maine Turnpike to Augusta, Exit 15, at Route 3. Follow Route 3 east through Ellsworth to the Trenton Bridge and Mount Desert Island. Once over the bridge, take Route 102 to Southwest Harbor and follow signs to The Claremont.

❧

Having had an excellent meal and a lovely evening,
I tucked myself in bed knowing I had sinned
but it did not seem to matter.

Olive Metcalf

The East Wind Inn
Tenants Harbor, Maine
04860

Innkeepers: Tim Watts and Ginny Wheeler
Address/Telephone: P.O. Box 149; (207) 372–8800
Rooms: 26, plus 3 suites and 1 apartment, in 2 buildings; 16 with private bath, all with phone.
Rates: $50 to $140, double occupancy, EP.
Open: All year.
Facilities and activities: Breakfast, lunch, dinner. Lounge with full liquor license, meeting room, deep-water anchorage for boats, sailboat charter. Nearby: golf, tennis, swimming, cross-country skiing.

The inn was built in 1890 and stood vacant for twenty years. Tim, a native of the town, watched the old house deteriorate and dreamed of restoring it so others could share the charm of "the country of the pointed firs." He's been able to do just that.

Today you can sit on the ☛ wraparound porch of the inn and enjoy the view. Tenants Harbor should be on a postcard, it's so beautiful. The inn is within walking distance of the village, where you will find a library, shops, post office, and churches.

The Meeting House is so nice for a relaxed conference or seminar. The guest rooms are very clean. Some have oak bureaus and Victorian side chairs, while others have brass beds. Almost all the rooms have good views of the harbor.

The lunch I had here was memorable because the view and the food were so terrific. My lobster salad plate was loaded with this king of fish. The chef's salad is also very good served with ☛ raspberry vinaigrette dressing. Dinner has marvelous offerings from the sea. One I really liked was New England crab and shrimp casserole—native shrimp and crabmeat baked in a mild white sauce and lightly breaded. Desserts—of course they are excellent.

The inn is open all year, so winter sports enthusiasts will find lots of snow for cross-country skiing. The Camden Snow Bowl is only a short drive away. ☛ The ketch *Izzy* sails twice a day from the pier at The East Wind. These are three-hour cruises on a 33-foot ketch with comfortable accommodations for up to six persons. The captain really knows these waters and can tell you all you want to know. Go and enjoy.

How to get there: From Route 1, just east of Thomaston, take Route 131 south for 9.5 miles to Tenants Harbor. Turn left at the post office and continue straight to the inn.

The Waterford Inne
Waterford, Maine
04088

Innkeepers: Barbara and Rosalie Vanderzanden
Address/Telephone: P.O. Box 149; (207) 583–4037
Rooms: 10; 7 with private bath.
Rates: $55 to $85, double occupancy, EP. No credit cards.
Open: May 1 through February 28.
Facilities and activities: Breakfast, dinner. BYOB. Nearby: hiking, hunting, fishing, swimming, bird watching, skiing.

This is a beautiful part of the world. It is secluded, quiet, and restful. The inn offers a fireplace in the parlor and a library full of books and good music for your relaxation. And when the weather is warm, you can while away your days in the rockers on the porch.

But if you're looking for activity, The Waterford Inne can offer that, too. The area provides hiking, hunting, fishing in the summer and winter, downhill and cross-country skiing, swimming, and bird watching.

This is a first for me, a mother and daughter who are the innkeepers. They bought the inn in 1978 and have done a masterful job of restoring and renovating it. There are antiques in all the rooms, nice wallpapers, and some stenciling. For your comfort there are electric blankets in the winter, and for your visual pleasure ☛ there are fresh flowers in the summer.

Rosalie, the mother, does the cooking. The dinner is a fixed price with one entree served each evening. She is a very good and creative chef. All baking is done right here and all the vegetables are grown in the inn's garden. Barbara does the serving, and you may be seated at a table for four in the ☛ attractive dining room with a fireplace or in a secluded corner just for two.

Tansey and Teasel are the two inn cats lucky enough to live in this beautiful part of the world.

How to get there: From Norway, Maine, take Route 118 west for 8 miles to Route 37. Turn left and go ½ mile to Springer's General Store. Take an immediate right up the hill. The inn is in about ½ mile.

❀

The crackle of an inn's hearth
can melt the chilliest of minds and bodies.

olive Metcalf

The Lawnmeer Inn
West Boothbay Harbor, Maine
04575

Innkeepers: Sylvia and Frank Kelly; Jim and Lee Metzger
Address/Telephone: P.O. Box 505; (207) 633–2544, (800) 633–7645
Rooms: 32; all with private bath, some with TV.
Rates: $55 to $110, double occupancy, EP.
Open: Mid-May to mid-October.
Facilities and activities: Full breakfast, dinner, Sunday brunch. Bar, lounge,
     croquet, badminton, lawn games, boat dock. Nearby: Boothbay
     Harbor activities, boat tours, aquarium, theater.

The inn is nicely located on the island of Southport in the
Boothbay Harbor region. As you sit on its porch, you are looking
at Townsend Gut and watching the masts of the moored sailboats
sway with the winds and tides.

The accommodations range from modern rooms in a new
wing to comfortable inn suites and rooms. Some have a television
and ☛ a sun deck overlooking the water. The views are really
lovely and tranquil.

There are delightful sitting areas. One has a fireplace to ward
off early spring or fall chills. Children enjoy the common room
that's full of games and a television—even children's videos. They
also like playing with Deacon, the inn dog. The bar and lounge add

to the inn's charm. The two dining rooms are attractive with their nice napery and tall ladder-back chairs. One has a fireplace.

A breakfast of hot oatmeal is nice, and the inn offers a full breakfast, too. I had orange French toast made with a hint of Triple Sec. It was very good. The brunch menu has quiches, crepes, eggs prepared many ways, waffles, and more.

For dinner, would you believe lobster prepared 🖝 five different ways? Even fried! There are baked, broiled, and fried seafood selections and plenty of them. The 🖝 native sea scallops are grand. Of course there are meat and chicken dishes for the landlubbers. Lawnmeer's Chicken Cordon Bleu with a sharp cheese sauce is a winner. So is the sautéed veal in wine and mushroom sauce. If you're worried about your health or weight, there is a light dinner menu offering steamed Maine shrimp, grilled chicken in fruit salsa, poached salmon, warm chicken salad, and more.

The inn has been operating since 1898. It is the oldest continually operated inn in the Boothbay area. Come see the puffins, craggy cliffs, coon cats, and lighthouses. It's all yours to enjoy.

How to get there: Take Exit 22 from I–95 onto Route 1. Just north of Wiscasset, turn on Route 27 south. Go through Boothbay Harbor onto the island of Southport. The inn is on Route 27, ³⁄₁₀ mile from the Southport Bridge.

❧

E: *The windjammers arrive every July, and I was lucky enough to be here then. What a treat.*

Olive Metcalf

The Squire Tarbox Inn
Wiscasset, Maine
04578

Innkeepers: Karen and Bill Mitman
Address/Telephone: RR/2, P.O. Box 620; (207) 882–7693
Rooms: 11; all with private bath.
Rates: $110 to $170, double occupancy, MAP. $65 to $125, double occupancy, continental breakfast.
Open: Mid-May through October.
Facilities and activities: Full license. Nearby: beaches, harbors, museums, antique shops.

Everyone knows how I feel about inns and animals. Well, here they are really different. Karen and Bill have 🖝 Nubian goats, which are very pretty animals. Much of the inn's baking is done with the milk, and the goat cheese is shipped all over the country. The barns are scrupulously clean, as these goats are fastidious. Their names—well, they are Cinnamon, Lacey, Jalapeño, Sugar, Spice, and Nice, watched over by B. C., the barn cat.

The inn is old, circa 1763, and is listed on the National Register of Historic Places. Many of the original boards and timbers remain today. There are eight fireplaces in the inn. 🖝 Four are in the bedrooms, which are nicely furnished and comfortable. If you'd like to bring your children to the inn, the innkeepers suggest you telephone first.

A five-course dinner is served at seven o'clock. There is one entree, and the menu changes daily; so stay a week or so, and you will never tire of the food. One dinner featured pear or cucumber soup, whey buns, roast pork tenderloin, Parmesan potatoes, broccoli, acorn squash, and chocolate cake with brandied strawberries. Another night: *potage Portugaise,* orange and grapefruit nut salad, whey buns, scallops Rebecca (scallops in a wine-Parmesan sauce), cranberried red cabbage, julienne of zucchini, carrots, nutmeg, and Sin Pie. As they say, it's the ultimate chocolate dessert.

The sitting areas are neat with a wood stove, books, and puzzles. The music room has a ☞ player piano with lots of rolls. Really nice.

You'll find much to do here. There are sand dunes, museums, and flea markets. I'd just sit and enjoy. It's beautiful here.

How to get there: From Route 1 between Bath and Wiscasset, turn onto Route 144 and follow it 8½ miles to the inn, which is on Westport Island.

E: *I just love the deck with its bird feeders. It's such fun to watch the many varieties of birds that come here.*

York Harbor Inn
York Harbor, Maine
03911

Innkeepers: Joe, Jean, and Garry Dominguez
Address/Telephone: P.O. Box 573; (207) 363–5119
Rooms: 32; 27 with private bath and all with air conditioning.
Rates: In-season, $65 to $125; off-season, $60 to $95; double occupancy, continental breakfast.
Open: All year.
Facilities and activities: Dining room open daily in summer and fall; after November 1, dining room open Thursday through Sunday. Lunch, dinner, Sunday brunch. Bar, cocktail lounge, entertainment on weekends, gift shop, large banquet facility, public beach, fishing, boating, golfing, tennis.

Wow! Three dining rooms with a 🖝 view of the Atlantic. This is a cozy and comfortable inn with good food and good grog. Sitting there looking over the Atlantic should be enough, but when you add the excellent food it is 🖝 heaven. Everything is made to order and baked right here. The appetizers are glorious. Tortellini, an Italian classic, is oh, so good, and there are several more. By his own words, Chef Gerry Bonsey creates incomparable homemade soups. You can imagine what the rest is like. I wish I had more space to tell you more. Do go, I know you will enjoy.

Chef Gerry was named chef of the year by the local Chapter of the American Culinary Federation.

The cellar, which once was a livery stable, is the lounge. A friendly bartender is at the beauty of a bar, made of solid unstained cherry wood joined with holly and ebony woods. The carpenter even put an inlaid tulip in a corner—out of tulip wood, of course. Happy hour is fun. The local people come in and I really enjoyed talking with them. The fireplace corner is so nice and cozy with the furniture clustered around the fireplace. There is listening-type music down here.

The inn is old; 1637 is the date for the room into which you first come. Originally a fisherman's house, it has sturdy beams in the ceiling, not for holding up the roof, but instead to hold up wet sails to dry before the large fireplace.

The rooms are comfortable, and from some you can see the sea. On a quiet night you can hear the sea breaking on the generous beach below the inn. The Carriage House next door is handsomely decorated. All the rooms over here have a private bath. There are two working fireplaces here. In the lovely new addition are twelve more rooms. The addition and the inn itself are fully air-conditioned and equipped with a sprinkler system.

When you arrive at the inn, you are given a book with information about the inn and area and a few poems, all lovingly put together. This is a really nice touch. Another one is the ☞ decanter of sherry in the hall for a thirsty guest. What I also liked was meeting Annie, the inn dog.

How to get there: From I–95 take the Yorks Berwicks Exit. Turn right at the blinking light, left at the first traffic light (Route 1A), and go through the village about 3 miles. The inn is on the left.

✳

E: York Harbor and all the areas around are beautiful. Be sure to bring your camera so you can remember it all at home.

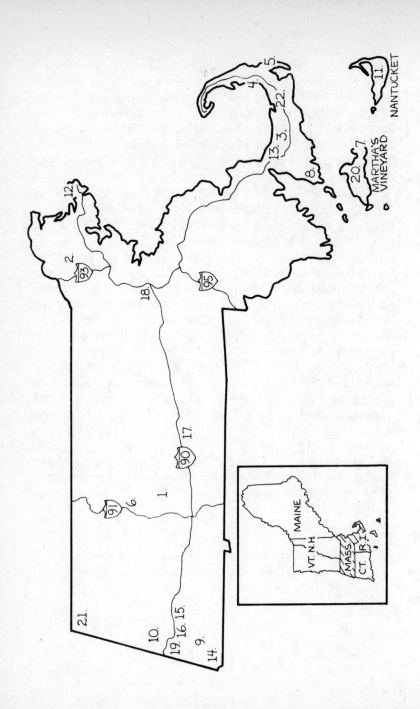

NANTUCKET

11.

MARTHA'S
VINEYARD

7.
20.

8.

22.

5.
4.
3.
13.

12.

2.
93

95

18.

17.
90

6.
91

1.

MAINE

VT. N.H.

MASS.

CT. R.I.

21.

10.

19. 16. 15.

9.

14.

Massachusetts

Numbers on map refer to towns numbered below.

The Lord Jeffery Inn
Amherst, Massachusetts
01002

Innkeeper: Lisa Freund, manager
Address/Telephone: 30 Boltwood Avenue; (413) 253–2576
Rooms: 50; all with private bath, TV, phone.
Rates: $70 to $120, EP.
Open: All year.
Facilities and activities: Breakfast, lunch, dinner, Sunday brunch. Elevator.
Nearby: skiing, golf, tennis.

The Lord Jeffery Inn, located on the historic common in Amherst, is named for Lord Jeffery Amherst, a hero of the French and Indian War. When you arrive here, you'll think the inn is so impressive with its whitewashed brick exterior.

The common rooms on the first floor are huge and comfortable. Cozy couches and chairs, beautiful flowers, and wonderful fireplaces are all around. An ☛ enormous walk-in fireplace is in the living room. There's a baby grand piano, circa 1876, a game table holding a backgammon board, and nice bookcases full of books. I also like the tavern with its small bar, tables, and windows looking out at the gardens. A patio is off the tavern.

A comforting thing to know about this old building is that its halls have sprinkler systems and that smoke alarms are everywhere. The rooms here come in all sizes, small, medium, and large. Some are small suites. All have new mattresses and box springs, television, and telephone. Some of the rooms look over the lovely Colonial gardens, and others have a view of the Amherst common. Eight of the garden rooms have porches.

The two large private dining rooms have their own fireplaces. The dining room has wrought-iron chandeliers, windows that overlook the lovely gardens, nice napery, and fresh flowers. A beautiful pink rose was on my table. The dining room is air-conditioned for your comfort. I had a ☞ seafood cream soup that was just loaded with delicious pieces of seafood. Believe me, it was a meal in itself. A very fresh and crisp salad was the only other thing I could eat. The food here is excellent. In summer lunch is served on the terrace.

There is much to do in this area. Besides Amherst College, many other colleges are in the area. Skiing, golf, tennis, and more are all nearby.

How to get there: Take I–91 to the Amherst exit (Exit 19), then go east 8 miles on Route 9 to Amherst.

∾

The good morning greeting
and the good night good wish
can only be found in a country inn.

olive Metcalf

Andover Inn
Andover, Massachusetts
01810

Innkeeper: Henry Broekhoff
Address/Telephone: Phillips Academy campus; (508) 475–5903
Rooms: 23, plus 6 suites; most with private bath and all with air
conditioning, TV, phone, wheelchair accessibility.
Rates: $79, single; $89, double; $130, suite; EP.
Open: All year except last two weeks of August.
Facilities and activities: Breakfast, lunch, dinner, Sunday brunch. Dining
room closed on Christmas Day. Bar, elevator, barbershop.

The Andover Inn is part of the campus of Phillips Academy. It
is privately owned and offers twenty-four-hour desk service, an
🖙 elevator, dry cleaning services, photocopying, and box
lunches. Room service is available, as are baby sitters, medical
services (a doctor is on twenty-four-hour call), safety deposit
boxes, taxis, and wake-up service. There is 🖙 limousine service to
and from the airports, and these stretched Cadillacs can be rented
for other activities such as weddings, proms, or an evening on the
town. Now that's the way to travel in style!

You expect ivy-covered buildings here, and you get them in
abundance. Upon entering the inn you are in the reception area
with a fireplace and comfortable couches. The bar is in the right

corner of this room, and it is one of the nicest I've visited. The stools with armrests are overstuffed, and honest, you hate to leave them.

The rooms have modern conveniences, such as color television, air conditioning, direct-dial phone, radio, and full bath. All of them have nice views.

The dining rooms are lovely and the china used is Villeroy and Boch Luxembourg. Siena is the pattern. It is porcelain and looks just like pink marble. The breakfast menu is extensive. Freshly squeezed orange or grapefruit juice is a nice way to start the day. Dinner selections include hot and cold appetizers, salads, and entrees from the sea or land. Try the specialty of the inn, shrimp flambé.

Sundays bring ☛ *Rijsttafel,* an original Indonesian dish served late in the day. It consists of dry steamed rice and an indefinite number of side dishes and sauces. The menu tells you how to eat it. I was overwhelmed and delighted by it. Do go and give it a try. It's worth a trip from anywhere, and reservations are a must.

How to get there: The inn is 25 miles north of Boston on Route 28, near the intersection of Routes 93 and 495.

E: *Monday through Saturday evenings guests enjoy light classical music on the grand piano.*

Olive Metcalf

Cobb's Cove
Barnstable Village, Massachusetts
02630

Innkeepers: Evelyn Chester and Henri-Jean
Address/Telephone: Powder Hill Road (mailing address: P.O. Box 208);
(508) 362–9356
Rooms: 6 suites; all with private bath.
Rates: $129 to $169, double occupancy, EPB. No credit cards.
Open: All year.
Facilities and activities: Dinner by reservation only to house guests. BYOB.

The moment you walk in the door and are greeted by Evelyn and Henri-Jean, you know you have happened on a distinctive and delightful inn. You are taken to your suite, and what a marvelous view you have. ☛ The third-floor suites have an immense dormer with glass on three sides and a million dollar view. There is a couch in front of this dormer where you can sit and see all of Cape Cod Bay, Sandy Neck, and all the way to Provincetown Light. The other suites also have grand views, deliciously comfortable beds, and all the extras you expect at an extraordinary inn. The baths all have ☛ whirlpools, so relaxing after a day of travel. The soaps and bubble bath are pear scented, a nice touch. Plenty of big towels and good, soft pillows.

The inn is on a very secluded and scenic piece of property. The bay is right at hand. The inn was built of 12-by-12-inch rough-cut timbers, and many of the walls are done in rough burlap. The keeping room has a large Count Rumford shallow fireplace, comfortable chairs, and wonderful smells that come from Henri's kitchen. There is a terrace full of bird feeders made by Harry Holl of the Scargo Pottery. Harry also made many of the kitchen things Henri uses, including a huge salad bowl that is a rare beauty. In summer, breakfast is served on the terrace, and it's quite a sight with all the birds on the feeders.

The dining room–library has a long hutch table that seats fourteen quite comfortably. Dinner is served in three or five courses. One night I was there it started with ☛ delicious mussels, then a special cauliflower dish done Henri's way. This was followed by a fish (cod, I believe, and you can only believe because Henri reveals no kitchen information at all) so white and so tasty you wonder why you had ever eaten meat. Next came a salad, and finally a creme caramel for dessert, topped off by a great cup of espresso coffee, an Henri specialty.

This is fine dining, and believe me, the innkeeper who joins you for every course is the reason this inn is such a success.

How to get there: Take Exit 6 off Route 6. Turn left on Route 132 North to Route 6A. Turn right, go about 3 miles, and pass through the light in the middle of Barnstable Village. After you pass the church on your left, turn left onto Powder Hill Road. Take the first driveway on the left marked "Evelyn Chester."

∽

E: *You can walk to a ship in Barnstable Harbor for whale watching. Meanwhile, back at the inn, ChaCha the chow waits for one and all.*

Olive Metcalf

High Brewster
Brewster, Massachusetts
02631

Innkeeper: Brian Sheehan
Address/Telephone: 964 Satucket Road; (508) 896–3636
Rooms: 4, plus 4 cottages, 1 barn; 1 room, cottages, and barn with private bath.
Rates: $80 to $160 per room, continental breakfast.
Open: All year.
Facilities and activities: Dinner every night in-season; Thursday through Sunday in winter. BYOB. Fishing. Nearby: biking, ocean, antique stores, state park with nature walks.

The main house is circa 1762. That's old, folks; and the way the floors tip and tilt upstairs, you know it's old. There are four rooms upstairs, and one has a private bath. The rest share. Glorious quilts are on the beds. These are quite small but adequate rooms.

Pond Cottage overlooks ☛ Lower Millpond and has one bedroom, a service kitchen, and a wonderful screened-in deck with a view of the pond. The living room in Brook House has a lovely fireplace, a dining table, and a picture window overlooking the pond. It also has two bedrooms and one bath and a deck, where you can sit and ☛ listen to the creek that goes down to the pond. A really restful sound for this inn creeper. Now there is also the barn, which sleeps five. It is a really good place for families to stay.

The grounds of High Brewster are beautiful. There are lush lawns, glorious flowers, and tables on the terrace overlooking the pond.

You have a choice of three dining rooms. Fresh flowers are on the tables year round. ☛ The kitchen is all new and a real pleasure to see. It's spotless. The food that comes from this kitchen is very good. The menu changes weekly and sometimes daily. When I was there, some appetizers featured on the menu were sea scallop bisque with fennel and grilled marinated shrimp with a red pepper butter. After a good salad, main course offerings may be grilled chicken breast with sage pesto, white and green asparagus and sweet potato chips, or grilled leg of lamb with a smoked port wine sauce, baby vegetables, and new potatoes. Dessert possibilities are apple crisp with walnuts and apple rum ice cream, white chocolate mousse, and homemade ice cream. Wow!

How to get there: Take Route 6 to Exit 11. Go left on Route 6A to a blinking amber light. Turn on Stony Brook Road and go about 1 mile. Just past the gristmill and creek, take the first left and turn into the inn's driveway.

⌒

E: *In spring the herring come up Herring Run Creek to spawn. There are walkways along the creek for you to walk on.*

> *Snug in a country inn, I have finally found*
> *the perfect topping to a windy Cape Cod day.*

The Captain's House Inn of Chatham
Chatham, Massachusetts
02633

Innkeepers: Cathy and Dave Eakin
Address/Telephone: 369 Old Harbor Road; (508) 945–0127
Rooms: 15, plus 1 suite; all with private bath.
Rates: $90 to $155, per room, EPB.
Open: February through November.
Facilities and activities: Dinner off-season by reservation only, afternoon tea. BYOB. Nearby: restaurants, swimming, sailing.

Cathy and Dave are the two very ambitious young innkeepers of this beautiful sea captain's house that dates back to 1839. They never stop making improvements, and this, of course, makes it very comfortable for you. They try to think of everything to make your stay perfect.

Breakfast is the important thing here, and it is one you will long remember. It is served in their lovely, light and airy dining room. Two or three live-in 🖙 English girls from the hotel management college in England are the staff, and they are so very pleasant. Good restaurants for lunch and dinner are in the area, and you will be given full directions on how to get there, plus a card introducing you to the restaurant signed by Dave or Cathy—very thoughtful.

Dave is a 🖝 licensed captain with the Coast Guard and, weather permitting, will take the guests out in their 23-foot Seacraft Sports Fisherman or 39-foot sloop. This is a wonderful way to see the Monomoy wildlife preserve.

The ambience of the whole inn is terrific. The rooms are named after ships that were sailed by Captain Hiram Harding who built the house. They are clean and well appointed with beautiful furniture. The Eakins are always adding "new" beds. They really are old, expensive, and beautiful four-poster canopy beds. The good mattresses and reading chairs ensure that your stay is comfortable. One room has a fireplace. Three of the rooms are in the Captain's Cottage, and one of these has a fireplace. Another building, the Carriage House, also has three beautiful bedrooms with private bathrooms, and one has a fireplace.

The inn dogs are Lily Marlene and Hallie. They are sometimes around for the formal afternoon tea.

This whole area offers many activities, fishing, swimming, boating, or just plain loafing. Whether you enjoy being relaxed or energetic, it's a nice place for it here.

How to get there: Take Route 6 (Mid-Cape Highway) to Route 137, Exit 11, and south to Route 28. Turn left to Chatham Center. Follow the rotary out of town on Route 28 toward Orleans. The inn is on the left in about a half mile.

✳

How good of you to have asked me in.

Olive Metcalf

The Queen Anne Inn
Chatham, Massachusetts
02633

Innkeeper: Guenther Weinkopf
Address/Telephone: Queen Anne Road; (508) 945–0394
Rooms: 30; all with private bath.
Rates: $105 to $212 per room, continental breakfast.
Open: All year except December to March.
Facilities and activities: Dinner. Dining room closed December 1 until mid-April. Tennis courts, meeting rooms. Nearby: swimming, boating. Fishing tours can be arranged.

Guenther has a fine inn. The rooms are so very comfortable. On the garden side the rooms have ☛ private balconies, which are a nice addition to the inn. Rooms looking south have a good view of Oyster Pond Bay.

There is a very pleasant lounge to relax in, and then there is the Earl of Chatham, the dining room, serving the most unbelievable food you can imagine. The help is beautifully trained. The chef has a briefing with them each night, so they can explain each course.

I have never seen appetizers presented this way. There were four different mousses. I tried sea bass and salmon mousse with lobster sauce. I really wanted them all. And such different soups.

I had cold leek and cream of carrot soup, thick and sumptuous. There is a very complete herb garden at the inn, and all the herbs are used in the kitchen.

Several different ☛ sorbets are served before the entree. Cantaloupe, grapefruit, and kiwi sorbets are but a few. I had lobster and medallions of veal, and oh, were they good. All this time you are looking at a magnificent dessert cart with an unbelievable array of sweets. I finally had to choose and had chocolate mousse topped with strawberries in Grand Marnier and real whipped cream. A snifter of Rémy Martin and I could hardly leave the table.

I needed a walk and there are pleasant places to go. The water is close at hand, and every Friday night band concerts are held in nearby Kate Gould Park. What a nice way to meet the other guests.

The inn has a 26-foot cabin cruiser, on which there are trips to Nantucket and Monomoy islands. Guenther is a Coast Guard–licensed skipper, and the boat is equipped with radio and radar. The inn also has ☛ three all-weather Har-Thu tennis courts in a beautiful parklike setting, a resident tennis pro, pro shop, and private lessons. Add to this a 6-foot television screen in the downstairs lounge, and your vacation is complete.

How to get there: From Route 6 take Exit 11, go south on Route 137 to its end, take a left on Route 28 to Chatham Center. At your first traffic light, in about 3 miles, go right on Queen Anne Road. The inn is on your right.

❀

E: *Imagine receiving this lovely place for a wedding gift. True. It happened in 1840.*

Olive Metcalf

The Town House Inn
Chatham, Massachusetts
02633

Innkeepers: Russell and Svea Peterson
Address/Telephone: 11 Library Lane; (508) 945–2180
Rooms: 24, plus 2 air-conditioned cottages; all with private bath, TV, refrigerator, phone.
Rates: $115 to $195, double occupancy, EPB.
Open: All year.
Facilities and activities: Dinner by reservation, full liquor license. Heated pool, spa. Nearby: Friday night band concerts, golf, tennis, beaches.

The front porch that overlooks Main Street beckons me. The Fourth of July parade, one of the summer's biggest events, goes right by the front door. Best seat in town is the porch of this inn.

The original structure dates back to the 1820s. Remains of the foundation still can be seen in the cellar, and some of the original woodwork is here. The carved moldings and wood trim depict harpoon and oar motifs. The floors are made of hemlock, and the original walls, recently exposed, have hand-painted scrolling. Check out the stencils in the rooms. Some of the shell stencils are really beautiful.

The rooms are immaculate; matter of fact, the whole inn is. The beds are queens and doubles. There are four-poster canopy beds in several rooms. All of the linens and towels are laundered right here by Svea. She likes to hang them out, when weather permits, for that ☛ lovely smell of fresh air. Each room has a television with HBO and a clock radio. Hair dryers are also in every room; this is a really nice touch. The cottages have a fireplace and air conditioning. Children are welcome in the cottages, and there are baby sitters available.

Breakfast is not a ho-hum thing here. Russ bakes the muffins and Svea does wonders with Scandinavian goodies. Favorites are Svea's ☛ Finnish pancakes with a fresh fruit mélange on top and her French toast with apricots.

The restaurant is called Two Turtles. Using her mother's recipes, Svea prepares Swedish pickled herring and Swedish meatballs as well as desserts. The chef provides a nice array of appetizers and main courses. Some specialties have been deluxe-cut Western lamb chops, scampi cooked with Svea's homegrown dill, and, of course, fresh fish. This is some meal!

How to get there: Take Route 6 (Mid-Cape Highway) to Exit 11, Route 137 south to Route 28 and east to the center of downtown Chatham. Watch for the Eldredge Library on your left. The inn is next door at 11 Library Lane.

Deerfield Inn
Deerfield, Massachusetts
01342

Innkeepers: Karl and Jane Sabo
Address/Telephone: Main Street; (413) 774–5587
Rooms: 23; all with private bath and air conditioning.
Rates: $137 to $156, double occupancy, EPB, tax and gratuity included.
   MAP rates available.
Open: All year except December 24 to 26.
Facilities and activities: Lunch, dinner. Cocktail lounge, two bars, elevator,
   color TV in lounge. Nearby: museum, Deerfield Academy, historic
   house tours.

   Some years back a serious fire did extensive damage to this
lovely old inn, but alumni of Deerfield and many others banded
together and rebuilt the inn. They did such an exquisite job the
federal government has designated the inn a ☛ National Historic
Site.
   ☛ The rocking chairs on the front porch somehow let you
know how lovely things will be inside. The parlors are beautifully
furnished with mostly twentieth-century copies or adaptations.
The Beehive Parlor, done in shades of blue, is a restful place for a
cocktail or two. The main dining room is spacious, serving the
kind of food befitting the setting. The chef prepares a daily special,

taking advantage of seasonal and local market offerings. He also does magical things with veal, chicken, and fish. Fresh fish is brought in three times a week.

The luncheon menu has some interesting and quite different offerings, such as a beautiful summer salad (the raspberry vinaigrette is glorious) and a very good casserole of fresh fish baked in wine and garden herbs. At dinnertime, try the gravlax with a sauce of honey mustard and dill. I thought it was yummy. There's also broiled venison on the menu.

The bedrooms are joys, Beauty-Rest mattresses, matching bedspreads and drapes, comfortable chairs and good lights for restful reading or needlework. The baths have been color coordinated with the rooms they serve. Little to nothing has been left to chance in this restoration.

There is a coffee shop on the lower level, which leads out to an outdoor garden. Perfect spot for informal meals, and a place the children will love.

How to get there: From I–91 take Exit 24 northbound. Go 6 miles north on Route 5. At the sign for Old Deerfield Village take a left. The inn will be on your left just past the Deerfield Academy.

❧

An unlit hearth in a good tavern is warmer by equators
than a blazing fire where there is no love.

The Charlotte Inn
Edgartown, Massachusetts
02539

Innkeepers: Gery and Paula Conover
Address/Telephone: South Summer Street; (508) 627–4751
Rooms: 25, plus 2 suites; 23 with private bath, some with fireplace.
Rates: In-season, $135 to $325; interim-season, $95 to $350; off-season, $85 to $350; double occupancy, continental breakfast.
Open: All year.
Facilities and activities: In-season, lunch and dinner. Off-season, dinner on weekends. Sunday brunch year round. Reservations a must. Gift shop and gallery. Nearby: sailing, swimming, fishing, golfing, tennis.

The start of your vacation is a forty-five-minute ferry ride to Martha's Vineyard. It's wise to make early reservations for your automobile on the ferry. There also are cabs if you prefer not to take your car.

When you open the door to the inn, you are in the 🖙 Edgartown Art Gallery, with interesting artifacts and paintings, both watercolor and oil. This is a well-appointed gallery featuring such artists as Ray Ellis, who has a fine talent in both media. The inn also has an unusual gift shop.

Four of us had dinner in the inn's lovely French restaurant named L'Etoile. The food was exquisite. 🖙 Capon breast stuffed with duxelles, spinach, and sun-dried tomatoes with coriander mayonnaise was the best I have had. I tasted everyone's food—nice occupation I have. Rack of lamb, served rare, with red wine–rosemary sauce, and accompanied by potato and yam gratin was excellent. They also have a special or two, but then everything is so special, the word does not fit. At brunch the cold cucumber soup was served with chives and followed by entrees like blueberry soufflé pancakes with creme fraîche. For breakfast I had a strawberry crepe that I can still remember vividly. Freshly squeezed juices and fruit muffins. . . . Heaven!

The rooms are authentic. There are early American four-poster beds, fireplaces, and the carriage house is sumptuous. The second-floor suite with fireplace I could live in. Paula has a touch with rooms—comfortable furniture, 🖝 down pillows, down comforters, and all the amenities. As an example, the shower curtains are of eyelet and so pretty. As a finishing touch, there are plenty of large towels.

Across the street is the Garden House, and it is Edgartown at its best. The living room is unique and beautifully furnished, and has a fireplace that is always set for you. The rooms over here are just so handsome. The Coach House is magnificent, furnished with fine old English antiques, a marble fireplace, and a pair of exquisite chaise longues in the bedroom. It is air-conditioned.

Paula, by the way, has green hands, and all about are gardens that just outdo each other.

How to get there: Reservations are a must if you take your car on the ferry from Woods Hole, Massachusetts. Forty-five minutes later you are in Vineyard Haven. After a 15-minute ride, you are in Edgartown, and on South Summer Street is the inn.

∾

E: *Gery and Paula are special innkeepers, but they do need the help of Andrew and Morgan, the dogs, and Oscar, Princess, and Cricket, the cats.*

Coonamessett Inn
Falmouth, Massachusetts
02541

Innkeeper: Marilyn Hughes
Address/Telephone: Jones Road and Gifford Street; (508) 548–2300
Rooms: 25 suites, plus 1 cottage; all with private bath.
Rates: $85 to $130, double occupancy, EP.
Open: All year.
Facilities and activities: Breakfast, lunch, dinner, bar. Parking.

In 1796, in a rolling field that sloped gently down to a lovely pond, Thomas Jones constructed a house and barn that was to become Coonamessett Inn (Indian, for "the place of the large fish"). The framework of the house is finished with wooden peg joints, and much of the interior paneling is original. Many of the bricks in the old fireplaces are thought to be made of ballast brought from Europe in the holds of sailing ships. Hanging in the inn are many paintings by the primitive American artist, Ralph Cahoon. They represent much of the history of the Coonamessett.

The food is excellent, offered from a large, varied menu, and served by friendly waitresses. Breakfasts are memorable.

Luncheons attract a lot of people, as the inn's food reputation travels far and wide. The famous ▶ Coonamessett Onion Rings are glorious. Dinner appetizers are many, including clams casino—

my favorite after lobster—and baked imported brie with basil pesto. A real winner, and judged to be the ☛ best in the East, is the lobster bisque, and I'll second it. It's really almost better than I make! And dinner entrees are great, with fresh lobster meat, Cape Cod lobster pie, or cold boiled lobster. There are other seafood dishes, and meat eaters are not forgotten either. There are beef, lamb, and veal entrees, plus the chef's special ☛ homemade fresh pasta of the day.

The guest suites have a sitting room, bedroom, modern bath, color television, and touch-tone telephones. They are furnished with period antiques and colonial pine and cherry reproductions. These are cottage suites, as there are no guest rooms in the inn itself.

I love the Cape in the off-season, and it is good to know that no matter what day I decide to come, I will receive a cordial welcome here. The inn grounds are beautiful and are kept in mint condition year round. All around you will see the loveliest array of grass, trees, flowers, shrubs . . . and peace. Don't forget the peace.

How to get there: Take Route 28 at the bridge over the canal, and go into Falmouth. Turn left on Jones Road, and at the intersection of Gifford Street you will see the inn.

✳

E: *I wish I lived closer, because I like the whole thing, starting with the flower arrangements, fresh every other day, that are done by a woman who really knows how to arrange.*

olive Metcalf

Windflower Inn
Great Barrington, Massachusetts
01230

Innkeepers: Barbara and Gerald Liebert, Claudia and John Ryan
Address/Telephone: 684 South Egremont Road; (413) 528–2720
Rooms: 13; all with private bath and many with fireplace and TV.
Rates: $80 to $95, per person, double occupancy, MAP. No credit cards.
Open: All year.
Facilities and activities: Full license. Reservations a must. Swimming pool.
   Nearby: golf, tennis, downhill and cross-country skiing, music, theater.

   Great Barrington was settled in the eighteenth century, and today it is a lovely resort town. The inn was built in 1820 and is Federal in style.
   I like the large living room. It has a white brick fireplace, couches, and a huge coffee table covered with magazines. Very conducive to ☛ loafing. There also is a reading or game room with a piano for anyone who knows how to play. There are tons of books to read.
   The guest rooms are spacious. All the beds are new and some have canopies. Fireplaces are in some of the rooms. The room on the first floor has its own entrance from the terrace and a large stone fireplace. It's a lovely room.

The dining room features Currier & Ives snow scenes on the walls and works done by local artists. One of them, by Gerald, is of his granddaughter holding a balloon. It's very dear.

Barbara and Claudia, mother and daughter, are the chefs. Every evening they give you a choice of three entrees, and each one is cooked fresh. Roast duck with plum sauce, salmon with sorrel sauce, and veal Marsala with peppercorns are just a few hints of what you might expect. The ☛ vegetable garden is a 70-by-90-foot spread of delights. John was ready to go out and pick raspberries when I saw him. He is the only one who picks them because he's so careful that they don't get bruised. ☛ Barbara makes any dessert you can think of with raspberries and chocolate (one of my favorite combinations).

The country club across the street is available for golf and tennis. The inn's own swimming pool is very relaxing, and in summer you have Tanglewood, Jacob's Pillow, and the Berkshire Theater nearby.

How to get there: The inn is on Route 23, 3 miles west of Great Barrington.

❋

E: *The wraparound porch is so nice. Dinner is served out here in summer and watched over by Libby and her children, Perri and Max, a bunch of springer spaniels.*

> *Our sympathy for the hardships*
> *of our forbears should be somewhat mitigated*
> *by the fact that they had the best*
> *of country inns.*

Appletree Inn
Lenox, Massachusetts
01240

Innkeepers: Aurora and Greg Smith
Address/Telephone: 224 West Street; (413) 637–1477
Rooms: 33; 31 with private bath, all with air-conditioning.
Rates: $50 to $190, double occupancy, continental breakfast.
Open: All year except mid-March to end of April.
Facilities and activities: Full breakfast available. Dinner daily, June 15
through Labor Day; rest of year, dinner Thursday through Sunday.
Sunday brunch, tavern. Heated swimming pool, clay tennis court.
Nearby: Tanglewood and other Berkshires attractions.

There are ☞ 450 varieties of roses here, which means the inn
has the second largest collection in New England. Believe me, this
is a sight to behold.

The inn is set up high and its view is magnificent. The lovely
heated pool is in an unbelievable setting on a high point of land.
When you are in the pool, all you see are the tops of mountains.
There are iris at the pool that smell like grapes. Honest. There are
twenty-two acres up here to wander about on. Tanglewood is
directly across the road from the inn.

The inn is more than a hundred years old. There are wonderful
country bedrooms, most with private baths. Some have a fireplace.

146

All the rooms are air-conditioned. Oh, the views from all the rooms and the wonderful comfort . . . I could go to sleep just thinking about them.

There is a circular dining room giving everyone ☛ a panoramic view of the surrounding hills and the lake in the distance called the Stockbridge Bowl. You can sit here and savor the view as well as the delicious food. Just a few of the dinner appetizers are shrimp vinaigrette (shrimp marinated in Dijon vinaigrette), fresh smoked trout, and half orders of selected pastas. There are five different pasta selections and entrees like Black Angus steak, veal Marseilles or florentine, crispy broiled fresh salmon, and of course much more. Daughter ☛ Lisa is the pastry chef. In the summer she makes as many as sixteen desserts a day. Chocolate mousse cake, fudge brownies, and baked lemon pudding are just a few. Do you want to have a wonderful wedding? This is the place. Lisa makes a wonderful wedding cake. The full breakfast menu with freshly squeezed orange juice is nice.

In the winter, dinner is served in the tavern around the huge fireplace. The room has oak beams; and on a cold winter night after a day of skiing, it's a pleasure to be here.

You know how I love animals. The inn dogs are Jonah, a wonderful Newfoundland, and Herbie, a mixed breed. It's fun to watch them play.

How to get there: Take the Massachusetts Turnpike to Exit 2. Outside of Lee, Route 7 joins Route 20. Turn left at the first traffic light onto Route 183 South, Lenox center. Go into the town of Lenox and when you come to the monument, bear left on Route 183 South (West Street) for 1½ miles. Just past the main gate of Tanglewood, bear right at the fork and you will see the inn sign.

The Gateways Inn
Lenox, Massachusetts
01240

Innkeeper: Vito Perulli
Address/Telephone: 71 Walker Street; (413) 637–2532
Rooms: 8, plus 1 suite with fireplace; all with private bath and phone.
Rates: $100 to $160, double; $295, suite; continental breakfast.
Open: All year.
Facilities and activities: Restaurant closed Sundays and Mondays in winter.
 In summer, dinner by reservation preferred. Nearby: Berkshires
 attractions.

The Gateways began as a mansion built for Harley Procter of
Procter and Gamble, the Ivory soap magnate. It is in the shape of
his favorite product, a cake of soap. It is square and flat on top.
 The chef, who 🐟 trained under former chef-owner Gerhard
Schmid for the last few years, learned his lessons well. The food is
still as glorious as ever. The Gateways rates four stars in the *Mobil
Guide.*
 Want a few hints of what to expect? Lobster cocktail, mussels
vinaigrette, and smoked salmon are some of the appetizers. Chilled
vichysoisse and bisques are some soups. These are followed by
wonderful salads and entrees like veal sweetbreads, veal contina,
steaks, salmon continental, rack of lamb, fish, game, poultry, and

specials of the house. The desserts are fabulous. I really cannot say enough about his creations. You'll have to try them for yourself. In summer you'll enjoy dining on a lovely side porch.

Two bedrooms, with their high ceilings, are perfect for the massive furniture with which they are furnished. The other bedrooms, equally lovely, have Colonial-style furniture. Color-coordinated towels add just the right final touch. The suite is called the Fiedler Suite because Arthur Fiedler stayed in it so many times. ☛ It is lavish in its appointments, and worth all it costs to spend a night in.

It is hard to believe that this lovely inn was once a girls' finishing school, a ballet school, a real estate office, and a boarding house. Lucky for us that it's now such a nice inn.

How to get there: Take Route 7 to Route 7A. The inn is on Route 7A, one block away from the intersection of Routes 183 and 7A.

❋

E: *The oval windows beside the front door and the magnificent stairway alone are worth a visit here.*

Hark, which are common noises
and which are the ghosts of long contented guests?

Seven Hills
Lenox, Massachusetts
01240

Innkeeper: Brian Butterworth
Address/Telephone: 100 Plunkett Street; (413) 637–0060
Rooms: 15; all with private bath, phone, air conditioning.
Rates: $150 to $200, EPB. MAP available.
Open: All year.
Facilities and activities: Dinner on weekends November through June, every night July through October. Meeting rooms with audio-visual equipment, banquet room, swimming pool, tennis, cross-country skiing. Nearby: Berkshires attractions.

It was a beautiful spring day when I visited Seven Hills. As I turned in the driveway, all I could see were tulips. What a glorious sight.

Seven Hills started life in 1885 and in 1911 was refurbished into a lush "Berkshire Cottage." It was called Shipton Court for many years.

There is much to do here. The inn has two all-weather tennis courts and a ☞ 60-foot swimming pool. Twenty-seven acres of property provide many opportunities for roaming about, jogging, or cross-country skiing. It is in the heart of the Berkshires with the Festival of Music all summer, Jacob's Pillow, and much more.

Two lovely sitting areas are provided for guests. One of these has a nice fireplace. There are meeting rooms of every size and a large banquet room. The private dining room has a huge old safe in the wall, and the large and lovely main dining room overlooks the lush landscaping and pool. I loved the ☞ enormous fireplace, open on both sides and adorned with hand-carved cherubs on each side. The plates on the tables are beautiful, and the food is glorious. The menu changes monthly. Green onion and chicken soup with smoked chicken is surely different. I had both the blackened shrimp with warm gazpacho and the ☞ grilled boneless quail with a juniper berry and red currant sauce. Fantastic! The menu also featured shrimp, lobster, and scallops sautéed with a light tomato-basil sauce on angel hair pasta, as well as tenderloin of beef with caramelized onions and a parsley, mustard, and green peppercorn sauce. The list goes on and on, and the desserts, well, why not come and try them for yourself.

The guest rooms are lovely. Five of them have working fireplaces, and three have whirlpool tubs. You'll find double beds, queens, and one king-sized four-poster. All of them have white bedspreads and feather pillows. They look and are very clean and comfortable.

All of this and a nice innkeeper and staff. Do come.

How to get there: Take the Massachusetts Turnpike to Exit 2. Turn right onto Route 20 west. Drive through the town of Lee. Pass the Cork & Hearth Restaurant on your left, then turn left onto Plunkett Street. The inn is in 1 mile on the left.

The Village Inn
Lenox, Massachusetts
01240

Innkeepers: Clifford Rudisill and Ray Wilson
Address/Telephone: Church Street; (413) 637–0020
Rooms: 29; 27 with private bath.
Rates: $60 to $150, double occupancy, EP. MAP rates available.
Open: All year.
Facilities and activities: Breakfast, afternoon tea, dinner Tuesday through
    Sunday, Sunday brunch. Late after-concert suppers on Friday and
    Saturday in July and August. Village Tavern. Nearby: skiing, tennis,
    golfing, swimming, horseback riding, fishing, hiking, Tanglewood,
    Jacob's Pillow.

There is a saying here at the inn, "If you can't be a house guest
in the Berkshires, be ours." This surely would be a fine choice. The
rooms are so clean and cheerful. The inn's walls are covered with
stenciled wallpapers, the maple floors have oriental rugs, and
antiques are found throughout the inn.

The Village Tavern, a British pub, was built in the old cellars
of this 1771 house. It is furnished with seats made from church
pews. On those blustery winter days, there is a cheery fire to go
with your drink. The living room, called the Common Room, is a
delightful place to sit and listen to the grand piano being played.
There is a nice television and reading room for your comfort.

A real first is an authentic English tea served from 2:30 to 4:30 every day with homemade scones, pastries, and small tea sandwiches. To make it perfect, you are provided with ☛ Devonshire-style clotted cream.

Breakfast is a thing of joy. Any inn that serves eggs Benedict with ☛ a glass of champagne gets my hearty applause. Another clap of the hands goes for their Irish coffee. There are many other good things to eat here. The dinner menu begins with such specialties as snails sautéed in brandy and white wine on toasted crusts with a shallot and garlic cream, and smoked Maine trout with horseradish cream. The summer menu offers your choice of cold fresh fruit soup (blueberry, raspberry, or strawberry), followed by fresh Columbia River poached salmon with a gingered hollandaise sauce, or ☛ fresh vegetable plate (steamed and lightly sautéed vegetables). This dish is not seen often enough on a menu.

The inn is near many activities, churches, shops, the library, and the bus stop.

How to get there: Take Route 7A off Route 7 and turn on Church Street in Lenox. The inn is on the right.

⤳

E: Once a month on Sunday afternoons in winter and spring the inn features chamber music concerts. All this and English tea. Oh my.

Ollve Metcalf

Wheatleigh
Lenox, Massachusetts
01240

Innkeepers: Susan and Linfield Simon
Address/Telephone: West Hawthorne; (413) 637–0610
Rooms: 17; all with private bath, air conditioning, phone.
Rates: $110 to $400, double occupancy, continental breakfast.
Open: All year.
Facilities and activities: Dinner served Tuesday through Sunday in winter and every night in summer. Lounge, swimming, tennis, cross-country skiing.

In the heart of the beautiful Berkshires, overlooking a lake, amid lawns and gardens on twenty-two self-contained acres stands the estate of Wheatleigh, former home of the Countess de Heredia. The centerpiece of this property is an elegant private palace fashioned after an Italian palazzo. The cream-colored manse re-creates the architecture of sixteenth-century Florence. You must read the brochure of Wheatleigh, for it says it all so well.

Patios, pergolas, porticos, and terraces surround this lovely old mansion. The carvings over the fireplaces, ☛ cupids entwined in garlands, are exquisite. In charming contrast, the inn also has the ☛ largest collection of contemporary ceramics in the New England area. There are many lovely porcelain pieces on the walls.

In the dining room are tile paintings weighing over 500 pounds. They are Doultons from 1830; this was before it became Royal Doulton. They are just beautiful.

There is a service bar in a lovely lounge, and boy, you sure can relax in the furniture in here. It has a wonderful fireplace, and the views from here are glorious. And imagine a ☞ great hall with a grand staircase right out of a castle in Europe. There are also exquisite stained-glass windows in pale pastels, plus gorgeous, comfortable furniture. From the great hall you can hear the tinkle of the fountain out in the garden.

The rooms are smashing with lots of white dotted swiss and eyelet material for the canopy beds. Do you long for your own balcony overlooking a lovely lake? No problem. Reserve one here. The facilities are not well suited to children under eight.

At the entrance to the dining room, the homemade desserts are beautifully displayed along with French champagne in six sizes from a jeroboam to a small bottle for one. This is very nice indeed. I chose grilled quail on young lettuce leaves and raspberries for a dinner appetizer; it was superb. Tartare of fresh tuna was so beautifully presented, just like a Japanese picture, and delicious. I also had chilled fresh pea soup with curry and sorrel, followed by monkfish coated with pistachios, sautéed, with red wine sauce. Homemade sorbets are very good, but then, so is everything here.

How to get there: From Stockbridge at the Red Lion Inn where Route 7 turns right, go straight on Prospect Hill Road, bearing left. Go past the Stockbridge Bowl and up a hill to Wheatleigh. From the Massachusetts Turnpike, take Exit 2, and follow signs to Lenox. In the center of Lenox, take Route 183, pass the main gate of Tanglewood, and then take the first left on West Hawthorne. Go 1 mile to Wheatleigh.

❋

E: *Susan's description of the inn is "elegance without arrogance," and Lin's is "the ultimate urban amenity." Mine is "a perfect country inn."*

Olive Metcalf

Jared Coffin House
Nantucket, Massachusetts
02554

Innkeepers: Philip and Margaret Read; manager, Don Terry
Address/Telephone: 29 Broad Street; (508) 228–2400
Rooms: 60; 11 in main house, 16 simpler rooms in Eben Allen Wing, 3
  rooms in Swain House connected to the Eben Allen Wing, 12 rooms
  in Daniel Webster House across the patio, 18 rooms in 2 houses
  across the street.
Rates: $60 and up, single; $100 to $150, double; EP.
Open: All year.
Facilities and activities: Breakfast, lunch, dinner, taproom. Eben Allen
  Room for private parties. Nearby: swimming, tennis.

It is well worth the 30-mile trip by ferry, or the plane trip from
Boston or New York, to end up at the Jared Coffin House. Built as
a private home in 1845, the three-story brick house with slate roof
became an inn only twelve years later. The inn passed through
many hands before it came to the extremely ☛ capable ones of
Philip and Margaret Read.

The public rooms at the inn reflect charm and warmth. The
furnishings are Chippendale and Sheraton; showing the results of
the world-wide voyaging by the Nantucket whalemen are Chinese
and Japanese objets d'art and furniture.

To add to the charm are many fabrics and some furniture that have been made right here on the island. In addition to the main house, there are several other close-by houses that go with the inn. All are done beautifully for your every comfort. The size and the quantity of the luxurious bath towels in the guest rooms please me greatly. The housekeeping staff does a wonderful job, and the exquisite antiques reflect their loving care.

☛ The taproom, located on the lowest level, is a warm, happy, fun place. Here you meet the local people and spin yarns with all. Old pine walls and hand-hewn beams reflect a warm atmosphere. Luncheon is served down here with good burgers and great, hearty soups. During the winter this is a nice spot for informal dinners.

The main dining room, ☛ papered with authentic wallpapers, is quiet and elegant. Wedgwood china and pistol-handled silverware make dining a special pleasure and reflect the good life demanded by the nineteenth-century owners of the great Nantucket whaling ships.

The inn is located in the heart of Nantucket's Historic District, about an eighth mile from a public beach, and 1 mile from the island's largest public beach and tennis courts. It's a pleasant 3-mile bicycle ride to superb surf swimming on the South Shore.

How to get there: To get to Nantucket, take a ferry from Hyannis (April through January) or Woods Hole (January through March and summer months). First call 617-540-2022 for reservations. Or take a plane from Boston, Hyannis, or New York. The inn is located 2 blocks north of Main Street and 2 blocks west of Steamboat Wharf.

Olive Metcalf

The Woodbox
Nantucket, Massachusetts
02554

Innkeeper: Dexter Tutein
Address/Telephone: 29 Fair Street; (508) 228–0587
Rooms: 3 doubles plus 6 suites in 2 buildings; all with private bath.
Rates: $110 to $170, double occupancy, EP. No credit cards.
Open: Memorial Day to Columbus Day.
Facilities and activities: Full breakfast, dinner, beer and wine license.
    Nearby: swimming, boating, biking.

For thirty-six years there has been a Tutein running this inn.
Built in 1709, it is the oldest inn on Nantucket Island. What a treat
to be here.

The suites are unique. In an old building like this, you cannot
change the structure to modernize it, so the bathrooms have been
very inventively fit in. Very pretty and comfortable. The suite I was
in had a 🖝 fireplace in the living room, two bedrooms, one with
a huge canopy bed, and a lovely little private patio. It was hard to
leave.

There are three dining rooms in the inn. I'm sure I had dinner
in what must be the oldest public dining room in New England.
The room has two "king's boards" on the wall of the immense,
almost walk-in fireplace. Today the fireplace holds an old cradle

with dried flowers. The china is old and there are nice touches on the tables like your own peppermill and cute little glass chicken salt holders. Tall candlesticks add to the charm of this inn.

They are famous for their 🖙 popovers and I believe it, having devoured quite a few. The food is truly gourmet. One of the appetizers was gravlax—fresh salmon in a fresh dill marinade. Naturally the entrees include the catch of the day; I had fresh sea bass that was delicious. My dinner companion had lamb noisettes, which were so tender and good. The house salad dressing is excellent. And for dessert, well, the best 🖙 white chocolate mousse I have ever had.

The inn's breakfast is a great way to start the day. A tent card lists "Our Morning Breakfast Bubbles—Mimosas and Champagnes." Oh my. The pancakes and waffles come with blueberries, strawberries, peaches, or apples. Those wonderful popovers come with any egg dish.

The powder room must be seen. There are no words to describe it.

How to get there: Take the ferry to Nantucket or fly from New Bedford. It's only 25 minutes. The inn is at 29 Fair Street. You can walk to it from the ferry.

> *"Drink wine, and live here blitheful while ye may;*
> *The morrow's life too late is, live to-day."*
> —Herrick

Yankee Clipper Inn
Rockport, Massachusetts
01966

Innkeepers: Bob and Barbara Wemyss Ellis
Address/Telephone: 96 Granite Street; (508) 546–3407, (800) 545–3699
Rooms: 27, plus 6 suites, in 3 buildings; all with private bath, air conditioning, phone.
Rates: $102 to $173, double occupancy, EPB; $45 more for MAP.
Open: All year except Christmas week.
Facilities and activities: BYOB, only wine allowed in dining room. Small function room, heated saltwater pool, tours in powerboat. Nearby: fishing, boating, shopping.

When you are lucky enough to be here and see a 🖙 sunset, you will be overwhelmed. It's a golden sea and sky, with the town of Rockport in the distance. No camera could truly capture this scene. Wait a while longer, and the moonlight on the sea is an awesome sight.

Three buildings make up the Yankee Clipper. The inn is an oceanfront mansion. Here the rooms have antique furniture, oriental rugs, and some canopy beds. Some rooms have porches. You're sure to enjoy the television lounge with cable television and a really big screen. All meals are served in this building.

The Quarterdeck has 🖙 large picture windows providing a

panoramic view of the ocean. Upholstered chairs are placed in front of the windows. Sit back and relax; it's almost like being on a ship that does not move. All of the rooms in this building are beautifully furnished. Some of the rooms in the Bullfinch House have waterviews. If you stay here you are on the EPB plan; the other buildings are MAP.

There is a function room, with a wonderful water view and just lovely for small weddings or executive meetings.

The 🖝 glass-enclosed dining room has marvelous views that are matched by the marvelous food. I started my dinner with an appetizer of chicken fingers served with a honey mustard sauce. Chilled melon soup was different, and Yankee clipper scrod is a young cod fillet topped with scallops, cheddar cheese, and Galliano sauce. Delicious. I was determined to make room for dessert. I had a hard time choosing, but chocolate won. I had the Grand Marnier soufflé, layers of chocolate cream molded on a base of chocolate cake and covered with a glaze of dark chocolate.

To work off some of the calories, you might want to swim in the heated saltwater pool at the inn. The inn also offers sightseeing tours in its powerboat. In the area there are whale-watching trips, fishing, and in the town of Rockport, fantastic shopping. It really is fun to walk around here.

How to get there: **Take Route 128 north and east to Cape Ann. Route 128 intersects Route 127 at two points. The second one is shorter. After taking the second one, go about 4 miles to the "corners" where you should see a sign for the inn.**

*

E: *Over the mantel is a portrait of Mehitable Lamon, Barbara's great-great-grandmother. That's really going back.*

The Dan'l Webster Inn
Sandwich, Massachusetts
02563

Innkeeper: Steve Catania
Address/Telephone: Main Street; (508) 888–3622
Rooms: 47, in 3 buildings; all with private bath.
Rates: $69 to $118, per person, MAP. $65 to $165, double occupancy, EP.
Open: All year except Christmas Day.
Facilities and activities: Breakfast, lunch, dinner, Sunday brunch. Bar, lounge, swimming pool, gift shop. Nearby: doll museum, glass museum, Heritage Plantation, beaches.

A 250-year-old linden tree, complete with bird feeders, stands outside the Conservatory, one of the inn's three lovely dining rooms. This is a glassed-in room, overlooking a beautifully landscaped courtyard and swimming pool. The Webster Room has china cabinets to display ☞ old Sandwich glass on loan from the museum. There's a portrait of Daniel Webster's second wife in here. The Heritage Room has a huge open fireplace and a grand piano on the stage for your entertainment. A ☞ dance band is here on weekends, and they surely sounded good to me.

These dining rooms provide the perfect atmosphere for the excellent food. Breakfasts are hearty, with eggs, six different omelettes, sausage, croissants, fruit, and much more. The lunch menu lists salads, sandwiches, and quite a few hot choices. Dinner is an adventure. The hors d'oeuvres list is extensive. I had clams casino and also tasted the escargots, which were served en croute with mushrooms, garlic, and herb butter. There are four veal offerings, chicken, ten different seafood specials, and, of course, beef. I had chateaubriand—very nice because it was served for one. It was very good. Desserts are sinful, and there are special coffees.

The Devil 'n Dan Tavern is a cozy spot, with stained glass windows and very nice wooden bar stools. There are tables and chairs here for those who are not barflies.

All the guest rooms are a little different. Most have Hitchcock furniture. Some have canopy beds. All of the beds are comfortable. The Webster Suite on the third floor of the inn has two bedrooms and two bathrooms. One bath has a Jacuzzi, and the other has a steam tub.

In the lovely Fessenden House next door are four suites. I was in the Captain Ezra Nye Suite. A ☞ whirlpool tub is in each of these suites, as is a marble fireplace. They are beautifully furnished with classic antiques. I had to go up two steps to get into bed. Oh my, I do like it here.

How to get there: Go over the Bourne Bridge to a rotary; go ¾ of the way around it, taking the Route 6A exit that parallels the canal. Stay on this road until you come to the third set of lights. This is Jarves Street. Go right, then right again onto Main Street. The inn is on the right, close to the corner.

❧

E: *A split of sparkling water is provided in each guest room. The beds are turned down in the evening, and a chocolate is left on the pillow. What nice touches.*

The Weathervane Inn
South Egremont, Massachusetts
01258

Innkeepers: Vincent, Anne, Robert, and Alena Murphy
Address/Telephone: Main Street; (413) 528–9580
Rooms: 10; all with private bath, 2 with wheelchair accessibility.
Rates: $80, per person, EP; $160, per person, MAP; $90, double occupancy, EPB.
Open: Closed 3 weeks in spring and from Thanksgiving to Christmas.
Facilities and activities: Breakfast, dinner, Sunday brunch. Bar, lounge, swimming pool, antique shop, outside games.

The Weathervane began its existence as a farmhouse in 1785. The original fireplace, which served as a heating and cooking unit, boasts a beehive bake oven. These are rarely seen today but were a real necessity in those early times. The inn has been included in the ☞ National Register of Historic Places.

The sign over the bar says, "Kiss the Cook." Anne is the chef, daughter-in-law Alena is another chef as well as the pastry chef, and they are both pretty enough to kiss. Some of Anne's specials are Rock Cornish hen with kiwi sauce, duckling with black cherries, and pork tenderloin Normandy (an apple and calvados concoction). There also are veal and fish entrees and ☞ vegetarian dishes if you let them know in advance. Alena turns out fresh fruit pies, cheesecake, and chocolate chip walnut pie. Sound good? Well, it's even better eating. The dining room is cozy and attractive with nice napery and candles.

The inn is so fresh and clean in every corner that you know you have good innkeepers at hand. One of the rooms is named the Norman Rockwell Room because Anne has three of his works on the wall. The first has two youngsters looking at the moon. The second has the youngsters, now a bit older, at the soda fountain, and in the last they are even older at the registrar's desk getting a license to marry. Anne has some other Rockwell paintings at various places in the inn. There are four-poster beds in the carriage house. The rooms are color coordinated, and finding cordials in them is a nice surprise.

There is ☛ one room that needs special mention. It is over the kitchen and has a tiny bathtub with a shower.

All the public rooms are comfortable, and there is so much to do in this area all year that you could stay and stay. Be sure to visit the antiques dealer in the barn.

Bear is the inn dog and is perfect for the part. He is an English cocker spaniel.

How to get there: Follow Route 7 to Route 23 west. You are now 3 miles from South Egremont. The inn will be on your left.

✻

Man's cruelty to man knows almost no horizons.
His continued existence, however, is justified
when he says to a stranger, ''Come in.''

olive Metcalf

Federal House
South Lee, Massachusetts
01260

Innkeepers: Robin and Ken Almgren
Address/Telephone: Main Street; (413) 243–1824
Rooms: 7; all with private bath and air conditioning.
Rates: $65 to $135, double occupancy, EPB.
Open: Every day of the year except Mondays.
Facilities and activities: Full breakfast in summer only; continental breakfast
    served during the rest of the year. Dinner, Sunday brunch, bar,
    lounge. Nearby: private club with golf and tennis privileges, skiing.

Ken is the innkeeper/chef of Federal House. He worked for
one of my favorite people, Albert Stockli, of the Stonehenge Inn in
Ridgefield, Connecticut, who has now gone to his reward.

The Federal House was built in 1824 by Thomas O. Hurlbut,
whose family came to America in 1635. It remained in this family
until 1948, when it became a summer home for family members
who resided in New York City. Today it has been restored to the
original country elegance it once had. Its architectural style is
Greek Revival.

The rooms are spacious, ☞ air-conditioned, and have large
windows. The wallpapers are lovely and so are the Victorian
couches. Some of the antiques came from the original Hurlbut

166

home, and some were handed down in the innkeepers' families.

Dinner, as well as Sunday brunch, is served in a choice of three lovely rooms—the original dining room, front parlor, or billiard room. No matter which one you choose, the tables are set with fine silver, tall candles, and ☛ fresh flowers that are just beautiful. The food, as you would expect in this elegant atmosphere, is glorious. No prepared foods are used. All the sauces and condiments are made right here. There are appetizers like seared yellowfin tuna with horseradish and soy sauce, Federal House smoked duckling with fresh peach chutney, and rabbit terrine. Dinner entrees always include fresh fish, duckling, chicken, sweetbreads, beef, and rack of lamb prepared in different ways depending on the season. To accompany your meal, choose a wine from the fine wine cellar. The inn also has a full license for other drinks.

Both Ken and Robin have had extensive training mostly in four-star restaurants, so it is no wonder this is a grand inn.

How to get there: South Lee is 4 miles from Lee and 1 mile from Stockbridge. The inn is on Main Street (Route 102).

E: *The food here is really something! Try the pâté of fresh salmon and flounder with sorrel sauce if you're here in the summer or fall.*

olive Metcalf

The Red Lion Inn
Stockbridge, Massachusetts
01262

Innkeeper: Betsy M. Holtzinger; Director of Lodging, Dennis Barquinero
Address/Telephone: Main Street; (413) 298–5545
Rooms: 110, plus 6 suites; 80 with private bath, all with wheelchair accessibility.
Rates: $51 to $180, winter; $64 to $250, summer; double occupancy; EP.
Open: All year.
Facilities and activities: Breakfast, lunch, dinner, bar. Heated swimming pool. Elevator. Pink Kitty Gift Shop.

The Red Lion Inn is a four-season inn. In summer you have the Berkshire Music Festival at Tanglewood and the Jacob's Pillow Dance Festival, both world renowned. The inn's own heated swimming pool is a nice attraction. Fall's foliage is perhaps the most spectacular in New England; in winter there are snow-covered hills; in spring come the lovely green and flowers. All go together to make this a great spot any time of year. And right down the street is the Corner House, the museum of Norman Rockwell's works.

The inn is full of lovely old antiques. The halls are lined with antique couches, each one prettier than the next. From a four-poster, canopy bed to beds with great brass headboards, all the rooms are marvelously furnished and comfortable as sin. Whether in the inn itself or in one of the inn's adjacent houses, Stafford House and Ma Bucks, you will love the accommodations. ☛ The wallpaper in Ma Bucks is a delight. All rooms have extra pillows, which I love.

The Lion's Den is downstairs with entertainment nightly, and it has its own small menu. In warm weather the flower-laden courtyard with its Back of the Bank Bar is a delightful place for food and grog. There's a wonderful collection of old birdcages out here. The chef really knows what to do with ☛ scrod. Another place to eat is the Widow Bingham's Tavern. There is an almost hidden booth designed for lovers in here.

More excellent food is served in the lovely dining room. The poached salmon is divine. The vegetable plate is a very nice touch. The inn also serves New England favorites like old-fashioned chicken pot pie and roast native turkey. The menu changes with the seasons. Do you still want to know more? Well, in the morning you'll find many breakfast choices starting with freshly squeezed orange juice.

Be sure you find an opportunity to visit The Red Lion Inn and listen to the authentic country-inn cricket in the lobby. Honest, he lives here.

How to get there: Take Exit 2 from the Massachusetts Turnpike and follow Route 102 west to the inn.

olive Metcalf

Colonel Ebenezer Crafts Inn
Fiske Hill, Sturbridge, Massachusetts
01566

Innkeeper: Pat Bibeau
Address/Telephone: Fiske Hill Road (mailing address: P.O. Box 187); (508)
    347–3313
Rooms: 6, plus 2 suites; all with private bath.
Rates: $79 to $99, double occupancy; $109 to $139, suites; continental
    breakfast.
Open: All year.
Facilities and activities: Afternoon tea. Publick House nearby for other
    meals. Small swimming pool. Nearby: Old Sturbridge Village.

In Colonial times the finest homes were usually found on the
highest points of land. Such a location afforded the owners
commanding views of their farmland and cattle. It also set them
above their contemporaries. So David Fiske, Esquire, a builder,
built this house in 1786 high above Sturbridge. The house was
magnificently restored by the management of the Publick House
and named after the inn's founder, Colonel Ebenezer Crafts.

Accommodations are wonderful. There are two 🖝 queen-
sized canopy beds that are real beauties. Some beds are four-

posters. ☞ Terrycloth robes are placed in your room for your comfort. The wallpapers are subtle and elegant. It joins the main inn by a short breezeway. It has a living room, bedroom, bath, and color television.

Provided for your relaxation is a nice living room with a baby grand piano, a color television with a videocassette recorder and movies, and a good library of books and *National Geographic* magazines that are always a pleasure to read or look through.

Your breakfast of freshly baked muffins, fresh fruit, juice, and coffee comes with a copy of the morning paper. In the afternoon, tea, sherry, and sweets are served. Or you can go 2 miles down the road to the famous Publick House in Sturbridge for a full breakfast. Here, too, you can have lunch and dinner and enjoy the lovely bar and cocktail lounge. You will find a gift shop and an incredible bake shop. Do not miss taking some treats home.

If you want to plan a business conference or family gathering, the entire house is available for up to twenty-two people.

How to get there: Take Exit 3 from I–86, and bear right along the service road into Sturbridge. Continue to Route 131, where you turn right. Turn left at Hall Road and then right on Whittemore Road, which becomes Fiske Hill Road.

∽

E: *Ask Pat to show you the Underground Railroad of Civil War days. The slave hole is still here.*

There is no definition of a proper inn.
Like night and day it either is or is not.

Olive Metcalf

Publick House
Sturbridge, Massachusetts
01566

Innkeeper: Noel Hennebery
Address/Telephone: P.O. Box 187; (508) 347–3313
Rooms: 17, plus 9 suites; all with private bath, air conditioning, phone.
Rates: $69 to $109, double occupancy; $99 to $139, suites; EP.
Open: All year.
Facilities and activities: Breakfast, lunch, dinner, bar. Wheelchair access to restaurant. TV in lounge, gift shop, swimming pool, tennis courts, jogging trail, shuffleboard, children's play area, petting farm. Nearby: Old Sturbridge Village, golf, fishing, cross-country skiing.

It's a real pleasure to me to keep coming back to the Publick House and finding it always the same, always excellent. As a matter of fact, very little has changed here in the last 200 years. The green still stretches along in front of it, and the trees still cast their welcome shade. The Publick House is still taking care of the wayfarer, feeding him well, providing a comfortable bed, and supplying robust drink.

The Publick House calendar is fun to read. Throughout the year there are special celebrations for holidays. They *do* keep Christmas here! All twelve days of it. The Boar's Head Procession is truly unique, complete with a roast young suckling pig, a roast goose, and plum pudding. Wow!

Winter weekends are times for special treats, with chestnuts roasting by an open fire, and sleigh rides through nearby Old Sturbridge Village, a happy step backward in time.

The guest rooms are decorated with period furniture, while the penthouse suite has the modern conveniences of a television and king-sized bed. The wide floorboards and beamed ceilings have been here since Colonel Ebenezer Crafts founded the inn in 1771.

The barn, connected to the main house with a ramp, has been transformed into a restaurant. Double doors, topped by a glorious sunburst window, lead into a restaurant that serves hearty Yankee cooking such as delicious lobster pie. There is a little musician's gallery, still divided into stalls, that overlooks the main dining room. Beneath this is an attractive taproom, where a pianist holds forth, tinkling out nice noises.

A blueberry patch and a garden that covers more than an acre of land provide the inn with fresh fruit and vegetables during the summer.

I found my way by following my nose around behind the inn to the Bake Shoppe, where every day fresh banana bread, sticky buns, deep-dish apple pies, corn bread, and muffins come out of the ovens to tempt me from my diet! Take some along for hunger pangs along the road.

How to get there: Take the Massachusetts Turnpike to Exit 9. The Publick House is located on the Common in Sturbridge, on Route 131. From Hartford, take I–84 to I–86, Exit 3, which brings you right into Sturbridge.

*

E: The inn's good jams, mustards, relishes, chowders, and more can now be enjoyed at home. They are beautifully packaged and mailed to you wherever you wish.

Longfellow's Wayside Inn
Sudbury, Massachusetts
01776

Innkeeper: Robert Purrinton
Address/Telephone: Wayside Inn Road; (508) 443–8846
Rooms: 10; all with private bath, air conditioning, phone.
Rates: $55, single; $60, double, EP.
Open: All year except Christmas Day.
Facilities and activities: Breakfast for house guests only, lunch, dinner, bar.
 Pets limited, horses boarded. Gift shop, museum.

Eight generations of travelers have found food and lodging for "man and beast" at the Wayside Inn. Route 20 is the old stagecoach road to Boston, now well off the beaten track. The inn looks much as it did 280 years ago and still supplies the traveler with hearty food and drink and a comfortable bed.

As with many old buildings, "improvements" were made to the inn in the nineteenth century, but a complete restoration in the 1950s afforded the opportunity to put many things back the way they were in the beginning. Now part of the inn serves as a museum with priceless antiques displayed in their original settings.

There are a large dining room and several smaller ones, a bar, a gift shop, and a lovely walled garden. At the end of the garden path is a bust of Henry Wadsworth Longfellow, who was inspired by the inn to link together a group of poems known to all schoolchildren as "Tales of a Wayside Inn."

Henry Ford bought 5,000 acres surrounding the inn in 1925, and since then this historic area has been preserved. A little way up the road stand a lovely chapel, the little red schoolhouse that gained fame in "Mary Had a Little Lamb," and a stone gristmill that still grinds grain for the rolls and muffins baked at the inn. I bought some of their cornmeal because ☛ the muffins I ate at the inn were exquisite. This is a most interesting building to visit as all of the equipment in the mill is water-powered.

As a final touch, the inn boasts of the oldest mixed drink in America. It is called ☛ "Coow Woow." You must taste it to discover how well our forefathers lived.

How to get there: From Boston, take the Massachusetts Turnpike to Route 128 North. Take Exit 49 West onto Route 20. Wayside Inn Road is 11 miles west, just off Route 20. From New York, take the Massachusetts Turnpike to Route 495, and go north to Route 20 East. It is approximately 8 miles to Wayside Inn Road.

Olive Metcalf

The Williamsville Inn
West Stockbridge, Massachusetts
01266

Innkeepers: Gail and Kathleen Ryan
Address/Telephone: Route 41; (413) 274–6118
Rooms: 13, plus 1 suite; all with private bath.
Rates: $90 to $170, double occupancy, EP.
Open: All year.
Facilities and activities: Breakfast, afternoon tea, dinner. Tavern, swimming pool, clay tennis court. Nearby: hiking, biking, skiing, golf, Tanglewood, Shaker Village.

Built in 1797 as a farmhouse, this inn is the second oldest house in the hamlet of Williamsville. It is a charmer, now run by a mother-daughter duo.

You will find 🔥 fireplaces all over the inn—so important in this part of the world where there is so much winter. The fireplaces in the dining rooms are raised hearth and especially warming. There also are fireplaces in two bedrooms, the sitting rooms, and the tavern.

The garden room is a lovely sitting room with a 🔥 puzzle going most of the time, books, television, and a music center with stereo and tapes. The comfortable chairs and couches make this such a cozy room for afternoon tea. Tom Ball's Tavern, which is a delight, has nice stencils on the walls.

The guest rooms and suite are so attractively styled and furnished with a sense for old-fashioned grace and comfort.

There are three candlelit dining rooms for your pleasure. Service is unhurried and the food is outstanding. Salmon mousse with green mayonnaise is yummy, and the onion soup is baked to perfection with Swiss and Gruyère cheese and croutons. Here are just a few ideas of the entrees: Boneless chicken stuffed with artichokes, mushrooms, and Gruyère cheese, or scallops baked in a delicately flavored cream sauce with stoneground wheat crumbs. And this is a real winner: ☛ boneless shell steak coated with crushed peppercorns and served with a brandy cream sauce.

Desserts, of course, are freshly made. Lemon angel pie is so good, and nice liqueur parfaits are always in order. Eating my way through New England is so much fun.

So much to do in this area, from skiing, theater, and antiques, to just loafing at this lovely inn.

How to get there: Take the Massachusetts Turnpike to Exit 1, which puts you on Route 41. Turn left toward Great Barrington. The inn is 4 miles south of the turnpike on your right. From the New York Thruway, follow directions for Berkshires Spur, Exit 33. Go south on Route 22 to Route 102, east on Route 102 to Route 41, south on Route 41 toward Great Barrington.

Lambert's Cove Country Inn
West Tisbury, Massachusetts
02568

Innkeeper: Ron and Kay Nelson
Address/Telephone: Lambert's Cove Road (mailing address: Box 422, RFD, Vineyard Haven, MA 02568); (508) 693–2298
Rooms: 15; all with private bath.
Rates: In-season, $105 to $130; off-season, $65 to $95; double occupancy, continental breakfast. 7-day stay in summer preferred, but 3-day minimum possible.
Open: All year except January.
Facilities and activities: Dinner daily in-season, Thursday through Sunday off-season. Sunday brunch. BYOB, tennis court. Nearby: swimming, cross-country skiing, ice skating.

At the end of a tree-shaded country road you will find this gem of an inn. The original house was built in 1790. Over the years it was enlarged and a carriage house and barn added. Today the carriage house and barn have been beautifully renovated for guest use, and half of the rooms are here.

One of the rooms in the carriage house has a 🖝 greenhouse sitting room at one end. Nice to have your cocktails in here and look up at the stars. All of the rooms in the inn are done with imagination. The mattresses are new, and there are plenty of 🖝 pillows and lush color-coordinated towels.

When you enter the inn, you are in an elegant center hall done in soft beige. Up a magnificent staircase and you are in a restful sitting area with wicker furniture and bookcases full of books. There also is a delightful library, a huge room with walls lined with volumes of books, and furnished with tables for games and really comfortable furniture. On a cold day a fire in the fireplace here feels great.

A big deck opens from the library and dining room and looks out on an apple orchard. There are five decks in all at this inn. The English garden is lovely, and flowers are everywhere you look. Princess, the inn cat, watches over it all.

🖝 Brunch is fun at a place like this. Cioppino is one of the dishes served. This Italian seafood stew is prepared here with salmon, scallops, scrod, swordfish, clams, and mussels. The omelettes are different, such as fresh salmon and tomato or asparagus, or tomato with smoked mozzarella. Maybe you'd like to come for dinner. Roast duckling is glazed with honey and Grand Marnier. Breast of chicken Francis comes with pine nuts and lemon butter. All the desserts are made right here. The one I had on my last visit was white and chocolate mousse with fresh raspberries. It was hard to make a choice, because they also serve Key lime pie and strawberries Romanoff. No matter what you order, it will be good.

This is real country. Walk twenty minutes to the Lambert's Cove beach, or just walk anywhere. It's just a beautiful part of the world, and it would be a wonderful spot for a wedding.

How to get there: Take the ferry to Martha's Vineyard from Cape Cod. After driving off the ferry, take a left, then a right at the next stop-sign intersection. Stay on this road for 1 ½ miles to Lambert's Cove Road, on your right. Three miles from this point look for the inn's sign, on the left.

olive Metcalf

Le Jardin
Williamstown, Massachusetts
01267

Innkeeper: Walter Hayn
Address/Telephone: 777 Cold Spring Road; (413) 458–8032
Rooms: 6; all with private bath.
Rates: $75 to $95, double occupancy, EP.
Open: March through November.
Facilities and activities: Breakfast, dinner, Sunday brunch, bar.

The grounds are so pretty at this inn. The backyard has picnic tables and in front are Hemlock Brook and a nice pond. There are a lot of sugar maples on the property, which Walter taps and then makes ☛ his own maple syrup.

The rooms are lovely. There are four working fireplaces with glass doors for safety. One of the rooms, the one where I always want to stay, has a whirlpool tub. What heaven it is to relax in. Another room has a deck extending into the woods.

Sports fans will love the ☛ 46-inch television screen in the bar and lounge. It's a most attractive room, with comfortable bar stools and tables.

Terry Perry is the manager of the dining rooms and she does a superb job. They are real beauties. Fresh, crisp napery, a fresh flower on each table, and plants hanging in the windows provide the perfect cozy, but still elegant, atmosphere for the magnificent food. The cuisine is French. Some of the hors d'oeuvres are snails in garlic butter, oysters baked with spinach and Pernod, and ☛ Beluga malossol caviar. I had the onion soup baked in a tureen. Very hot and good. The frog legs were done to perfection. There also are jumbo shrimp baked with a hint of garlic and crisp Long Island duckling with apples. A real zinger is sirloin flamed in cognac and laced with coarse black pepper. Rack of lamb is beautifully served with tender vegetables and fresh mint sauce. There's a wonderful and extensive wine list. It's so nice when both the food and the wine are exceptional.

And the desserts . . . well, just imagine a French restaurant. I'm not about to spill the beans and tell you what to expect. Come on up and see for yourself.

How to get there: The inn is right on Route 7, just 2 miles south of Williamstown, on the right.

&

*Who can refuse the beckoning
of a cozy country inn?*

Olive Metcalf

Old Yarmouth Inn
Yarmouth Port, Massachusetts
02675

Innkeepers: R. Karl Manchon, Brian and Stephen Harriman
Address/Telephone: 223 Main Street; (508) 362–3191
Rooms: 5, plus 2 suites; all with private bath.
Rates: $60 to $85, double occupancy, EPB.
Open: All year.
Facilities and activities: Lunch, dinner, bar. Nearby: theater, beaches.

Whenever I get the feeling that I want to step back in time, I go to the Old Yarmouth Inn. It is the oldest inn on Cape Cod. Built in 1696 as a wayside staging inn, it has had many owners, but it maintains its charm. The building sags a bit, and when you come in it is like savoring a bit of yesterday, with old leather suitcases, quaint, papered hat boxes, dusty coats, hobnail boots, and ancient horse brasses, all combining to carry you back to the olden days.

There is salt air here, flowers, sunshine, and on some days a little fog. You can dine indoors or out at the Old Yarmouth Inn, and seafood is, of course, a specialty of the house.

I love eating here because the food is excellent. Besides seafood, they have prime rib, veal, duck, and steak au poivre. Flaky pastries, rich cakes, and hot breads burst from the ovens. Let me tell you about one recent holiday menu. Fresh fruit cup or piping hot French onion soup were among the appetizers. Oven-roasted fresh New England turkey with country dressing and hot cranberry sauce, roast prime ribs of beef from ☞ rare to medium, or roast leg of lamb were three of the entrees you could have. All dinners included a garden salad, potato or vegetable, and a bread basket. All this plus a divine dessert and coffee. What a nice place to come for any holiday. Just be sure you reserve well ahead. The Stagecoach Lounge has its own bar menu.

You are only 4 miles from the famous Cape Playhouse at Dennis, one of the original "straw hat" theaters. There are several fine beaches nearby, and fishing, boating, and day trips to Nantucket and Martha's Vineyard can be arranged.

How to get there: Leave Route 6 (Mid-Cape Highway) at the Yarmouth Port Exit to Route 6A. Turn right, and 1 mile will bring you to the Old Yarmouth Inn.

✺

The aroma of freshly baking bread told me surely
I was awakening in a good country inn.

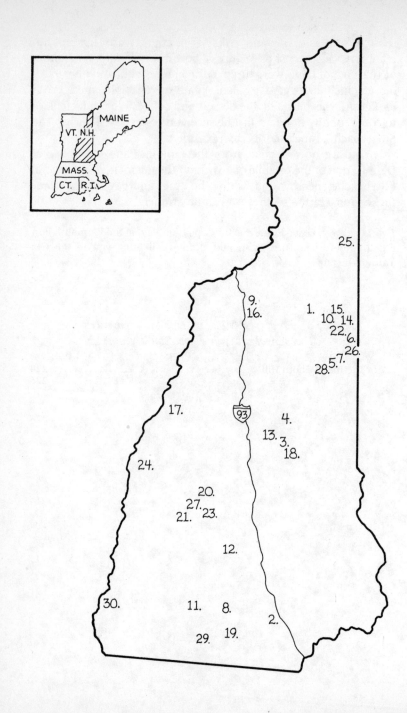

MAINE

VT. N.H.

MASS.

CT. R.I.

25.

9.
16.

1. 15.
10. 14.
22. 6.
26.
28. 5. 7.

17.

93

4.
13. 3.
18.

24.

20.
27. 23.
21.

12.

30.

11. 8.
2.
29. 19.

New Hampshire

Numbers on map refer to towns numbered below.

The Nolchland Inn
Bartlett, New Hampshire
03812

Innkeepers: John and Pat Bernardin
Address/Telephone: Route 302; (603) 374–6131
Rooms: 11, plus 4 suites; all with private bath.
Rates: $52 to $78, per person, double occupancy, MAP.
Open: All year.
Facilities and activities: BYOB. Trout pond for fishing and ice skating.
  Nearby: hiking, skiing, swimming, canoeing, fishing, bicycling.

The inn was built in 1862 by a wealthy Boston dentist, Samuel Bemis. He used native granite and timber, and you can bet that the construction of this building was some job.

☛ Seventeen fireplaces are in the inn, and all of the rooms have working fireplaces. There are high ceilings and beautiful mountain views. The dining room looks over the pond, which is ☛ stocked with trout. Yes, you may catch your own. There's a raised hearth fireplace in here that has a frame around it dating back to 1790.

Pat is a gourmet chef. The menu changes daily, but it always offers a choice of three or four entrees. The soups are all home-made, like curried cream of tomato bisque and cream of fresh asparagus. An appetizer I loved was leek, onion, and spinach tart.

One entree Pat makes is beef Wellington. Her Cajun-style chicken is boned chicken baked on a bed of ham, pan-fried potatoes, and mushrooms, dressed with béarnaise sauce and a touch of Cajun seasonings. Chocolate raspberry torte wins a star in my book. What a delightful combination of tastes.

There's so much to do in this area you may have a hard time deciding where to start. Hiking is by far the nicest you'll find almost anywhere. There are beautiful waterfalls and granite cliffs to scale. The Saco River is the place for swimming, fishing, or canoeing. ☛ Whitewater Class III and IV are here in the spring, so come on up with your canoe. Or bring your bicycle, as biking is fun here. Skiing of all kinds is very close by—or do you want to try snowshoeing? This is the place for it, or you can go ice skating on the inn's pond. If more sedentary activities suit your fancy, rocking chairs on the porch are ideal for reading and needlework. And by the way, there are two llamas, angora goats, a flock of endangered sheep (Karakuls), a white duck named Reggie, and a golden retriever, Ruggs.

How to get there: Follow Route 302 from North Conway to the inn. It is 20 miles north of North Conway.

olive Metcalf

The Bedford Village Inn
Bedford, New Hampshire
03102

Innkeeper: Jack Carnevale
Address/Telephone: Route 101; (603) 472–2602; restaurant, (603) 472–2001
Rooms: 12 suites, plus 2 apartments; all with private bath.
Rates: Suites, $85 to $175; apartments, $225 to $275; double occupancy, continental breakfast.
Open: All year.
Facilities and activities: Full breakfast, lunch, dinner, Sunday brunch, tavern. Conference areas.

Country elegant is the way to describe this inn. It was a farmhouse built before the American Revolution, and it still retains the original wide fireplaces and wide pine boards. There are cows who live here. Four white Charolais cattle are in the meadow.

In what was the hayloft, there are sumptuous suites, each with a bathroom of ☛ Spanish marble and a Jacuzzi. The fixtures are gold finish—very pretty. The suites are well furnished. There are nice lamps with three-way switches, a too-often forgotten detail. Each suite has three telephones, one at the desk, one by the bed, and one in the bathroom. A deck off the luxury suite in the barn's peak overlooks the meadow. One of the apartments has two bedrooms.

The original milking room has become a common area for inn guests, furnished with couches, lounge chairs, and a nice table for games or whatever. It is a very comfortable room.

If you decide you want a full breakfast, you'll find it has all of the usual items plus banana pancakes, frittered French toast, and a different poached egg every day from an inventive chef. ☛ The sticky buns are beautiful and come straight from the inn's own bakery. The tavern has its own menu. There are seven dining rooms, each one lovely. The oldest dates back to around 1700 and has a huge fireplace. Lots of windows make it light and airy. The luncheon and Sunday brunch are ambrosia, and dinner is a delight. Traditional New England foods are served here, and the menu changes every two weeks. There are special dinners. Christmas Eve is very special and includes a ☛ Christmas goose. There are also wild-game feasts.

How to get there: The inn is on Route 101, just west of Manchester.

*

E: *Oriental carpets, antique four-poster beds, and a 40-inch television set all add up to a wonderful country inn.*

Olive Metcalf

Red Hill Inn
Center Harbor, New Hampshire
03226

Innkeepers: Rick Miller and Don Leavitt
Address/Telephone: Route 25B and College Road; (603) 279–7001
Rooms: 21, in 4 buildings; all with private bath.
Rates: $65 to $125, double occupancy, EPB.
Open: All year.
Facilities and activities: Lunch in season, dinner, Sunday brunch. Television
   and VCR, gift shop, cross-country skiing, hiking. Nearby: sailboat
   rentals, swimming, tennis, golf.

Traveling along Route 25B, you glance up a hill, and sitting
there is this lovely old restored country inn. Not very long ago,
Rick and Don waded through waist-high snow to begin a project
that was destined to become a showplace of New Hampshire's
Lakes Region. What they had to do to make the inn what it is
today is just incredible. Their crew consisted of themselves plus
two others. Rick and Don alone sanded the floors of twenty-five
rooms.

Oak paneling is in the living room. A huge bay window
affords you a view of Squam Lake and the Squam mountain range,
the foothills of the White Mountains. There is an immense
fireplace here that sure felt good one cool July night.

The rooms, all named after mountains, are different. Two of them have a sun room and balcony, and three have their own fireplace. That same July night I lit a fire in the fireplace in my room; it felt and looked great. Most of the rooms are large and very comfortable, with grand views. During the inn's restoration, they discovered 🖝 nursery rhyme characters that had been painted on the walls and covered by panels. Of course they are here for you to see.

One of their buildings has hand-hewn beams, brick hearths, and fifteen rooms with fireplaces and telephones (five with Jacuzzis). The runabout lounge is very interesting; half of a 22-foot Chris Craft is the bar. Don's collection of license plates adorns the walls.

The dining rooms are lovely. Both have fireplaces and views, and the food that is served here is sumptuous. I had a garlic night—escargots, then garlic dressing on my salad, and finally the best 🖝 shrimp scampi around. Of course I had to taste my dinner companion's lamb, and boy was it good. Sunday brunch's menu is unusually large. Something for everyone from lamb chops, omelettes, and eggs Benedict to cool salads. The luncheon menu is the same, just a joy—lobster salad, diet tuna salad, and on and on. The desserts at every meal are glorious. All are baked here. I had 🖝 the best lemon meringue pie I've had in many a country mile.

There are more than 150 acres for cross-country skiing or hiking. It's a nice ten-minute walk down a hill and through the woods to the beach on Squam Lake. All this plus an inn cat named Kir, the innkeeper's collections, and utter peace. Do I like it here? You bet.

How to get there: Take Exit 23 off Route 93. Follow Route 104 east toward Meredith. At Route 3, go left, and follow Route 3 north about 4 miles to its junction with Route 25B. The inn is ⅛ mile off Route 3 at the corner of 25B and College Road.

✳

E: *The herb path is outside the sun porch–dining room. All hearty for the cold New Hampshire weather, all used in the kitchen, and so pretty to see.*

Corner House Inn
Center Sandwich, New Hampshire
03227

Innkeepers: Jane and Don Brown
Address/Telephone: Route 113; (603) 284–6219
Rooms: 4; 1 with private bath.
Rates: $60 to $70, double occupancy, EPB.
Open: All year.
Facilities and activities: Lunch, dinner, full liquor license. Nearby: skiing, hiking.

This is a very interesting and different town. The inn is centrally located so you can walk to everything. The ☞ New Hampshire League of Arts and Crafts is here, as well as pottery shops, galleries, and museums. There are five major ski areas within a short driving range.

The inn has been in business for more than one hundred years. To keep pace with its history, the waitresses are in colorful period pinafores. The food they serve is excellent. The kitchen is famous for its ☞ crepes, and several different ones are prepared each day. I have tried a few and, wow, are they good. They also do fabulous things with soups. Another great inn specialty is ☞ dessert; apple crisp and apple pie stand out, and I dare you to eat just one of their cookies and not go back for more.

192

Of special note is the inn's house salad dressing. It is a buttermilk-dill combination. One of my party usually hates salad, but he ate it down to the last wisp of lettuce.

Roast duck is unusual. It is glazed with a variety of fruit sauces. And a new one on an old "inn creeper" like myself is a crab and scallop pie topped with puff pastry. Well, that tells enough about this good New Hampshire food.

The rooms are very comfortable. Bay windows in the living room, a spinning wheel, and plants give that touch of comfort you love in an inn. The carriage house is now the main dining room. Good inn animals are here. The cat is Anna, and the dog, a golden retriever, is Cousteau.

How to get there: Up I–93 to Exit 24, thence Route 3 to Route 113. Route 113 goes directly to Center Sandwich.

❧

For one night at least
let me escape from all those things
the Puritans tell me I must face.
Let me find a friendly inn.

Stafford's in the Fields
Chocorua, New Hampshire
03817

Innkeepers: Ramona and Fred Stafford
Address/Telephone: P.O. Box 270; (603) 323–7766
Rooms: 17, including 3 in cottages; 11 with private bath.
Rates: $60 to $90, per person, double occupancy, MAP.
Open: All year.
Facilities and activities: Liquor license, trail lunches available. Clay tennis
  court, cross-country skiing.

At the end of a quiet country lane sits a really lovely country
inn. It comes with a babbling brook, has forests at hand, and
overlooks some rolling fields. You will also find a barn with truly
unusual acoustics. ☛ Square dancing is fun here in the summertime.

Ramona Stafford likes to cook in a sort of French-country
style with wine and herbs and spices and, best of all, with great
imagination: pork tenderloin with prunes, and stuffed chicken
breast with almonds and raisins. Most of Ramona's recipes are
included in the inn's own cookbook. How nice. Now we can try to
repeat some of her good cooking in our own homes.

Breakfast is the way to start your day. Omelettes are
different—sour cream with green chives, mild country cheddar, or

cheddar and salsa. For Sunday brunch a real special is 👉 eggs hussard with *marchant du vin*. It translates to a wine merchant or a wine sauce in the vernacular. You could also try eggs Benedict or blueberry pancakes. You will not go wrong. Ramona serves well-balanced meals. No smoking is permitted in the dining room.

The inn is immensely comfortable with cross-country skiing right on the fields, and just utter peace. As Fred Stafford says, there is an inexhaustible supply of "nature things to do." Just sitting, watching the swallows swoop or a leaf spin slowly to the ground restores what you may have lost in the hustle and bustle of today's world.

Turn in the lane some snowy evening and see Stafford's glowing in the field, waiting to welcome you from a world well left behind. Bhuelah, a Brittany spaniel, and Lautreck and Celeste, the geese, will be waiting to greet you.

How to get there: Take Route 16 north to Chocorua Village, then turn left onto Route 113 and travel 1 mile west to the inn. Or, from Route 93, take Exit 23 and travel east on Route 104 to Route 25, and then to Route 16. Proceed north to Route 16 to Chocorua Village.

Darby Field Inn
Conway, New Hampshire
03818

Innkeepers: Marc and Marily Donaldson
Address/Telephone: Bald Hill Road (mailing address: P.O. Box D); (603) 447–2181
Rooms: 17, plus 1 suite; 14 with private bath.
Rates: $60 to $80, per person, double occupancy, MAP. $40 to $60, person, double occupancy, EPB. Package plans available.
Open: All year.
Facilities and activities: Bar, television, library, swimming pool, skiing, hiking.

Set high atop Bald Hill in New Hampshire's White Mountains with spectacular views of this wonderful country is Darby Field Inn. Located 1,000 feet above Mount Washington Valley and only 3 miles from Conway Village, the inn delights wanderers adventurous enough to leave the beaten path.

The inn borders the ☛ White Mountain National Forest, where guests are welcome to cross-country ski, snowshoe, hike, or walk to nearby rivers, waterfalls, and lakes. The inn dogs, Lupo and Chuska, are Malamutes who love this beautiful country.

Rooms are charming, some with four-poster beds, patchwork quilts, and braided rugs. Most rooms have private baths, and they

196

are tucked away wherever space was available. How do you feel about an L-shaped shower stall?

Downstairs the inn's huge ☛ cobblestone fireplace is the center for warm conversation. If you want a bit livelier time, come into the pub, which sometimes features local singers.

Candlelit dinners begin with fine wine and a smashing sunset view up the valley. The food reflects the careful preparation of the chef. You'll always find a chef's special and fresh fish du jour. Whatever you order up here will be excellent. Desserts are interesting. You must try Darby cream pie, quite different. The ☛ Irish Revolution will really end your day nicely.

Darby Field, a notorious Irishman, was the first white man to ascend Mount Washington. Had the inn been here in 1642, it is doubtful whether Mr. Field would ever have passed the pub.

How to get there: Turn on Bald Hill Road a half-mile south of the Kancamagus Highway on Route 16, then go 1 mile up the hill and turn right onto a dirt road. The inn is 1 mile beyond.

> *A good innkeeper, a good cook,*
> *and an affable barkeeper*
> *are as standard in a country inn*
> *as a fire engine in a fire house.*

Olive Metcalf

The Inn at Crystal Lake
Eaton Center, New Hampshire
03832

Innkeepers: Walter and Jacqueline Spink
Address/Telephone: Route 153, Box 12; (603) 447–2120
Rooms: 11; all with private bath.
Rates: $56 to $65, per person, double occupancy, MAP.
Open: All year.
Facilities and activities: Bar, lounge. Nearby: skiing, swimming, hiking,
theater.

The inn was built in 1884 by Nathaniel G. Palmer and was
known as the Palmer House until the Spinks bought it and
completely remodeled it. Because of its commanding views of the
lake, they renamed it The Inn at Crystal Lake. This is truly a
Victorian inn.

You enter the inn on a ☛ marble floor with fossils embedded
in it. While you're at the inn, make sure you examine Walter's
fossil and rock collection, or ask him about the geology of the area.
Fascinating. Walk through the Victorian parlor complete with a
237-year-old grandfather clock, mauve carpet, and Victorian
fireplace and sofa. The next room is a lovely three-level dining
room featuring ☛ Walter's metal sculptures.

Walter is the chef. He has worked for some of the finest

restaurants and inns. The emphasis is on unhurried, relaxed dining with a variety of international cuisine. Some things you may find are marinated mushrooms, good soups, and salad with the inn's own piquant French dressing for starters; chicken brie (chicken sauced with brie cheese and sprinkled with sesame seeds) and Walter's own duckling (sautéed boneless and skinless duck breast with a veal demi-glace sauce flavored with caramelized honey, orange, and lemon juice) for dinner entrees.

All of the rooms are named after gemstones. The beds are queens and doubles and have beautiful brass and iron headboards. The showers are ☛ nice and large.

A game and television room is tucked away in one area, and a lounge and bar is in another area. This inn really roams about. The patio in back is brick, with tables in summer that are watched over by the inn cat, B. W. The balconies beckon me, and so does the porch with its wicker rockers and chairs.

How to get there: From I–95 take Route 16 to Conway. Turn right on Route 153 to Eaton Center and the inn.

Olive Metcalf

The Inn at
Crotched Mountain
Francestown, New Hampshire
03043

Innkeepers: John and Rose Perry
Address/Telephone: Mountain Road; (603) 588–6840
Rooms: 13; 8 with private bath, 4 with fireplace.
Rates: $50 to $60, per person, double occupancy, MAP.
Open: All year except first three weeks in November, weekdays in winter, and after ski season until Mother's Day.
Facilities and activities: Bar, tennis, swimming pool, cross-country skiing. Nearby: golfing, fishing, summer theater.

This 150-year-old Colonial house is located on the northern side of Crotched Mountain. There is a 40-mile view of the Piscataquog Valley, complete with spacious skies. Both innkeepers have gone to 🐎 school to learn their trade, and what a charming house to practice it in. They are both pretty special themselves. Rose is from Singapore, and John is a Yankee.

Come and stay, there are many things to do. There are three golf courses in the nearby valley, fishing is great, and there is a wading pool for the young, as well as a 30-by-60-foot pool for real swimmers. Two areas provide skiing, one at the front door, and another down the road. Two clay tennis courts eliminate that tiresome waiting for a playing area. And come evening there are two summer theaters, one at Peterborough and another in Milford.

There are two English cockers who live here, Winslow and Anan. There are numerous streams, ponds, and lakes for fishing and mountains for hiking. Golf is nearby. Come and enjoy this wonderful countryside with Winslow and Anan. They would love to have you.

How to get there: Take 101A from Nashua to Milford, Route 13 to New Boston, and Route 136 to Francestown. Take Route 47 2½ miles, then turn left onto Mountain Road. The inn is 1 mile up the road.

᷄

E: *Any house that has nine fireplaces needs a wood lot and a man with a chain saw.* ☛ *Four of the bedrooms here have a fireplace, so remember to request one when you reserve.*

The register of a country inn
is a treasure of the names of good people.

Olive Metcalf

Franconia Inn
Franconia, New Hampshire
03580

Innkeepers: Richard and Alec Morris
Address/Telephone: Route 116; (603) 823–5542
Rooms: 34, including 1 suite; all with private bath, 1 with Jacuzzi.
Rates: $135 to $150, double occupancy, MAP. EP rates available.
Open: All year except April 1 to May 25 and mid-October to December 15.
Facilities and activities: Bar, lounge, game room, hot tub, swimming, four tennis courts, cross-country ski center, ice skating, sleigh rides, soaring center, horseback riding. Nearby: downhill skiing, golf.

This is an inn in the fine tradition of old New England hostelries. The inn is the fourth for the Morris family. It is run by third-generation innkeepers. The inn welcomes children. Never a dull moment any season of the year. While the children play Ping-Pong or watch a movie, you can relax in 🖙 the lounge and listen to selected classical and popular music by the glow of the fireplace.

A card room and a library are here for your enjoyment, as is a screened porch overlooking the pool and the mountains. And they have something a bit unique: a game room for children, no adults allowed. Another entertainment for you is horseback riding. There are 🖙 trail rides through Ham Branch stream and around the hay fields.

The living room is paneled with old oak and, with the fireplace, is very warm and cozy. A lovely candlelit dining room, with pink and white napery, serves glorious food. The chef has treated escargots in an innovative way. They are marinated, baked in butter, garlic, and Ouzo, and sealed in a puff pastry shell. Superb! Bouillabaisse a la Provençale is really a winner, and so is spicy ginger and soy sauce sauté. A vegetarian pastry is delightful for vegetarians. ☛ Breakfast in bed? It's here, if you wish, complete with a pitcher of mimosas. I could stay forever.

There are 65 miles of cross-country trails right at hand, and they also have facilities so that you can ski from inn to inn on connecting trails. Downhill skiing is but 10 miles away. Horse-drawn sleigh rides in this beautiful winter wonderland are my idea of heaven. Do come and enjoy.

How to get there: Take I–91 north to the Wells River-Woodsville Exit. Go right on Route 302 to Lisbon, New Hampshire. A few miles past Lisbon, go right on Route 117 to Franconia. Crossing the bridge into town, go right to the Exxon station. There, take another right to Route 116, and you're 2 miles from the inn. Or, if you have a single-engine plane, the inn has its own F.A.A.-listed airfield with a 3,000-foot-long runway.

Olive Metcalf

The Horse and Hound
Franconia, New Hampshire
03580

Innkeepers: Bill Steele and Jim Cantlon
Address/Telephone: Wells Road; (603) 823–5501
Rooms: 8, plus 2 suites; all with private bath.
Rates: $40 to $80, double occupancy; $110, suites; EPB.
Open: All year except a few weeks in April and November.
Facilities and activities: Dinner, Sunday brunch Mother's Day through
    foliage season. Skiing, soaring, biking, hiking. Nearby: swimming,
    boating, fishing, golf, tennis.

The Horse and Hound is located at the base of Cannon
Mountain just north of Franconia Notch. Tucker Brook rushes
down from the top of the mountain just past the edge of the inn's
property. In winter you can set off from the door of the inn on your
cross-country skis. In other seasons, ☞ bicycling is a big thing
here at the inn. There is a 7-mile circle for you to try. Should be
fun up here in these beautiful mountains.

You also can go soaring in a plane or just take an airplane
ride. What a way to enjoy the fall foliage. I did it once in a
helicopter and it was sublime.

There are three fireplaces to warm you whether you are in the
living room or the dining rooms. The library lounge has ☞ lots of

books that are well organized in categories such as bike books, children's books, and classics. There is music in here also. They play a lot of old and new jazz and classical jazz; this is such a fine sound. A miniature pool table is tons of fun, or you can enjoy checkers and other games. You might enjoy playing with Fred and Rusty, the inn's yellow Labs.

Comfortable accommodations are here. The rooms are bright and airy and have lovely views.

The terrace in summer is so lovely for Sunday brunch or cocktails. The menu is good and the food is excellent. Under appetizers, escargots *en croute* are good. I liked the baked French onion soup, but there also is a soup du jour. Entrees include filet mignon, Trafalgar Grill (a petite fillet with two jumbo scampi-style shrimp), lamb chops, veal, fish, the chef's Vegetarian Fancy, and daily specials. For Sunday brunch, there are a number of starters in the continental buffet, and six entrees are made to order. The desserts and pastries all are made here and are so good.

How to get there: Take I–93 north, exit at Route 18, and turn left. The inn is on the left, several miles down the road. It is on Wells Road.

Lovett's by Lafayette Brook
Franconia, New Hampshire
03580

Innkeepers: Sharon and Anthony Avrutine
Address/Telephone: Route 18; (603) 823–7761
Rooms: 31, in inn, barn, cottages; 25 with private bath. No smoking inn.
Rates: $86 to $146, double occupancy, MAP. EP rates available.
Open: All year except November.
Facilities and activities: Bag lunches available, bar, game room, heated swimming pool. Nearby: tennis, golf, riding, bicycling, fishing, skiing.

There are a lot of reasons for coming to the White Mountains and Franconia Notch, and one of the reasons is this inn. It was constructed circa 1784, even before a road was built through Franconia Notch.

Sharon and Anthony are the new innkeepers at this fine inn. They work hard to have the best table and the best cellar in the North Country. The menu changes daily and includes a variety of real temptations. On my most recent visit, I had 🖝 Wild White Mountain Blueberry Soup, and it was glorious. Other appetizers were marinated herring in wine sauce and chilled vichyssoise. I also had a moist and yummy Boston scrod. Guests at the next table ordered tenderloin of beef stroganoff, and they reported it to be excellent. The next time I visit here I hope to have the roast loin of pork with fresh applesauce, or maybe I'll choose the mild curried lamb with Lovett's chutney. The chef also puts up his own pickles, and they are great. The inn has its own 🖙 herb garden. At last count there were thirty-seven different herbs at hand. No wonder the food is so good. Desserts, as you would expect, are heavenly.

There is a lovely terrace overlooking the mountains and the pool. Actually there are two pools. One is to the rear of the inn, and the other is fed from mountain springs. Oh, to be that hale and hearty for the latter.

Try to visit the New England Ski Museum, an excellent review of a sport that goes back 5,000 years. It is important to preserve these rare artifacts. It is right in the area.

There is no smoking in this inn. Benjamin, the inn dog, does not like smoke. Neither do I.

How to get there: Take I–93 north, exit at Route 18, and turn left. The inn is on your right.

❁

E: *The bar, the bar! From the staircase in a Newport Mansion, the marble bar is the most inviting spot I've run into in a month of Sundays.*

> *I never thought of business when awakened at an inn*
> *by the three o'clock chime of a nearby church.*

Sugar Hill Inn
Franconia, New Hampshire
03580

Innkeepers: Jim and Barbara Quinn
Address/Telephone: Route 117; (603) 823–5621
Rooms: 10, plus 3 cottages; all with private bath. No smoking inn.
Rates: In summer, $40 to $55, per person, double occupancy, EPB. Fall
    foliage season, $75 to $85, per person, double occupancy, MAP. In
    winter, $65 to $75, per person, double occupancy, MAP.
Open: All year except April and November.
Facilities and activities: Dinner in summer Thursday through Saturday;
    dinner daily rest of year. Full license. Nearby: skiing, riding, fishing,
    canoeing, tennis, golfing, hiking.

The White Mountains are so beautiful and majestic, it is a joy to find the Sugar Hill Inn tucked into this loveliness. It is a charming inn. It was built in 1789 as a farmhouse by one of Sugar Hill's original settlers, and it was converted to an inn in 1929.

The inn has been carefully restored. The innkeepers have made the most of the beautiful old beams and floors and the handsome fireplaces. They have two charming common rooms, each with original fireplaces. Each has comfortable furniture, reading materials, board games, and puzzles. A television is in one of these rooms. In the living room is an antique 🐾 player piano with a lot of rolls. Really fun for a sing-along.

Guest accommodations in the inn and in the three country cottages are lovely. Nice spreads, good mattresses, lovely antiques, and all super clean. The closets are ☞ scented with potpourri. The rooms in the inn are not well suited to children under twelve. The cottages are used from the middle of May through October and are ideal for families. Each cottage has two bedrooms, two bathrooms, and a front porch. Smoking is permitted in the cottages but not in the inn itself.

Jim prepares all the meals. The breakfasts are full country ones and may include super walnut pancakes or Swiss eggs with croissant. Be sure to try the fresh muffins. I had the ☞ pumpkin-raisin muffins.

Dinner starters might include a choice of mushroom dill soup or New England clam chowder. Try the chicken Washington (chicken breast stuffed with crabmeat and covered with hollandaise) or veal Oscar with béarnaise sauce. Two entrees are always offered each evening. Desserts are delicious; raspberry pie, pecan bourbon pie, and chocolate mousse might be available when you're here.

How to get there: Follow Route 18 through Franconia. Turn left on Route 117. The inn is ½ mile up the hill on the right.

☙

E: ☞ *Hot cider on the woodburning stove for skiers is so nice.*

Bernerhof Inn
Glen, New Hampshire
03838

Innkeeper: Rick Spencer; owners, Ted and Sharon Wroblewski
Address/Telephone: Route 302; (603) 383–4414, (800) 548–8007
Rooms: 11; 9 with private bath, 4 with Jacuzzi.
Rates: $75 to $117, double occupancy, EPB.
Open: All year.
Facilities and activities: Lunch July through October, dinner, bar. Sauna, swimming pool.

The bar and lounge of the inn is fondly called the Zumstein Room for Claire and Charlie Zumstein who once owned the inn and introduced Swiss specialties here from their native land. Almost thirty years later the restaurant still features some of them. This is a lovely oak room, done in the style of a European pub. It has its own menu. You can sip some real Gluh Wein or espresso made from freshly ground beans.

Rooms are light and airy and individually decorated. There are two king-sized brass beds and four Jacuzzis. One is in a sensational window alcove. There is a sitting room with a television for your enjoyment. Or perhaps you'd like to unwind with a visit to their ☞ Finnish sauna.

☞ A Taste of the Mountains, a cooking school run by the

innkeepers, is designed for lovers of fine food. If you want to know more, do call or write for a brochure.

Food here is something else, as you might expect from anyone who runs a cooking school. Shrimp remoulade and fettucine aux herbs Provence are good, but the *delices de Gruyère*—a smooth blend of Swiss cheeses, delicately breaded and sautéed and accompanied by a savory tomato blend—is superb. Swiss entrees include *emince de veau au vin blanc,* Weiner schnitzel, and, of course, fondues. Veal ragout is a stew made with braised veal, simmered slowly with vegetables and "old world" spices. Spaetzle is served with it. Noisettes of pork tenderloin are so tasty. The portions served are very generous.

You'll want to leave room for dessert, it's so good. Pot de creme, chocolate fondue, or profiteroles au chocolat—tiny pastries filled with ice cream and topped with chocolate. ☛ The soufflé Grand Marnier is outrageous. I could go on, but I'm getting hungry.

How to get there: From North Conway take Route 16 north. At Glen, turn left onto Route 302. The inn is on your right.

❀

E: *A free champagne breakfast in bed is yours on the third morning of your stay. It comes with eggs Benedict and fresh flowers. My, my.*

The John Hancock Inn
Hancock, New Hampshire
03449

Innkeepers: Glynn and Pat Wells
Address/Telephone: Main Street; (603) 525–3318
Rooms: 10; all with private bath.
Rates: $72 to $75, double occupancy, EP.
Open: All year except one week in early spring, one week in late fall.
Facilities and activities: Breakfast, lunch, dinner, Sunday brunch, lounge.
  Parking. Nearby: swimming, hiking, antiquing, summer theater,
  skiing, tennis.

Operated as an inn since 1789, the John Hancock has been owned by Glynn and Pat since 1973. What a great job they do.

This is a nice old inn. Carefully preserved is ☞ The Mural Room, believed to date back to the early years of the inn. The Carriage Lounge is very unusual, with tables made from giant bellows from an old foundry in Nova Scotia. Seats are made from antique buggy seats. The name stems from the fact that John Hancock, the founding father, once owned most of the land that comprises the present town of Hancock. Set among twisting hills with a weathered clapboard facade, graceful white pillars, and a warm red door, the inn represents all that is good about old inns. Warm welcomes, delicious food, sound drinks, and comfortable beds, set in a quiet town that hasn't changed much in the last two centuries.

Sunday brunch is very popular with the townspeople as well as inn guests. They serve a variety of egg dishes, crepes, and quiche.

Dinner is served by candlelight, and when winter storms howl through the hills the fireplace in the bar has a crackling fire to warm your heart and toes. Braided rugs cover part of the wide-board floors, and primitive paintings hang on the walls. ☛ There is a pastel of the inn, done in 1867, that the Wells were able to acquire. Dinner entrees are excellent. Prime rib, veal, lobster Alfredo, good fish choices, and the chef's choice of the day are some of what you may find. Three of the dining rooms are smoke-free.

Swim in summer in Norway Pond, within walking distance of the inn. Climb mountains, or just sit and listen to the church chimes during foliage time. Alpine and cross-country skiing are nearby in winter. Or browse in the antique shops on a cool spring morn.

The inn dog is a Lhasa named Nay-Daak Poo, which means "little innkeeper."

How to get there: From Boston take Route 128, then Route 3 to 101 west. Hancock is located just off Route 202, 9 miles above Peterborough.

❈

We sat together around a single table and talked
and heard each other in the quiet of the inn.

olive Metcalf

The Meeting House
Henniker, New Hampshire
03242

Innkeepers: June and Bill Davis; Cheryl and Peter Bakke
Address/Telephone: Flanders Road; (603) 428–3228
Rooms: 6; all with private bath.
Rates: $63 to $93, double occupancy, EPB.
Open: All year.
Facilities and activities: Dinner, Sunday brunch. Bar, lounge, hot tub, sauna. Nearby: white-water rafting, downhill skiing, antiquing, theaters.

You can sit in the bar and lounge area of this inn and watch the skiers coming down the hill. Now that's fun. This old barn that houses the restaurant and lounge is 200 years old.

Hanging on the walls are ☞ plastic bags in which people from all over the world have collected shells, stones, sand, and volcano dust, and sent here for display. A nice thing to do. Little white Christmas lights are all over this area. They are so pretty and so unique. Only in a country inn.

When you want breakfast, it is ☞ delivered to your room in a basket, and what a surprise awaits you! (No, I'm not going to tell; you'll have to see for yourself.) The brunch menu is fun. Beaten-egg cookery are seven different omelettes. Whole-egg cookery is just that: eggs with ham or eggs with steak. Their no-egg cookery features banana pancakes, apple pancakes, chicken, and beef. Do come and try it. Brunch is another popular and ample meal.

And dinner. . . . Well, I had ☛ Bermuda lobster. It was sautéed in butter, dark rum, and sherry peppers, and finished with heavy cream. Divine. The other seafood offerings also were ones you don't find very often, and the veal and chicken dishes looked great. Their salad dressings are super. I had an excellent hot bacon dressing. The fried cinnamon apples with ice cream, flavored with apple brandy, were the perfect ending to my dinner.

The rooms are filled with treasures from June's and Bill's former homes. I was delighted to find plenty of books and magazines and plump pillows for reading in bed, a favorite pastime of mine.

After a day of skiing, try the sauna and hot tub in the greenhouse. Sheer luxury!

White-water activities are on the Contoocook River. Antique shops are nearby, and two summer theaters are in neighboring towns. This really is a nice area.

How to get there: In Henniker take Route 14 south for about 2 miles to Pat's Peak sign. Turn right onto Flanders Road. The inn is in about ½ mile on the right.

olive Metcalf

The Manor
Holderness, New Hampshire
03245

Innkeeper: Andy Lamoureux
Address/Telephone: Box T; (603) 968–3348, (800) 545–2141
Rooms: 24, plus 3 housekeeping cottages and 2 housekeeping chalets; all
  with private bath.
Rates: In-season, $142 to $208; off-season, $128 to $178; double occu-
  pancy, MAP. Cottages and apartments rented by week or month.
Open: All year.
Facilities and activities: Sunday brunch. Bar, lounge, swimming pool,
  tennis, boating, ice skating. Nearby: downhill and cross-country
  skiing.

From the moment you drive up the long driveway to the inn,
you are enchanted with the surroundings. Then The Manor comes
into view and your enchantment is complete, the inn is just so
lovely. Built in 1903 by a wealthy Englishman, Isaac Van Horn,
the house still has its original rich wood paneling, beautiful doors
(some with mirrors), magnificently carved moldings, marble fireplaces, and old pedestal sinks. Thankfully, all details have remained unscarred over the years.

There are two handsome library–living rooms with fireplaces.
The Tapestry Lounge is elegant. There also is a cocktail porch
overlooking the lake, so nice on a moonlit night.

The dining rooms are lovely. Beautiful stemware, courteous staff, and good food. From where I had lunch, I could look down on Squam Lake, made famous as the lake in ☛ *On Golden Pond.* Oh my, I do like it here. I had the ☛ best grilled corned beef and Swiss cheese sandwich I ever had. The inn's tangy dressing and homemade pumpernickel bread made the sandwich memorable. Everything on the menu sounded so good, it was hard to choose. Dinner— I wouldn't know where to begin to describe it. The menu is extensive, so even the fussiest person would find it hard to complain. I hate to mention the desserts, they are sinfully good. I think I'll lose ten pounds and go back for a week.

The guest rooms are exceptional with handsome wall-coverings and good beds and chairs. Some have ☛ lovely old pedestal sinks, and nine have fireplaces. The cottages are elegant.

There is everything to do here: swimming pool, tennis, shuffleboard, croquet, Ping-Pong, and much more. The Manor's own canoes, sailboat, and fishing dinghy are free for your use. The *Lady of the Manor* is a luxurious 28-foot pontoon craft, which is available for guided tours of "Golden Pond," parties, picnics, and transportation to Church Island for Sunday services in an outdoor setting. There are thirteen acres for you to play in and 300 feet of sandy beach frontage for you to sunbathe on. If it rains, there are many games to play inside, Bogie the inn dog to visit with, or many places to just relax in at this beautiful mansion.

How to get there: Take Route 3 into Holderness. Cross the bridge, and on the right you will see the signs for The Manor.

The New England Inn
Intervale (North Conway),
New Hampshire
03860

Innkeeper: Kathy Whitbeck
Address/Telephone: Route 16A; (603) 356–5541
Rooms: 25, plus 10 cottage suites and 3 private cottages; all with private
 bath, some with fireplace.
Rates: $65 to $96, per person, double occupancy, MAP. Hiking and tennis
 packages available.
Open: All year.
Facilities and activities: Entertainment on weekends and holidays, conference room, three clay tennis courts, swimming and wading pools,
 skating rink, sleigh rides, cross-country skiing and lighted trails for
 nighttime.

"If you enjoy the charm of an authentic country inn where
cozy intimacy has been carefully preserved over the centuries by
conscientious innkeepers . . . if you relish the warm feeling of a
gracious country inn with a reputation for hospitality and friend-
liness . . . if you enjoy savoring hearty New England regional
foods, selected wines, and hearty drinks . . . if you like sports and
outdoor recreation . . . if you prefer just plain quiet and relaxation
. . . you'll love the village at The New England Inn."

218

It is said so well in their brochure, I just stole it.

When you arrive at the inn in any season, the sight is glorious, a white rambling country inn in the shadows of the White Mountains. The living rooms are gracious, with plenty of chairs and couches. Nice to curl up in with a good book, or, as I am prone to do, with needlework. The guest rooms are smashing, and all have recently been done over. After a full day they are a real pleasure to return to. Besides the rooms in the inn, there are ten suites (each with a fireplace) in village houses and four one-room cottages with fireplace and cable television.

This is an all-American inn. The food and wine are as ☞ all-American as apple pie, and they have that, too. Try New England chicken and shrimp sauté, New England chicken pot pie, or Shaker cranberry pot roast. I've had the pot roast, and it's glorious. The wines, all-American, are served in crockery pitchers. A nice change from the ordinary.

They are involved with the ☞ Intervale Nordic Center. Between the inn and the Forest Inn next door are 35 kilometers of marked trails. Start off right by being outfitted in proper-fitting equipment, next take a lesson from a PSIA-certified instructor, and then go and enjoy cross-country skiing. The Intervale Tavern at the inn, with a blazing fireplace, serves skiers lunch and après-ski. A good hot chili is nice when you are cold.

Plan on a week at a time at this lovely inn. There is so much to do inside and out, and in any season.

How to get there: The inn is at the Gateway to the White Mountains, a Resort Loop, Route 16A, 3½ miles north of the village of North Conway.

✱

E: Tuesday night is Hoot Night, with local entertainment.

olive Metcalf

Christmas Farm Inn
Jackson, New Hampshire
03846

Innkeepers: Bill and Sydna Zeliff
Address/Telephone: P.O. Box 176; (603) 383–4313
Rooms: 37, including suites and cabins; all with private bath.
Rates: $68 to $90, per person, double occupancy, MAP. Special weekly
   and package rates.
Open: All year.
Facilities and activities: Pub, swimming pool, game room, putting green, 80
   kilometers of cross-country trails, golf, tennis, sauna, complimentary
   movies. Nearby: downhill skiing, alpine slide, canoeing on Saco
   River.

Yes, Virginia, there is a Christmas Farm Inn, and they have
the Mistletoe Pub and the Sugar Plum Dining Room to prove it.
The food is fit for any Santa and his helpers, from the hearty, full
country breakfast, which includes ☛ homemade doughnuts,
muffins, and sticky buns, to gracious dinners that include three
entrees each evening, two homemade soups, a full salad bar,
homemade breads, and a complete dessert menu. Children age
twelve and under have their own special menu.

The food is excellent. The ☛ medallions of pork MacIntosh
are glorious and have a hint of brandy. Veal and chicken are so

tender. Treats from the seas are real treats. The desserts do indeed make visions of sugarplums dance in your head, and all are made right here. How about apple pie, carrot cake, or the Christmas Farm special sundae? From here take a quick trip to the Mistletoe Pub for a nightcap.

Separate from the main building is the Christmas Farm function center. Perfect spot for not only medium to small business meetings, but also weddings, anniversaries, and the like. At one side of the room is a 12-foot-wide fieldstone fireplace. There are games of all sorts, a sauna, bar, and four nice suites that are ideal for families.

Also separate are the cottages, each with living room, fireplace, two bedrooms, and two baths. The rooms in the main building have Christmas names: Holly, Dasher, Prancer, Vixen, Donner, Cupid, Comet, and Blitzen. There are two deluxe rooms with Jacuzzi tubs.

Jackson is in the heart of the White Mountains, so bring your skis, or come in the summer for the annual Christmas-in-July Week. ☛ There's a magnificent gala Christmas party Wednesday night with an outside buffet and Christmas tree, as well as live entertainment, dancing, shuffleboard, and golf tournaments. Santa must live nearby, because he never fails to arrive in a most unusual manner. And when he comes, he's eagerly greeted by the inn dog, Daffodil.

How to get there: Go north on Route 16 from North Conway. A few miles after Route 302 branches off to your left, you will see a covered bridge on your right. Take the bridge through the village and up the hill ¼ mile, and there is the inn.

෴

E: *Making memories is something Bill and Sydna and their staff know all about.*

olive Metcalf

Dana Place Inn
Jackson, New Hampshire
03846

Innkeepers: Harris and Mary Lou Levine
Address/Telephone: Route 16; (603) 383–6822, (800) 537–9276
Rooms: 35; 31 with private bath.
Rates: $55 to $85, double occupancy, EPB. $110 to $135, double occupancy, MAP. Special weekend package rates.
Open: All year.
Facilities and activities: Picnic lunch available. Bar, lounge, facilities for small conferences, hot tub, swimming pool, cross-country skiing, two all-weather tennis courts. Nearby: golf, downhill skiing.

The inn is nestled at the foot of magnificent Mount Washington in a beautiful valley next to the Ellis River. The mountain alone draws hikers and climbers and skiers who brave the big spill to ski Tuckerman's Ravine each spring, and visitors who journey to the top of the mountain via the Cog Railway or the auto road. All of this plus this beautiful inn to stay in.

The inn was built in the mid-nineteenth century and surely must have been a stagecoach stop. We know it was once a farmhouse, set in an apple orchard, and built by Antwin Dana. Set your own pace along lawns, gardens, streams, meadows, and woodland trails. Walk through the orchard, pass the swimming pool, take the country road past the tennis courts along a mossy tree-shaded path, through a clearing, and you'll be at a 🖙 crystal-clear, rockbound pool in the Ellis River. Peace here is beyond description. There are five rooms in Tree House, which is by the river. A tree grows right through the deck. If you want to go off for the day for other activities, you'll find golf, canoeing, kayaking, racquetball, family attractions like Storyland, outlet shopping in North Conway, as well as skiing.

The interior of the inn has been beautifully updated. The hot tub is in a room by itself and an indoor swimming pool is in its own room. The dining rooms with pink napery and flowers are restful, and the food is good. 🖙 A good way to start your dinner is with the spinach and mushroom ravioli, smoked salmon, or seafood bisque. These are followed by good salads and wonderful entrees. Salmon fillet comes wrapped in puff pastry and served with a spinach and herb beurre blanc. Veal saltimbocca, five beef favorites, rack of lamb, veal Oscar, roast duck, and chicken Gloria are more dinner possibilities. Their Dana Garden Scampi is shrimp sautéed with garlic, julienne vegetables, and wine. Desserts are wonderful. All baking is done right here. If you're too full to move after dinner, the inn shows a movie every evening at eight o'clock.

You wake up to a very good breakfast. The menu has Disney toast. I won't tell you how it's made, so you'll have to come and try it. The list goes on to include pancakes, johnnycakes, waffles, cereals, and more. Do come up and try this lovely inn.

How to get there: Take I–95 north to Portsmouth, then the Spaulding Turnpike to Route 16 north at Rochester. Follow Route 16 north past Jackson Village for about 4½ miles.

❋

E: *The hammock on the lawn overlooks the Ellis River. Lovely spot.*

The Inn at Thorn Hill
Jackson, New Hampshire
03846

Innkeepers: Peter and Linda La Rose
Address/Telephone: Thorn Hill Road; (603) 383–4242
Rooms: 16, in 2 buildings, plus 3 cottage suites; all with private bath. No smoking inn.
Rates: $55 to $96, per person, double occupancy, MAP.
Open: All year except April.
Facilities and activities: Bar, swimming pool, cross-country skiing. Nearby: downhill skiing, golf club.

Over the Honeymoon Bridge to The Inn at Thorn Hill you go, and when you get there you will find a Victorian beauty. Mountains are everywhere you look from this inn. Relax on the 🖙 porch in a New England rocking chair and enjoy the view. Even on a bad day it is spectacular.

I loved the Victorian parlor and the spacious drawing room with a wood stove and an unbelievable view. A pair of 🖙 Victorian ladies in their finery stand at the windows next to the lovely old Victrola. There are board games, cards, and books for you to enjoy. A cozy pub with a fireplace and five bar stools has lots of cheer.

Elegant country dining by candlelight is what you get, and the

224

food is good. The menu is revised nightly to offer variety and popular seasonal dishes. Rosemary smoked shrimp with black beans is an example of their good appetizers. The soups and salads are interesting. And the entrees are grand. Mahi-mahi with lobster and dill sauce. Shrimp with fresh pea and ginger sauce. Breast of duck with two sauces. Grilled lamb chops with roasted garlic butter. The list goes on. The desserts that follow are excellent.

There is a Victorian flair to all the inn rooms. A variety of beds is available—canopies, singles, doubles, kings, and queens—and all rooms have wonderful views of the mountains. The carriage house next door has a ☛ 20-by-40-foot great room with a fireplace and seven guest rooms, so bring a gang and have some fun. This is the place to be. The cottages are very nice and just great for those who want more privacy. The inn's facilities are not well suited to small children.

There is much to do here. The inn has its own swimming pool; hiking and downhill skiing are close at hand; and cross-country skiing begins at the doorstep and joins the 146-kilometer Jackson touring network.

How to get there: Go north from Portsmouth, New Hampshire, on the Spaulding Turnpike (Route 16) all the way to Jackson, which is just above North Conway. At Jackson is a covered bridge on your right. Take the bridge, and just 1 block this side of the village center on the right is Thorn Hill Road, which you take up the hill. The inn is on your right.

> *"And now once more I shape my way*
> *Thro' rain or shine, thro' thick or thin,*
> *Secure to meet, at close of day*
> *With kind reception, at an inn."*
> —William Shenstone, 1714–1763
> (written at the Inn at Henley)

Olive Metcalf

Nestlenook Farm
Jackson, New Hampshire
03846

Innkeeper: Roger Bintliff; owners, Robert and Nancy Cyr
Address/Telephone: Dinsmore Road (mailing address: P.O. Box Q); (603) 383–9443
Rooms: 5, plus 2 suites; all with private bath and Jacuzzi. No smoking inn.
Rates: In-season, $105 to $216, double occupancy, EP. Off-season, $85 to $140, double occupancy, EPB.
Open: All year.
Facilities and activities: Full breakfast, dinner for inn guests only. Pub, full liquor license, game room, pool, sleigh rides, cross-country skiing, ice skating, fishing.

Wend your way through a covered bridge and down a country lane to this wonderful Victorian farmhouse complete with
☛ lots of gingerbread. It's truly a feast for the eyes. Walk up the walk to the porch with rockers and wicker furniture—oh, this is a good place to sit and relax—and on into the 200-year-old house, where you'll see a Victorian settee and chairs, a small wood stove, and a Victorian birdcage full of finches. A bit farther and you are in an intimate pub. There is a comfortable parlor with good couches, and the stone fireplace is the original one. A game room is downstairs, full of lots of things to do, even movies to watch.

All of the rooms are named after well-known local artists and include original paintings as part of the decor. There are four-poster queen- and king-sized canopy beds. Eighteenth-century parlor stoves are in all but one room, which has a Count Rumford fireplace. Each room has a wonderful view. One suite occupies the entire third floor and has a ☞ separate Jacuzzi room with a wet bar. It accommodates up to four people.

The dining room, as expected, is lovely. It looks into the original kitchen, which has a beautiful new, old-fashioned stove that is only to be looked at. You can choose from three or four dinner entrees like poached salmon with dill sauce, steak au poivre done tableside, and various veal dishes. Desserts are made right here, such as flaming crepes, and—I like this one—there is the cake of the evening.

The inn sits on sixty-five acres of land. A real ☞ Victorian swimming pool is here, surrounded by comfortable hammocks and wonderful flowers. There are miniature horses from Switzerland and reindeer from Japan. Winter brings sleigh rides, ice skating on the pond, and cross-country skiing from the door. The trails are part of the world-class Jackson Ski Foundation, which has more than 150 kilometers of tracked and groomed skiing. If you're looking for something else—well, as they say here at the inn, romance and relaxation is what the inn stands for.

How to get there: Go through the covered bridge at Jackson and take the first right turn at their sign. Go about ¼ mile to the inn, which is on the right.

Olive Metcalf

Whitney's Village Inn
Jackson, New Hampshire
03846

Innkeepers: The Tannehill and Kelley Families
Address/Telephone: Route 16B (mailing address: P.O. Box W); (603) 383–6886, (800) 252–5622
Rooms: 33, including 2 cottages; all with private bath.
Rates: $60 to $80, per person, MAP. EP rates available.
Open: All year.
Facilities and activities: Lunch in season or box lunch. Bar, lounge, TV and VCR with movies, skiing, ice skating, tennis, swimming, summertime hayrides.

I've always liked this inn but now I like it even more. Three generations of innkeepers now run the inn, and they all are concerned about personalizing the service and watching out for your every need. Terry and Judy Tannehill were the original innkeepers. They have been joined by their daughter, Tara, and her husband, Scott Kelley; their grandson, P.J., born in 1989; and their son, Mitch, who is responsible for the dining room. One of them is always on hand to greet you when you arrive, and many weekday evenings they have an Innkeepers' Reception with hors d'oeuvres.

Dinner is superb in a casually elegant dining room. Mauve

and tan are the napery colors. They have a new chef who is really good, but they still prepare their excellent Jackson-style duckling. Every night a pasta of the evening, a veal of the evening, and the innkeepers' choice are offered. The innkeepers highlight a very country-oriented dish such as roast loin of pork or roast turkey, which is always a very popular selection on the menu. In the summer a lobster cookout is held by the brook once a week.

This is an authentic mountain hideaway nestled in among New Hampshire's White Mountains. It's pretty nice to be able to crawl out of bed, dress, have a sumptuous breakfast, and ☛ walk across to the lifts, trails, ski shop or ski school, all just a snowball's throw away. It is a real treat not to have to drive the car anywhere after you get here. Black Mountain, with its own snowmaking equipment, is right here. The lifts can handle about 3,000 skiers per hour, so there is hardly any waiting. There are many trails that serve the mountain, and all are kept in the best condition possible. A lighted skating rink is right beside the inn. Bring your own skates or borrow some here. The inn also has sleigh rides.

Summer fun is the inn's own swimming pond, which is in such a pretty setting on the lovely grounds. There are also all sorts of lawn games. Inside is a game room, well equipped with Ping-Pong, television, and all sorts of games. One of the parlors has puzzles in the making, nice comfortable furniture, a Steinway piano, and lovely old oriental carpets. There are Hunter fans all over the inn. Then there is the Shovel Handle Pub for après-ski fun and entertainment on weekends. Lunch in season is served out here.

Most of the guest rooms have new finishing touches with antiques, country wallpapers, and quilts. Some of the rooms have nice wingback chairs. Try it here. You will like it.

How to get there: Go north from Conway 22 miles on Route 16. Take a right on Route 16A through a covered bridge into Jackson Village. Take Route 16B to the top of the hill to the inn.

✳

E: *A really nice touch for families in the summer and on school vacation weeks is a special children's table. Dinner at six o'clock is followed by a movie. Parents and children both can enjoy themselves.*

The Wildcat Inn
Jackson, New Hampshire
03846

Innkeepers: Pam and Marty Sweeney
Address/Telephone: Route 16A; (603) 383–4245
Rooms: 12; 10 with private bath.
Rates: $40 to $45, per person, EPB.
Open: All year.
Facilities and activities: Lunch daily in-season, weekends off-season. Dinner, bar. Music in lounge. Downhill and cross-country skiing, hiking, tennis, riding.

The brochure here at Wildcat says it so well, I'm just going to repeat it. "Everything you need for a perfect vacation is within ☛ walking distance of the inn, so leave your car out back and save gas, money, and time. Begin in the Tavern Gardens, where you will be well fed and properly wined from breakfast through last call. Tennis, your choice of one hard and three clay courts. Golf at the beautiful Wentworth Hall course. Riding lessons, shows, and trail rides through mountain forests. There are package deals for all of the above. Fishing, hiking, or just meandering through town; good shopping is up here. And both downhill and cross-country skiing are nearby."

The tavern has two big fireplaces and nice couches, and on

weekends and holidays there is music. Accommodations are comfortable. All the rooms are different and each one has a view.

The Wildcat is a very popular dining spot. In fact, some years ago the big old front porch had to be converted into a dining room to make more dining space for all the people who wanted to eat here. The food here will ☞ titillate your taste buds. All meals are made to order and, as the chef says, patience is a virtue. Breakfasts are full, with all pastries baked right here. There are tavern specials at lunch. ☞ Lobster Benedict is different. I had it for lunch one day. Another day I tried one called Salmagundi; enough food for an army and delicious. Also, lovely lox on a bagel! Marvelous salads, six of them, all accompanied by homemade breads. Be sure to read the sign with the rules of the tavern. It's very funny.

And at dinnertime good appetizers and soups. One entree is baked seafood platter, which is different every day. Wildcat chicken is chicken wrapped in puff pastry. Tempura is so good. A few of their desserts are sour cream apple pie, rhubarb pudding cake, frozen raspberry soufflé, so what are you waiting for?

How to get there: Take Route 16 north from North Conway. Take Route 16A to your right, through a covered bridge, and into Jackson. The inn is in the center of town.

✸

E: There are a lot of inns in Jackson, but only this one serves lunch.

The Ammonoosuc Inn
Lisbon, New Hampshire
03585

Innkeepers: Laura and Steve Bromley
Address/Telephone: Bishop Road; (603) 838–6118
Rooms: 9; all with private bath.
Rates: $50 to $85, double occupancy, continental breakfast.
Open: All year.
Facilities and activities: Dinner, Sunday brunch, full license. Privileges at
   Lisbon Village Country Club—golf, swimming pool, cross-country
   skiing, sledding, tennis. Nearby: fishing, canoeing, downhill skiing.

The inn was constructed as a farmhouse in 1888. It has been restored and remodeled into an inn with a fine restaurant called Cobblers.

The inn sits up high and overlooks the Ammonoosuc River, which flows peacefully along. ☛ Fishing is great. Tubing down the river would be fun. The Lisbon Village Country Club is right next door and offers many activities. Its golf course was designed by ☛ Ralph M. Bartin, a renowned golf architect. The club has its own clubhouse and lounge.

Relaxing at the inn after a day of fun is easy. The lounge has a wood stove, and the parlors are comfortable. Everything is aimed at your comfort. There is satellite television for you to enjoy. The guest rooms are lovely and very tastefully decorated.

The dining room has its original wood paneling and beams. Breakfast has Danish and other pastries. For dinner there are traditional New England entrees and a lot more. Steamed mussels, Greek sausage, calamari, and good soups are nice for a start. There are four chicken dishes. ☛ Chicken Grand Marnier gets my vote. Barbecued pork ribs is another good dish. The seafood medley is served on linguine, and the combos take care of two taste treats—ribs and shrimp or steak and shrimp. Of course there are veal dishes and steak. This is a really nice menu. Sunday brunch is just as good with a variety of dishes.

There is so much to do here, you should be sure to come for more than one day. If you like skiing, the inn is fifteen minutes from Cannon Mountain. I, for one, would love to go sledding on the golf course. In warmer weather the porch with rockers is my idea of peace. Just sit back and rock and watch the river. Of course, Tasha, the inn dog, is here, too.

How to get there: From I–91, take Exit 17 (Woodsville–Wells River). Go east on Route 302 to Lisbon. Two miles past Lisbon take a left on Lyman Road for about ½ mile, then left onto Bishop Road for about ¾ mile. The inn is on the right.

*

*The time between sunset and the completeness of night
should be spent around a well-laid board
with assurances of a warm bed to follow.*

olive Metcalf

Lyme Inn
Lyme, New Hampshire
03768

Innkeepers: Fred and Judy Siemons
Address/Telephone: Route 10; (603) 795–2222
Rooms: 14; 12 with private bath.
Rates: $96 to $150, double occupancy, MAP. $66 to $120, double occupancy, EPB.
Open: All year except two weeks in late spring and the Sunday after Thanksgiving to Christmas.
Facilities and activities: Dining room closed Tuesdays. Bar. Nearby: Dartmouth College, golf course, canoeing, fishing, skiing.

Lyme was the most productive sheepraising town in New England during the mid-1800s. Now it is mainly a quiet residential town and close to Dartmouth College and Mary Hitchcock Regional Hospital in nearby Hanover. The inn dates back to 1809 and sits at the end of the common.

All of the inn's original rooms have been restored in keeping with the age of the building. The wide pine floorboards are handsome. The rooms are different in size and are full of antiques, quilts, four-poster beds, and hooked rugs. Judy's beautiful handmade quilts are for sale in the inn. The inn is not well suited to children under eight.

The tavern—a really nice place to meet new friends—has a small fireplace. Great on a cold night. There are antique tavern tables in here.

Dining rooms wander about the inn. Good food is served in them. ☛ Deep-fried mushrooms or escargots are always a favorite. Fresh homemade soups are a plus, with a different one each day. The inn offers a light supper, which is nice when you are not very hungry. However, for the hungry, entrees like Alaskan King Crab legs or beer-batter shrimp are good seafood choices. Hunter-style veal is veal stuffed with Swiss cheese and ham, served with a delicious herb sauce. Desserts, naturally, are good.

There is an extensive library for guests to enjoy. You are ☛ encouraged to take home a partially read book and return it when you are finished. This is nice.

There is much to do in the area. Great walking, great hiking, and wonderful skiing. Many people who stay here enjoy going over to Dartmouth College for its Ivy League sports competitions and fine cultural events. Locally you have a golf course, and there is canoeing on the Connecticut River. There are many secluded ponds for the fisherman to try his luck. And, of course, you have antique shops all about.

And do try a hot dog at the general store just on the other side of the common. Rare treat. So is Duffy, the real inn dog.

How to get there: Take Exit 14 from I–91. The inn is located east of the interstate on Route 10, right at the village common.

❋

You cannot hide a good country inn.

Olive Metcalf

The Inn at Mill Falls
Meredith, New Hampshire
03253

Innkeeper: Kathy Cummings
Address/Telephone: Route 3; (603) 279–7006
Rooms: 54; all with private bath, cable TV, phone.
Rates: $90 to $140, EP.
Open: All year.
Facilities and activities: Full breakfast, lunch, dinner, Sunday brunch, bar
   and lounge. Indoor pool, sauna, whirlpool spa, shops, art gallery.
   Boating, swimming, and fishing in lake. Nearby: tennis, racquetball,
   golf, skiing.

The inn is in what was once an old mill. It straddles an
underground canal that runs from Lake Waukewan in the hills
above to Lake Winnipesaukee below. Through a window near the
lobby you will see a sluice that is solid ice in winter.

The inn can accommodate banquets, seminars, conferences,
and special events. Everything is here: mooring for your boat,
newspapers, indoor pool, whirlpool spa and sauna, video rentals,
safety-deposit boxes, and boating on beautiful Winnipesaukee, the
🖝 sixth largest natural lake entirely within the United States. It is
28 miles long and 9 miles wide. The M.S. *Mount Washington* is an
excursion ship that will take you on a 50-mile cruise. Or sail the

Queen of Winnipesaukee, a 46-foot sloop. There are others to choose from. You prefer sports on solid ground? Golf, jogging, skiing, hiking, tennis, and racquetball are all in the area, too. And twenty shops and an art gallery are right here if you'd rather do something less active.

The enclosed walkway leading from the lobby spans the tumbling falls and connects the inn with the Mill Falls Marketplace. This 180-year-old restored mill building is the setting for the inn's full-service tavern and restaurant. Millworks has great breakfasts, both large and small ones. At luncheon there is a good selection of sandwiches. The ☛ brandied onion soup offered at dinner is glorious. The salads are very choice, and the entrees are excellent. You must try it here. Mame's is a small restaurant with many interesting things on the menu. Sunday brunch is served here, and the eggs Benedict are perfect.

The accommodations are yummy with wall-to-wall carpets, telephones, and cable television. ☛ Well-lighted areas are provided for reading or for work (if you must). This is a wonderful vacation spot and well run by Kathy, who is a very nice person.

How to get there: From I–93 take Exit 23. Go east on Route 104 to its end. Go left on Route 3 north. The inn is in 1 mile, down the hill, on the left.

The Ram in the Thicket
Milford, New Hampshire
03055

Innkeepers: Andrew and Priscilla Tempelman
Address/Telephone: Maple Street; (603) 654–6440
Rooms: 9; 3 with private bath.
Rates: $60 to $75, double occupancy, continental breakfast.
Open: All year.
Facilities and activities: Dinner, bar. Hot tub, indoor swimming pool, horseback riding, hiking. Nearby: summer theater.

The unusual name of the inn is taken from the old Bible story of Abraham and Isaac. As a substitute for his son Isaac's death, Abraham finds "a ram caught in the thicket" sent by the Lord. Andrew and Priscilla founded the inn as a substitute for a life in the Midwest from which they wanted a change.

Luckily for all inn lovers, the Tempelmans' move has resulted in another better-than-nice inn. This old Victorian mansion has been carefully restored and now has lovely dining rooms with crystal chandeliers, ▰ a hand-carved fireplace, and many other Victorian touches. One dining room has lovely blue delft tiles. The innkeepers are Dutch. The New Hampshire lounge has plants hanging from the ceilings.

You will surely love the inventive and interesting dinners.

238

Pork Nyama is tenderloin of pork, marinated with garlic, mint, and cloves, and served with a hot African carrot relish. Camay Chicken is chunks of chicken breast in spiced rum and orange juice, then sautéed with rum-saturated orange slices, dates, and pine nuts. These are just an example of what you can expect. The menu changes every three months. In the summer, all this good food can be savored on the screened porch.

This good inn is set in eight acres of wonderful country for roaming. Horses and sheep are in the lower pasture and you also have Jaws II, the cat, and her friends. Summer theater is close by. If you love to walk, there are many trails right at hand.

How to get there: Take Route 3 and just about at Nashua take Exit 7 west on 101A to 101 about 15 miles to Wilton. Watch for the inn's signs. The inn is 200 yards from the Wilton line.

When life dwindles thin and you wonder
if the sun will rise on another day,
seek perhaps an unfamiliar but rejuvenating bed
in a nearby country inn.

New London Inn
New London, New Hampshire
03257

Innkeepers: John and Maureen Follansbee
Address/Telephone: P.O. Box 8; (603) 526–2791, FAX (603) 526–2749
Rooms: 30; all with private bath.
Rates: $55 to $75, single; $75 to $95, double; EPB.
Open: All year.
Facilities and activities: Lunch, dinner, bar. Nearby: skiing, theater, golf,
    two public beaches, water sports.

This college-town inn has been restored back to the grandeur
it had in 1792 when it began serving the traveler. The Follansbees
have been faithful to detail, even right down to the new 🖙
Federal-period sign that hangs in front of the inn. This restoration
has been a tremendous job for them, and I applaud them for their
effort. And their gardens are lovely.

As you enter the inn you immediately appreciate the long
veranda. There's also another one upstairs with the rooms. Do
come up and try the 🖙 rockers. Rooms in the inn are large, airy,
and comfortable. Each one is decorated differently from another.

Cool cream and green are the colors of the dining room. It has
large windows and the original fireplace is still working. For an
almost 200-year-old fireplace, that's a lot of fires! The dining

room's gracious ambience is well suited to the wonderful food.

The dinner menu features such enticing appetizers as warm asparagus strudel with light wine and herb sauce, and lemon pepper pasta with fresh vegetables and Italian bacon. For soups they have ☛ bisque of New England spring vegetables and chilled tomato lime and scallop soup, among others. Oh, I love interesting soups. Entrees are innovative, like grilled marinated monkfish served with red and yellow pepper coulis, grilled smoked duck breast served with spicy white beans and corn crepes, and spiced beef medallions with lime-cilantro butter and avocado sauce. Boy, it's hard to choose which one to eat! Desserts are very good and prepared daily. Breakfasts feature freshly squeezed orange or grapefruit juice.

The town of New London, home of Colby-Sawyer College, still has the feeling of a nineteenth-century village. From its wide main streets, fields, fences, and gracious houses to the beautiful mountains, it's just a lovely place to be. Its location in the Mount Sunapee lake region means there are three lakes close by that offer all the water sports. Golf is nice because there is no waiting, and there is good skiing.

Living here in the inn are an American short-haired cat named Loco and an Abyssinian named Zuni.

This is a beautiful part of the world any time of the year, so come on up.

How to get there: Take Exit 8 at Ascutney, Vermont, from I–91. Follow signs to Claremont, New Hampshire. Take Route 11 east to Newport, Sunapee, Georges Mills, and New London. There is bus service via Vermont Transit from Boston, and from White River Junction, Vermont.

Pleasant Lake Inn
New London, New Hampshire
03257

Innkeepers: Grant and Margaret Rich
Address/Telephone: Pleasant Street; (603) 526–6271
Rooms: 10, plus 1 suite; all with private bath.
Rates: $65 to $85, double occupancy, EPB.
Open: All year.
Facilities and activities: Dinner for houseguests by reservation, bar. Swimming, boating, fishing, and all winter sports.

Pleasant Lake Inn is the oldest operating inn in this area. It began as a farm in 1790 and became an inn almost one hundred years ago.

Inn guests today are given privileges at the Slope and Shore Club on Pleasant Lake, just across the road, which offers tennis, boating, fishing, and swimming. There are iceboating and cross-country skiing here in the winter. The inn also has a nice pond for ice skating on the property, and downhill skiing is close at hand. King Ridge is five minutes away. Mount Sunapee and Whaleback are fifteen minutes away, Pat's Peak is twenty-five minutes away, and many more are within an hour's drive. Back at the inn, spend some time at the bumper pool table in the family room. It's a favorite game of mine.

The view from the inn's front windows is magnificent, and in the fall, it's ☞ spectacular. The inn looks right out onto Pleasant Lake, and beautiful Mount Kearsarge is just on the other side of the lake.

There are antique furnishings, warming fireplaces, nice views, and very comfortable guest rooms throughout the inn. Two cockatiels are here. One is gray and one is white. They sure are pretty.

The food served in the pleasant dining rooms is good. Breakfast is hearty and includes a longtime favorite of mine, blueberry pancakes. Dinner appetizers include a beauty: ☞ escargots in mushroom caps with herbed garlic butter, baked in a pastry shell. All sauces and soups are prepared with fresh ingredients, ☞ no artificial agents, and sauces are thickened by natural reduction instead of with heavy starches. Entrees include steaks, chops, veal, chicken, and fish. They have nice liqueur parfaits for dessert and, as they say, if you have a favorite, they will try to make it.

How to get there: From I–89 take either New London exit. Halfway through New London, turn at the New London Trust Company. This is Pleasant Street. Go about 2 miles, and the inn is on your left.

☙

When the stars are lost and rain seeps coldly
upon the ground, how wonderful to find a lighted inn.

Olive Metcalf

The Inn at Coit Mountain
Newport, New Hampshire
03773

Innkeepers: Dick and Judi Tatem
Address/Telephone: Route 10; (603) 863–3583 or (800) 367–2364
Rooms: 5; 1 with private bath, 2 with fireplace, all with refrigerator.
Rates: $85 to $150, double occupancy, EPB.
Open: All year.
Facilities and activities: Lunch and dinner for houseguests only and by reservation only. BYOB. Sleigh rides. Stoneagle Frame Studio.

The history behind this inn is so interesting that I will share it with you from the inn's brochure. "Built in 1790 by a farmer named Taylor, the white Georgian home was purchased in 1878 by Austin Corbin II as a wedding present for his daughter Mary and her French-born husband, René Cheronette-Champollian. René's family had a distinguished history on the continent. This was their summer home until 1910 when their son André and his wife moved in full time. They added the 35-foot, two-story library and well-lit studio. André, an American, served France in World War I and died a hero. Their only son, René, lived here until his death in 1959. A closet door still records his growth chart as a young boy."

The huge library has a massive granite fireplace and oak paneling. It's so nice to read, knit, or just sit and relax in this room. Just off the library is the ☛ Stoneagle Frame Studio, a custom picture-frame shop. You can't miss its large arched window designed to resemble the window in Independence Hall in Philadelphia.

Two of the rooms have fireplaces, and one room has a balcony. All the rooms have a small refrigerator. There is a bathtub with a ☛ Victorian lampshade over it so you can read in the tub. Honest, you should see it.

A full gourmet breakfast is served. Fresh juice, pecan waffles, muffins, bacon and eggs, eggs Benedict, and more make this quite a breakfast. The dinners are also gourmet. One entree is served each night. You might find roast lamb, lemon chicken, Greek stew, pork roast, chicken tarragon, and chicken divan. They have their own garden, so you know the vegetables are the best possible. Desserts are sinful. French silk pie and lemon pudding cake are just a few of the choices. It's nice here. Come and visit.

How to get there: The inn is on Route 10, just north of Newport.

olive Metcalf

The Scottish Lion Inn
North Conway, New Hampshire
03860

Innkeepers: Michael and Janet Procopio
Address/Telephone: Route 16; (603) 356–6381
Rooms: 7; all with private bath.
Rates: $25 to $45, per person, EPB.
Open: All year except Christmas Eve and Christmas Day.
Facilities and activities: Lunch, dinner, bar. Parking.

When you come down the road and see the magnificent flag streaming out in the wind, you just can't go by. Stop for a drink, if you can't stay the night. You'll love it.

The rooms at The Scottish Lion Inn are cozy. One has an eyelet-trimmed canopy bed, another a spool bed with a patchwork quilt. All are charming. The whole inn is full of fine ☛ Scottish paintings. Do not miss any of them.

Food, of course, features the best of Scottish touches. A hearty Scottish breakfast is served to houseguests. Dinner is rated three stars in the Mobil Guide. Highland game pie, which is venison, beef, hare, and fowl simmered in wine and baked in puff pastry, may sound strange, but a gentleman who had had it the night before reported to me, "Delicious." Hot Scottish oatcakes are served instead of bread or rolls. A marvelous dish named ☛

Rumbledethumps is one of the potato choices; what a taste. I must tell you one more: Lobster Lady Tweedsmuir, tender pieces of lobster in a delicate cream and Drambuie sauce, stuffed in the shell. You must try this dish.

For dessert, Scottish trifle or Scots crumpets with fresh fruit and honey are but a few. The inn also serves a very special coffee. The pub has a long list of tantalizing pleasures, such as Hoot Mon cocktail, St. Andrews Hole-in-One, or Loch Ness Monster.

How to get there: Take Route 16 to North Conway. The inn is 1 mile north from the center of town, on the left.

✴

> *I was lost, I was tired, I was discouraged,*
> *and then I found a friendly inn.*

olive Metcalf

The 1785 Inn
North Conway, New Hampshire
03860

Innkeepers: Charles and Rebecca Mallar
Address/Telephone: Route 16; (603) 356–9025
Rooms: 16; 11 with private bath.
Rates: $55 to $110, double occupancy, EPB.
Open: All year.
Facilities and activities: Dinner, bar, lounge. Nearby: golf, tennis, swimming pool, canoeing, fishing, skiing.

The 1785 Inn is one of the oldest houses in all of Mount Washington Valley. It was built in 1785 by Captain Elijah Dinsmore. Records indicate that Captain Dinsmore received a license to "keep a Publik House" in 1795. In addition to being a public house, the lovely old inn served as a stagecoach stop. The chimney and dining room fireplace with brick oven are original to the house. They form a beehive structure the size of an entire room in the center of the inn.

Guest accommodations are ample. The Mallars have completely refurbished the inn. What a large undertaking! They have done such a fine job. There is a ☛ sink in all the rooms. I find this a very nice feature in rooms with shared baths.

There are two living areas; both have fireplaces, and one has a television set. They are furnished with attractive chairs and couches for your comfort. An old oak icebox is in here. It surely makes a beautiful piece of furniture. The tavern has a large bar, a woodburning stove, and good sitting areas. There is light classical music here at times.

The views from the porch–dining room are just lovely. The food is inventive and very good. I had a salad here once: ☞ crab and shrimp served on top of spinach and alfalfa sprouts, tomatoes, and herbed dill dressing. Wow, it was good. Another dinner dish is raspberry duck: duck roasted with a brandy-laced raspberry sauce and served on wild rice. There are several veal selections, and, of course, fish, chicken, and beef. The desserts are wild. ☞ Deep-fried ice cream. Honest, and it's great. So is the chocolate velvet. Becky does wonders with raspberry desserts.

This is a nice inn surround by many activities, good food— what more can you want?

How to get there: Take Route 16 north. The inn is on the left just before you come to Route 16A.

❀

> *"Enough," he cried*
> *and left with all speed*
> *for the neighborhood inn.*

Stonehurst Manor
North Conway, New Hampshire
03860

Innkeeper: Peter Rattay
Address/Telephone: Route 16; (603) 356–3113
Rooms: 16 in the manor, 10 in the annex adjoining the manor; 24 with
  private bath, air conditioning, cable TV, radio.
Rates: $50 to $135, double occupancy, EP. MAP and package rates
  available in summer and fall.
Open: All year.
Facilities and activities: Breakfast, dinner. Bar, meeting room for up to 50
  persons, limousine service available. Pool, tennis, shuffleboard, vol-
  leyball.

This turn-of-the-century mansion is a fine country inn. Set
back from the highway among stately pine trees, it makes you
think you are going back in time, and in a way you are.

The front door is huge. Once inside, you see beautiful oak
woodwork and a wonderful wall-to-wall carpet. The room to the
left is all wicker and all comfort. Ahead of you is the warm living
room, with walls full of ☛ books and a huge fireplace. The
unusual screen and andirons were made in England. To the right
of the fireplace is a 12-foot, curved window seat of another era.
The lounge area has a two-seat bar, just the right size.

Relax in a high-back wicker chair in one of the inn's four dining rooms that have been awarded three stars in the Mobil Guide and also won the silver spoon award. Enjoy the fine gourmet dining with appetizers like lobster ravioli (I never had this one before; it's delicious) and wonderful soups. For entrees there are three veal dishes. The veal *péche* won my vote: it's medallions of veal sautéed with peaches, cream, and cumin and finished with peach brandy. Needless to say, there are many more, and all are divine.

The manor staircase is a beauty, and its large rooms are beautifully appointed. ☛ Fantastic wallpapers and beautiful carpets all add to this great inn. The third-floor rooms have windows at odd angles, dictated by the roof line of the house. Some rooms have porches, and one has a stained-glass door going out to its porch. There is a lot of lovely stained glass throughout the inn. On the second floor, in one of the hall bathrooms, is a wood-enclosed steel bathtub. Be sure to take a look at it. It is quite a sight.

Their pool, the largest in the Mount Washington area, is made of ☛ wood, the only wooden one I have ever seen. You swell it in the spring, just as you would a wooden boat. Cocktails are served around the pool in the summer. There are tennis courts and shuffleboard and volleyball courts. Plenty of things will keep you busy, or, like me, you might want to just sit and relax.

How to get there: The inn is on Route 16 just a short distance north of North Conway.

᳇

E: *The inn was the country estate of the Bigelow carpet family, so the inn cat's name is Mrs. Bigelow.*

olive Metcalf

Follansbee Inn
North Sutton, New Hampshire
03260

Innkeepers: Sandy and Dick Reilein
Address/Telephone: P.O. Box 92; (603) 927–4221
Rooms: 23; 11 with private bath. No smoking inn.
Rates: $70 to $90, double occupancy, EPB.
Open: All year except two weeks in April and two weeks in November.
Facilities and activities: Dinner for houseguests by reservation, lounge. Cross-country skiing from the inn, swimming, boating, Ping-Pong. Nearby: downhill skiing, golf.

The Follansbee Inn is an 1840 New England farmhouse located on Kezar Lake. It has its own pier and private beach. A sailboard, paddleboat, rowboat, and canoe are provided for your pleasure. Or perhaps you'd like to take a 🐟 swim in this lovely lake?

A wood-burning stove makes the living room cozy and homey. The lounge has a small bar, and a Ping-Pong table is ready for use. Guests are encouraged to play the piano or guitar. The rooms are newly refurbished and are nice. The innkeepers have thoughtfully purchased very good mattresses. The upstairs halls are wide enough to have space for some interesting furniture. There are plants all over the inn and lots of books. The inn's facilities are not well suited to children under ten.

The dining room has comfortable captain's chairs and touches of chintz and linen. These are very pleasant surroundings in which to relax and savor the food. One entree is served each evening. It might be rack of lamb, a chicken dish, roast pork, their special crab-and-shrimp casserole, or something else equally delicious. The desserts are homemade. How about some chocolate cheesecake, chocolate eclair tart, or baked Alaska pie?

There is much to do in the area. You can go play a game of tennis or golf, take a hike or bicycle ride, or go picnicking. In winter alpine skiing is nearby, and cross-country skiing is from the door of the inn.

How to get there: Take I–91 north to Ascutney, Vermont. Follow Route 103 to Route 11 east, to Route 114. Proceed to North Sutton. The inn is behind the church.

✳

E: *North Sutton's old church is right next door. You might want to set your watch by its chiming clock.*

Home Hill Inn
Plainfield, New Hampshire
03781

Innkeeper: Roger Nicolas
Address/Telephone: River Road; (603) 675–6165
Rooms: 7, plus 2 suites; all with private bath.
Rates: $85 to $120, double occupancy, continental breakfast. Fall season
 and holidays slightly higher.
Open: All year except Sundays and Mondays, two weeks in March, and
 two weeks in November.
Facilities and activities: Dinner, bar, lounge. Swimming pool, tennis court,
 cross-country skiing, fishing in Connecticut River.

Roger's brochure said Home Hill Country Inn and French
Restaurant, and I could hardly wait to get there.

Roger was born in Brittany in northwest France, and he
speaks with a pleasant French accent. He has an ☛ authentic
French restaurant here. The food presentation is picture perfect
and the taste is elegant. No gravies, only sauces, and no flour,
cornstarch, or fillers are allowed. Roger believes in innovative
French cooking.

I started with a ☛ fresh fish mousse with lobster sauce. I have
never had better. Next, cream of onion soup, then veal slices, very
thin and young with French mushrooms. You may have the salad

before, with, or after dinner and the house dressing is gorgeous. Roger joined me at dinner and had duck prepared with white plums. I tasted it and it was very moist and delicious. Another dish served occasionally is veal stuffed with kiwi. Desserts, as would be expected, are superb. The wine list features both French and California wines.

In the kitchen is a lovely, long pine table where breakfast is served. What a homey spot at which to enjoy the continental breakfast of juice, ☛ croissants, butter, jams, and coffee.

The rooms are charming. The cottage is large enough for eight persons. There are French and American antiques, reproductions, and comfort. The lounge-library is lovely; in fact, you will find it hard to find any fault with this inn.

Roger's Great Dane is Bacchus. The inn is on twenty-five acres, only 500 yards from the Connecticut River. There are a swimming pool (a bar is out here), tennis courts, and cross-country skiing. Any season, any reason, head for Home Hill.

How to get there: Take I–89 to Exit 20. Follow Route 12A south to River Road and turn right. In 3½ miles you'll find the inn on the left.

❧

E: *Herman, the automatic tennis ball shooter, is a neat exercise encourager.*

Olive Metcalf

Philbrook Farm Inn
Shelburne, New Hampshire
03581

Innkeepers: Connie Leger and Nancy Philbrook
Address/Telephone: North Road (mailing address: Star Route 41, Gorham, NH 03581); (603) 466–3831
Rooms: 19, plus 5 cottages with housekeeping arrangements; 10 rooms and all cottages with private bath. Pets welcome in cottages.
Rates: $50 to $60, per person, double occupancy, MAP. Cottages $300 weekly. No credit cards.
Open: All year except April and October 31 to December 26.
Facilities and activities: Lunch, BYOB lounge. Library, pool table, Ping-Pong, swimming pool, horseback riding, cross-country skiing, snowshoeing, hiking. Nearby: downhill skiing.

When you're traveling along Route 2, take a look across the fields, and there you'll see this lovely inn that is listed on the National Register of Historic Places. And rightly so. In 1861 Philbrook Farm started as an inn. Today it is still an inn and still has ☛ Philbrooks living here, running it in fine New England tradition.

Everything you eat here is prepared from scratch in their kitchens. The baked goods are made daily. A huge garden provides good vegetables. One entree is served each night. Roasts of everything you can want—pork, beef, turkey—and on and on. The New England boiled dinner is also a favorite.

The downstairs playroom has Ping-Pong, a pool table, shuffleboard, puzzles, and fun. A lot of reading material can be found all over the inn. Fireplaces are also all over the inn. ☞ The inn has a wonderful selection of Philbrook Farm puzzles made by Connie's grandfather. They have large, ¼-inch-thick pieces and are just beautiful. A player piano, an old pump organ—where else can you find such unique things except in an inn?

Rooms are furnished with a lot of old ☞ family treasures. There are some nice four-posters and a wonderful collection of old bowl and pitcher sets. All the cottages are different. They sure are nice if you want to linger here awhile. Some have dining rooms, some have fireplaces, and some have porches. If you are staying in a cottage, you may bring along your pet.

With more than 1,000 acres, the inn has plenty of room for you to roam any season of the year. Look across their fields to the Carter-Moriah and Presidential mountain ranges. Behind the inn rises the Mahoosuc Range. This is the Androscoggin Valley. Horseback riding lessons and trail riding are available at the Philbrook Farm stables. What a heavenly place for a horseback ride. I saw a foal about two weeks old when I was here. A real little beauty. The inn cats are Cobweb and Fuzzy, and the inn dog, Leibschen, is a German shorthair pointer.

How to get there: The inn is 1½ miles off Route 2. Going west, look for a direction sign on your right, and turn right. Cross the railroad tracks and then a bridge. Turn right at the crossroads and go ½ mile to the inn, which is on North Road.

Snowvillage Inn
Snowville, New Hampshire
03849

Innkeepers: Frank, Peter, and Trudy Cutrone
Address/Telephone: P.O. Box 176; (603) 447–2818
Rooms: 18; all with private bath, 4 with fireplace.
Rates: $65 to $90, per person, double occupancy, MAP. Special package
    rates available.
Open: All year except April.
Facilities and activities: Bar, lounge, sauna, cross-country skiing, tennis,
    nature trails. Nearby: swimming, fishing, canoeing, hiking, downhill
    skiing.

    The view from the inn is breathtaking. Mount Washington
and the whole Presidential Range, plus the rest of the White
Mountains, greet your eyes everywhere you look. In summer at
the top of Foss Mountain, right at the inn, you can eat your fill of
wild blueberries.
    When I arrived at the inn this time, my car died in the
driveway. The Cutrones were so helpful and made me feel right at
home while finding someone to work on the car. We found out in
the morning how sick my car was . . . oh, dear. Remember, these
innkeepers would be just as welcoming and helpful to you, too.
    The guest rooms, which are not well suited to children under

eight, are comfortable and spacious, with 🖝 tons of towels in luscious colors. Each room is named after a favorite author of the innkeepers. The living room, with its huge fireplace and nice couches all around, makes this an inn for rest and relaxation. There are a service bar and a lounge, and plants are everywhere. The game room has a television, and there is an extensive library. A huge porch surrounds the inn. I could sit here all day and enjoy the incredible view.

The cooking has an 🖝 Austrian flavor. One entree is served each evening. You may find pork tenderloin with sauerkraut, 🖝 curried chicken with peaches, beef tenderloin, chicken or veal piccata, and shrimp scampi, just to name a few. All breads and desserts are made here, and the soups also are homemade. This does make a difference. Cookies, made right here, are placed in your room in a cookie basket as a welcome to the inn.

Nice animals are here. The cats are Skunk, Elvira, and Virginia. Boris and Natasha, the inn dogs, are Samoyeds. Igor is a gorilla (he's stuffed) who holds the menu outside the restaurant.

How to get there: Out of Conway on Route 153, go 5 miles to Crystal Village. Turn left, go about 1½ miles, turn right at the inn's sign, and go up the hill ¾ mile to the inn.

E: *Peter, the son, makes the best darn chili in the world. He sent some home with me and wow, it was good and hot. He also makes a mild-flavored one.*

Olive Metcalf

Dexters
Sunapee, New Hampshire
03782

Innkeepers: Frank and Shirley Simpson; Holly and Michael Durfor
Address/Telephone: P.O. Box P; (603) 763–5571, (800) 232–5571
Rooms: 17, plus 1 cottage; all with private bath.
Rates: $125 to $165, double occupancy, MAP. Package rates offered in off-season.
Open: May 1 to October 31.
Facilities and activities: Lunch in July and August, bar. Tennis, swimming pool, recreation barn.

The main house was built in 1801 by an artisan, Adam Reddington. He earned his living by carving from the huge knurls of the many fine maples on the grounds the bowls in which sailing ships carried their compasses. In 1948 the house became a small country inn.

Dexters is a nice family inn that welcomes children. The Simpsons, their daughter, Holly, and her husband, Michael, run the inn. They also have two young innkeepers, Hartwell and Hayley-Marie, born in 1985 and 1988. Never too soon to start learning.

Your day starts with 🖝 juice and coffee served in your room at a time you set the night before. Or you can be really spoiled and have a New England breakfast tray in bed. How about some eggs Benedict, French toast, or pancakes to start your day right? These are rooms you'll want to linger in. They are a bit above average, with marvelous wallpapers, heavenly pillows made of ☛ feathers, and fresh fruit and flowers. Most of the antique beds have come down through the Simpson family.

The living room library has over 500 books, magazines, and newspapers. It offers lots of comfort and charm along with a fireplace. There are two television rooms and a breezy screened porch. For dinner, one special is Frank's scallops Françoise, or try chicken piccata, swordfish, lambchops, or steak.

Outdoor sports? You name it. Tennis is taken seriously here. Three all-weather ☛ Plexicushion tennis courts with a pro and shop are provided for your enjoyment. Tournaments for seniors are just a few of the happenings going on up here. After a game there is a lovely outdoor swimming pool to cool off in. Croquet, a horseshoe pit, and shuffleboard are also available. In springtime the lake trout and salmon are close to the surface and hungry, so come all you fishermen. Spring is always late up here, so you have a longer season. For a good summer or fall activity, there are some of the loveliest walking and hiking trails right on the inn's property.

There is a special recreation room in the barn for all ages, but it is keyed to those under seventeen who need a place of their own when the five o'clock cocktail hour begins.

How to get there: Take I–89 out of Concord and follow Exit 12 to Route 11, to 103B in Sunapee. Or take I–91 out of Springfield and follow Exit 8 to Claremont, New Hampshire, to Route 103. The turn to the inn is marked by a sign 200 yards south of the intersection of 103 and 11. The inn is about 1½ miles off Route 103.

The Inn at Sunapee
Sunapee, New Hampshire
03782

Innkeepers: Ted and Susan Harriman
Address/Telephone: Burkehaven Hills Road (mailing address: P.O. Box 336); (603) 763–4444
Rooms: 16, plus 5 suites; all with private bath.
Rates: $55 to $75, single; $65 to $79, double; $110 to $130, suite; EPB.
Open: All year except two weeks in November and April.
Facilities and activities: Dinner every night but Monday and Tuesday. No smoking in dining room. Bar, lounge, full license. Pool, tennis, hiking, cross-country skiing. Nearby: downhill skiing.

The Inn at Sunapee, an 1800s farmhouse with a classic wraparound porch, is nicely situated on a hilltop that overlooks beautiful Lake Sunapee and historic Sunapee Harbor. The lake is the second largest in New Hampshire, and it's a great spot for sailing, fishing, and water-skiing. The inn is also located at the base of Mount Sunapee. You can go skiing for the day or you can sit and watch the skiers from the warmth of the inn.

Attached to the house is a barn, which has been turned into a lounge with a fieldstone fireplace and good couches. The views from the windows in here and in the dining room are spectacular any season of the year. If you like animials, you'll especially like watching the 🖝 cows in the field across the road. Most of all you'll enjoy the good food served here. The menu changes quite often. When I was here, there were 🖝 Maryland crabcakes and Vietnamese spring rolls with spicy dipping sauce as appetizers. Grilled tuna, a daily veal special, beef, and chicken are but a few of the foods served here. Holidays, I'm told, are really special.

Ted and Susan lived in the Far East and Southeast Asia for more than twenty-five years, and their wonderful collection of furnishings is used throughout the inn. Rooms are decorated with oak and iron furniture. Some rooms have wide-board pine floors. There is a separate honeymoon cottage, which is cute and small. Everything about this inn is very gracious.

Children are welcome here. They'll enjoy the swimming pool, tennis court, and ten acres of woodland for cross-country skiing or hiking. They also will want to curl up with the inn cats—all six of them, including a calico and a coon cat. A sign on the door reads: "Don't let the inn cats out."

How to get there: Coming from Boston, take I–93 north to Concord, New Hampshire. Then take I–89 north to Exit 12 and follow Route 11 west to Sunapee. At the blinking light by Bankeast, turn toward Sunapee Harbor. At the harbor, you will see a park with a bandstand. Take the first right after the bandstand and go ½ mile up the hill to the inn.

≈

*With its swinging sign near
the hills it stands,
Vine-clad and filled with cheer.
'Tis a place to laze through
fresh, golden days
with sunlit peaks so near.
So good-bye to cares,
this spot is rare,
and we thank kind fate
for having brought us here.*

Olive Metcalf

Seven Hearths
Sunapee, New Hampshire
03782

Innkeepers: Marianne Morse Callahan and Miguel Ramirez
Address/Telephone: Route 11; (603) 763–5657
Rooms: 10; all with private bath, some with fireplace, and 1 with
  wheelchair access.
Rates: In-season, $118 to $138, per room, double occupancy, EPB. In
  winter, $78 to $98, per room, double occupancy, EPB.
Open: All year except April and November until Thanksgiving.
Facilities and activities: Dinner, Sunday brunch. Restaurant open Wednesday through Sunday, July through October; rest of year, Thursday
  through Saturday. Full license. Swimming pool, cross-country skiing
  from inn door.

The inn was built in 1801 and remained in its original family
for almost one hundred years. It is nestled in a quiet and tranquil
part of the lovely area of Sunapee. The name Seven Hearths came
about from the fact that the inn has seven working fireplaces.

Five of these fireplaces are in the rooms. Some rooms have
wide-board floors and exposed ceiling beams. Two rooms downstairs have an outdoor terrace overlooking the lake. ☛ Fresh
flowers and bowls of fruit are set out to welcome you. There are
plants all over and lots of books to read.

264

The living room has a massive fieldstone fireplace, a baby grand piano just waiting to be played, and a library full of books and board games. ☛ Afternoon tea is served in here.

Breakfast and dinner are served in a lovely room that has another one of the seven fireplaces. This one has a beehive oven. A bay window overlooks the peaceful countryside. Hors d'oeuvres are served in the hearth room. The soups are divine. Creamy scallop bisque St. Jacques, and spring fiddlehead cream bisque are only two. They have more tasty offerings. Roast duckling with raspberry glaze, or seven-pepper pork tenderloin medallions with cumin and serranos, followed by good salads and desserts. One I love is ☛ chocolate raspberry torte. But I also love the fresh fruit tart with chantilly cream. Oh, it's hard to choose between them. This is a prix fixe dinner, by reservation only.

The inn has a nice screened porch with rockers and a lovely swimming pool with a wooden deck all around it. The smell of the tall pines is heavenly. Care for croquet? It's here. And in the winter you can go cross-country skiing right from the door. The innkeepers own twenty-five acres of land and are surrounded by many more acres of conservation land. This is a great place to get away from it all.

How to get there: Take Exit 12 from I–89 and turn west on Route 11. In 4.2 miles, on the right, is a sign for the inn, which is in a few yards.

❋

E: *In the living room is an album with menus going back to the 1930s. Thanksgiving dinner, five courses, $1.50. Wow.*

The Tamworth Inn
Tamworth, New Hampshire
03886

Innkeepers: Phil and Kathy Bender
Address/Telephone: Main Street; (603) 323–7721
Rooms: 14; all with private bath.
Rates: $80 to $115, double occupancy, EPB.
Open: All year except the first two weeks of April.
Facilities and activities: Lunch on Saturdays in summer, Sunday brunch, dinner. Bar, lounge, swimming pool, fishing, skiing, hiking. Nearby: downhill skiing, Barnstormer's Theater.

Built in 1833, The Tamworth Inn is a rambling building in a lovely New England town across from the Congregational Church and a thoroughbred horse pasture.

The Swift River flows swiftly behind the inn. If you're looking for a memorable spot for your wedding, the riverside gazebo is great; if you're inclined toward fly-fishing, this is the place for you. The hale and hearty might want to walk about a quarter-mile to the swimming hole. Anyone less adventuresome will find the inn's swimming pool just right.

The main attraction in the summer is the Barnstormer's Theater down the street, the oldest summer theater in New England. An "equity house," there are eight different professional performances each summer. It certainly is nice to stay at the inn, have a tasty dinner, and walk to good theater.

There are lots of hiking trails in this area, which are maintained by the Appalachian Mountain Club, the Tamworth Outing Club, and the Wonalancet Outing Club. They are within walking distance of the inn. In winter these trails become cross-country ski trails.

Back at the inn, guests enjoy sitting by the fireplaces, reading a book, patting Misty the cat, or watching a movie from the extensive video collection. The bar and lounge has a dart board—anyone for a game of darts?—as well as a large collection of old sleds on display. You can order a light meal in here. Full dinners are served in the lovely dining rooms. The menu changes monthly. You might find chilled cucumber soup and crab bisque among the appetizers and fettucine Alfredo, sole Florentine, beef, and veal among the entrees. Do save room for dessert; they're delicious.

The guest rooms are all different, and all of them are comfortable. One room has a huge canopied bed, so high it needs steps to climb into it. As Phil says, Kathy is the key person here and takes charge of the rooms beautifully. She makes sure all the amenities are here, including your morning coffee being left at your door.

How to get there: Tamworth is on Route 113, 3 miles northwest of the intersection of Routes 25 and 16.

The Birchwood Inn
Temple, New Hampshire
03084

Innkeepers: Judy and Bill Wolfe
Address/Telephone: Route 45; (603) 878–3285
Rooms: 7; 5 with private bath.
Rates: $55 to $70, double occupancy, EPB. No credit cards.
Open: All year except three weeks in April.
Facilities and activities: Dinner served Tuesday through Saturday. BYOB.
   Nearby: trout fishing, hiking, hunting, golf, summer theater, lakes.

   The inn is in the Mount Monadnock region of New Hampshire, so there is plenty to do and see here. From the top of the mountain you can see four states, a nice reward for you hikers. There are trout waiting for the fisherman, much game for the hunter, plus golf, summer theater, horseback riding, and walking. If you really like being sedentary, go outside and watch the sheep grazing in the meadow. This is a very peaceful scene.
   Bill and Judy are the owner-chefs and are very good at what they do. I understand from my spies that their ☛ stuffed lobster is better than anywhere else. Chicken piccata and shrimp Parmesan served on green noodles are two more examples of their good food. They have she-crab soup, which is hard to find north of South Carolina. It is excellent. The dining room walls are covered with beautiful Rufus Porter murals.

Bill is an avid collector of model trains. I'm a train buff myself, so I got a real kick out of seeing Bill's collection all over the inn.

The inn has an ☞ 1878 square Steinway grand piano that is kept in perfect tune. The inn history stretches back some two centuries to circa 1775. During this time many people have come and gone, one notable personage being Henry David Thoreau. A room at the inn is named for him. Other rooms have rather different sort of names such as "The Bottle Shop" and "The School Room." The innkeepers will entertain you with the stories of how the rooms became so named.

How to get there: Take Route 3 out of Boston to Nashua, New Hampshire, Exit 7W. Follow Route 101 to Milford to Route 45 to Temple.

∽

*The chill of a wood stove–warmed bedroom
evaporates in the crisp smell of bacon for breakfast.*

The Chesterfield Inn
West Chesterfield, New Hampshire
03466

Innkeepers: Judy and Phil Hueber
Address/Telephone: Route 9; (603) 256–3211, (800) 365–5515
Rooms: 7, plus 2 suites; all with private bath, air conditioning, refrigerator, phone, and 4 with fireplace.
Rates: $99 to $149, double occupancy, EPB.
Open: All year.
Facilities and activities: Dinner Wednesday to Sunday. Full license. Ice skating. Nearby: fishing, boating, skiing, swimming.

The inn was a tavern from 1798 to 1811, and then it became a farm. In 1984 the inn opened after extensive renovations by architect ☞ Rod Williams of The Inn at Sawmill Farm, and he is the best around. Exposed beams, many of them part of the original structure, and walls paneled with boards that came from an old barn make for a warm and friendly atmosphere.

The guest rooms are spacious. Some rooms have balconies, others have a fireplace, and all are scrumptious. They are done in soft shades of blues, greens, and pinks. They are air-conditioned and have clock radios and telephones (all different), including one in the bathroom. Good fluffy towels and an assortment of toiletries are here. To top it all off, each room has a ☞ refrigerator with juice, bottled spring water, beers, and wine. I found a welcoming split of champagne in mine. Oh my.

The foyer has a large fireplace holding a bright red wood stove, and nice couches. It's a good place for cocktails. The entrance to the dining room is ☞ through the kitchen. It was designed this way as a tribute to the chef, Carl Warner. It shows he is proud of his kitchen and his staff. He is a four-star chef, and when you dine you will believe it. The menu changes often, and many unusual dishes are served. Country pâté is made right here. Fettucine with four cheeses is unbelievable. So are grilled vegetables with aioli. A different soup is featured every day. Duck is served with homemade mango chutney; coho salmon comes with garlic, ginger, and tomatoes; and lamb tenderloin is stuffed with leeks and Vermont goat cheese. The chef always has a fish of the day. Desserts are wonderful. Come and try this food. There are three dining rooms to choose from, all with wonderful views.

The inn's grounds are full of perennial, herb, and vegetable gardens. The beautiful Connecticut River is a short walk from the inn, so bring along your canoe or fishing pole. Lake Spofford has boats for rent. Pisgah Park has hiking trails and two spring-fed ponds for swimming. In winter skiing is close at hand, and the inn's pond is lighted for night skating under the stars. (Watch for Ellie, the inn cat.) And all year, you'll find good antique shops and arts and crafts shops.

How to get there: Take Exit 3 off I–91. Take Route 9 west, going over the border from Vermont to New Hampshire. The inn is in 2 miles on your left.

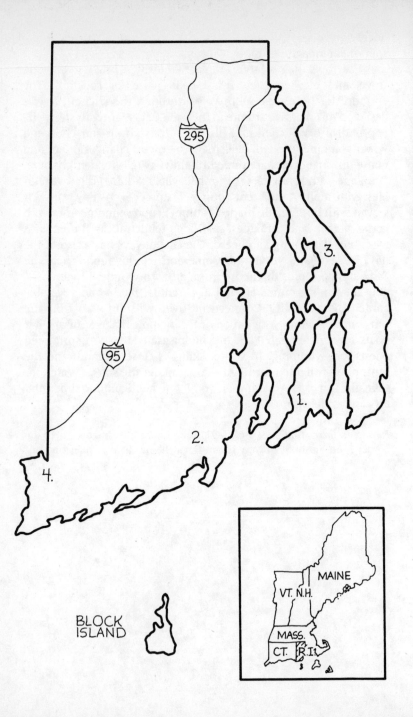

295

95

3.

1.

2.

4.

BLOCK
ISLAND

MAINE

VT. N.H.

MASS.

CT. R.I.

Rhode Island

Numbers on map refer to towns numbered below.

olive Metcalf

The Inn at Castle Hill
Newport, Rhode Island
02840

Innkeeper: Paul McEnroe; general manager, Jens Thillemann
Address/Telephone: Ocean Drive; (401) 849–3800
Rooms: 10; 7 with private bath.
Rates: Depending on the season, rates range from a low of $50 to a high
   of $242, double occupancy, continental breakfast.
Open: All year.
Facilities and activities: Restaurant closed from second week of November
   through March. Lunch daily May through October. Dinner and
   Sunday brunch April through early November. Bar, entertainment,
   live jazz on Sunday afternoons, private ocean beach.

   Newport is a fabulous place to visit any time of the year. And
to be able to go to Newport and stay at The Inn at Castle Hill is a
rare treat. I have always loved the warm atmosphere of this inn. It
was built as a private home in 1874 and has been little changed
over the years. Thirty-two acres of shoreline right on the entrance
of Narragansett Bay offer a natural setting for almost anything a
person could desire. The views from any place, in or about the inn,
are breathtakingly beautiful. ☛ The Atlantic Ocean and the bay
are at your feet.
   As for things to do, there is the Tennis Hall of Fame, and

Newport is famous for its great "cottages" lining the waterfront.

The inn has four dining rooms. The small one with only six tables, each set with different serving plates, is very special. Another is a light and airy oval room, which, like the others, looks over the water. The chef is very good, and the food he creates is delicious. The menu changes seasonally. Veal, beef, lamb, fowl, and seafood are prepared many ways and are beautifully served. Every day there are three homemade soups, together with an endless variety of appetizers. The inn has always had a 🖙 sumptuous ten-course New Year's Eve dinner, which is now held the first Saturday in November with all their old fanfare of December 31. It's called the Harvest Food Ball.

The Tavern is a different room, with a beauty of a bar and a view unmatched, if you love the sea. There are Chinese teak and marble tables in the living areas, and the banister on the staircase is its own delight.

Almost all the rooms are quite large and beautifully furnished. The paneling is magnificent, as are the oriental rugs that have been left here.

Innkeeper McEnroe has refurbished the entire inn with wallpapers that are color coordinated with spreads and drapes, plus thick towels. Here the view outside is not enough for our innkeeper. He cares about the interior look, too.

How to get there: From the north take Route 138 into Newport, and follow Thames Street about 4½ miles to Ocean Drive. Look for the inn's sign on your right. From the west come across the Newport Bridge and take the scenic Newport exit that goes into Thames Street.

*

E: *The 10-mile ocean drive is among the most strikingly beautiful areas in New England. And do remember that Sunday brunch is very active with jazz.*

Olive Metcalf

Larchwood Inn
Wakefield, Rhode Island
02879

Innkeepers: Francis and Diann Browning
Address/Telephone: 521 Main Street; (401) 783–5454
Rooms: 19, in 2 buildings; 12 with private bath, some with phone.
Rates: $30 to $85, double occupancy, EP.
Open: All year.
Facilities and activities: Breakfast, lunch, dinner, bar, tavern. Nearby: swimming, fishing, skiing.

Over the fireplace in the homey bar is carved "Fast by an Ingle Bleezing Finely," a quotation from the Scots' Robert Burns. The Tam O'Shanter Cocktail Lounge serves up a delectable lunch that includes huge sandwiches, good salads, hamburgers, and quiche.

There are four other lovely rooms for dining or private entertaining. Dinner ideas are rack of lamb for one or two, lots of fresh fish, and a 🐖 beefeater's special, a thick slice of prime rib Angus. Breakfast is very ample. I really like their special French toast topped with either sour cream or whipped cream and warmed strawberries. Perhaps you'd enjoy croissants or poached eggs with hollandaise and mushrooms artichoke hearts. Come summer the meals are served on the covered patio in the garden.

Some of the rooms are in the Holly House across the street. It is the same age as the inn; both were built in the 1830s. It is so well done. ☛ Diann has a real touch. The wallpapers are glorious and one room is an especially lovely salmon color. All of the inn's guest rooms have been individually decorated and are beautifully furnished. Butch, the inn cat, is a beauty; maybe you can rent him for a night.

The inn is situated in the heart of Rhode Island's beautiful South County. Saltwater beaches for bathing, fishing, and sunning are close by. In the winter it is only a short drive to Pine Top and Yawgoo Valley for skiing.

Rhode Island isn't all that big, you know, so it's never very far from anywhere to the Larchwood Inn.

How to get there: Take I–95 to Route 1. Exit from Route 1 at Pond Street, follow it to the end, and the inn will be immediately in front of you.

༺⚬༻

E: *Monday night is cabaret night in summer—This is a really fun time and includes a sing-along.*

> *When you have but one night to spend,*
> *which inn to choose is as difficult*
> *as the choice you had years ago*
> *at the penny candy counter,*
> *and equally rewarding.*

Olive Metcalf

Nathaniel Porter Inn
Warren, Rhode Island
02885

Innkeepers: Paulette and Robert Lynch
Address/Telephone: Water Street; (401) 245–6622
Rooms: 3; all with private bath.
Rates: $70, single or double occupancy, continental breakfast.
Open: All year except Christmas Eve, Christmas Day, July 4, and Labor Day.
Facilities and activities: Dinner. Tavern. Nearby: boating and swimming at town beach.

   The inn is named after Nathaniel Porter, who, at the age of twelve, established his place in history when he was among the seventy-seven minutemen who stood on Lexington Green and fired the first shots of the American Revolution in 1775. The present owners are direct descendents of that young man.
   The restored inn dates back to 1795, when it was built by a wealthy sea captain. Some of the earliest documented stencils were discovered under numerous layers of paint and wallpaper. The ☞ parquet floors, dating back to the early 1800s, are just beautiful, and so are the wide-board floors. The inn is listed on the National Register of Historic Places. The French mural in one of the parlors dates from about 1810, and all the window glass was hand-blown in Germany.

278

The front parlor has nice romantic tables for two, and there are five fireplaces in the dining rooms. The waitresses here are called hostesses. They describe everything on your plate to you. Very professional. The menu changes twice a year and is extensive, offering more than enough choices for all tastes. There are seven appetizers as well as a soup of the day. ☛ I had grilled shrimp in a strawberry-thyme sauce. What a nice and different flavor it had. I also tasted the smoked mussels and the excellent seafood chowder. I get hungry just thinking about the entrees. I had filet mignon with roasted hazelnuts, flamed with cognac. It was tender and delicious. The next time I visit the inn, I'm going to try the whiskey cream shrimp. The shrimp are sautéed in butter, flamed with Jim Beam, finished with cream and Dijon mustard, and served in puff pastry. Everything is spectacular and well presented. Need I mention desserts? Ambrosia. Add to this a wonderful wine list with some interesting Australian wines.

So off to bed. Two rooms have ☛ canopied double beds with lovely antiques, and the other has twins. At night the inn is lighted by window candles and chandeliers.

How to get there: From Providence, take Route 195 east to Route 114. Go south on Route 114 to Warren. At the first traffic light in town, go right onto Water Street. The inn is in 4 blocks on the right.

olive Metcalf

Shelter Harbor Inn
Westerly, Rhode Island
02891

Innkeepers: Jim and Debbye Dey
Address/Telephone: Route 1; (401) 322–8883
Rooms: 24; all with private bath, TV, phone, and some with fireplace and private deck.
Rates: $68 to $92, single; $86 to $102, double occupancy; EPB. Corporate rate available.
Open: All year.
Facilities and activities: Lunch, dinner, Sunday brunch, bar. Private ocean beach, two paddle tennis courts with night lighting, hot tub, croquet court. Nearby: golf, boat-launching area, tennis, summer theater, Block Island ferry, Mystic Seaport, Mystic Marinelife Aquarium.

If you would like a 3-mile stretch of uncluttered ocean beach located just a mile from a lovely old country inn, find your way to Rhode Island and the Shelter Harbor Inn. Bring the children. When they're not playing in the ocean surf, there's a salt pond near the inn for them to explore.

Eight of the guest rooms are in the restored farmhouse, and ten more are located in the barn. The rest of the rooms are in the coach house, which is a lovely addition to the inn. There is a large central living room here that opens onto a spacious deck—how ideal for families. Or if your business group is small, have a meeting right here. There is also a library with comfortable leather chairs where you can relax with a book.

The menu reflects the location of the inn, and at least half the items offered are from the sea. ☛ The finnan haddie is specially smoked in Narragansett. You can choose your place to eat—the formal dining room, the small private dining room with a fireplace, or the glassed-in terrace room. The sun porch has been turned into a pub bar and Debbye's plants are everywhere. If weather permits, take a drink out to the secluded terrace. On a clear day you can see Block Island from the third floor of the inn. There's a hot tub up here, plus a barbecue grill.

If you can tear yourself from the beach, there is much to see around here. You are about halfway between Mystic and Newport. The ferry to Block Island leaves from Judith Point. It is an hour-long ride, and when you arrive on Block Island you will find it a super spot for bicycling. You can charter boats for fishing or stand at the edge of the surf and cast your line into the sea. In the evenings there are Theater by the Sea in nearby Matunuck or the Colonial Theater in Westerly.

How to get there: Take I–95 to Route 1. Follow Route 1 out of Westerly for about 5 miles. The inn is on the right side of the road when you're heading northeast.

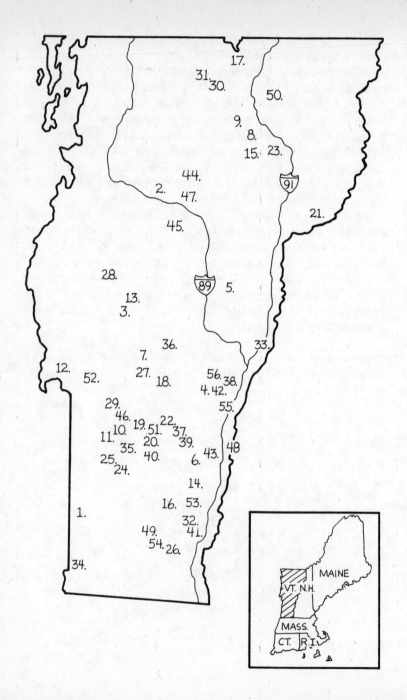

Vermont

Numbers on map refer to towns numbered below.

Olive Metcalf

The Arlington Inn
Arlington, Vermont
05250

Innkeepers: Paul and Madeline Krozel
Address/Telephone: Route 7A; (802) 375–6532
Rooms: 13; all with private bath.
Rates: $58 to $125, double occupancy, continental breakfast.
Open: All year.
Facilities and activities: Lunch, summer and fall; dinner, Sunday brunch.
     Bar, lounge, tennis court, fishing in Battenkill River.

If you want to go back in time, this is the inn to do it in. You can recapture the gracious living of the Victorian period in this historic Greek Revival mansion. It was built in 1848 by Martin Chester Deming. The lovely rooms in the inn are named after Deming family members. There are Sylvester's study, Pamela's suite, Martin Chester's room, Sophie's room, Mary's room, and (I love this name) Chloe's room. The rooms are beautifully furnished and very comfortable. One guest room has a working fireplace.

The parlor or sitting room has a wonderful red oriental rug on the floor and, in the winter, a fire roaring in the fireplace. The whole inn is magnificent.

The dining rooms are well appointed. There is a 🐷 solarium for dining that's perfectly lovely. Plants, fountains, and beautiful landscaping outside. The best part, of course, is the food. There are eight appetizers. I love garlic and the ☞ escargots are divine. So is the fettucine *alla parma*. The soups and salads are very special. They have a house dressing I would love to steal, it is so good. The main courses vary from day to day. Salmon, baked with tomato and spinach butter cream sauce, or stuffed with shrimp and topped with a creamy dill sauce. Get the idea? It's great. Sunday brunch is inventive, with a really super menu. Spinach and mushroom salad with a lemon and Pommery mustard dressing is just one selection. You really must go.

How to get there: The inn is located on Route 7A in the middle of Arlington.

❧

E: *The tavern has live entertainment on Friday and Saturday nights. If you get tired, there's a huge oversized rocking chair out on the porch.*

In the autumn, especially as one ages,
a firelit tavern in an excellent inn cannot be bettered
by the smallest mansions in Christendom.

Olive Metcalf

West Mountain Inn
Arlington, Vermont
05250

Innkeepers: Mary Ann and Wes Carlson
Address/Telephone: P.O. Box 481; (802) 375–6516
Rooms: 13, plus 3 suites and 1 apartment; all with private bath, 1 with
  wheelchair accessibility.
Rates: $120 to $165, double occupancy, MAP.
Open: All year.
Facilities and activities: Bar, hiking, cross-country skiing, fishing, swim-
  ming.

Wes and Mary Ann are really the ideal innkeepers. From the
minute you arrive until you leave you feel at home.

The inn is always being updated. There is a new lovely suite of
rooms with a fireplace. There also is a room and bath with complete
facilities for the handicapped. The nicest touch is the thought. There
are too few people who care enough to spend a bit more for other
people's comfort. The apartment has housekeeping facilities.

Wes loves ☛ exotic goldfish. They are in the ponds around
the inn and in a huge aquarium inside that is so nice to watch.
You'll find a pair of peace doves in the inn, too. Wes also raises
African violets. He puts one in each room and invites you to take
it home with you. The bowl of fruit, chocolate bar, and trail map
are also for your pleasure.

The rooms, all named for famous people, are quite different. I have stayed in the Norman Rockwell Room, which is up in the treetops. Icelandic comforters and wool blankets are provided to keep you toasty warm.

The inn prepares great dinners. Wes has some excellent wines in an extensive wine cellar. They are the perfect complement to the meal.

This inn is truly in the country, with 150 acres of trees, trails, pastures, and ponds, all on the mountainside overlooking the village of Arlington. Cross the trout-filled Battenkill River, wind your way over the bridge, which is flower-laden in summer, go by the millhouse, up past the main cottage and spring-fed rock quarry, to the seven-gabled inn. ☛ The grounds around the inn are reputed to have more species of evergreens than any other place in New England. There are lovely trails for hiking, jogging, or cross-country skiing, depending on the season.

How to get there: Midway between Bennington and Manchester, the inn is ½ mile west of Arlington on Route 313. Turn onto River Road, cross the river, and go up the hill until you come to the inn.

The Black Bear Inn
Bolton Valley, Vermont
05477

Innkeepers: Sally and Dennis Turpin
Address/Telephone: Bolton Valley Road; (802) 434–2126
Rooms: 24; all with private bath and color TV.
Rates: $59 to $119, double occupancy, EP.
Open: All year.
Facilities and activities: Breakfast, dinner mid-December to mid-April, bar, lounge. Heated swimming pool, cross-country skiing, hiking. Nearby: tennis, fishing, downhill skiing, golf.

Four miles up twisting, curving Bolton Valley Road you come across this contemporary country inn, nestled in the mountainside as if it had been here forever. Once inside, you are greeted by the warmth of a woodburning stove and the aroma of ☞ freshly baked breads and muffins that fills the air.

Everything is homemade. ☞ You could stay here for two weeks and not be served the same thing twice, and that even includes the breads and muffins. You can begin your dinner with some good soups, like cream of broccoli or chilled gazpacho. There are always three entrees offered, one of which is seafood. You might find rack of lamb, sea scallops baked with mushrooms and herbs, and vegetarian pasta on the menu one evening.

The rooms are well appointed, with color televisions, good beds, and lovely balconies where in summer you may sit and smell the good clean air and enjoy the views. They are spectacular this far up in the mountains.

In summer the grounds are covered with wildflowers. The heated pool beckons you, comfortable lawn furniture is all around, and the beautiful blue skies are yours to enjoy. The inn's 54 miles of cross-country ski trails make good paths for a hike, and you may also borrow a canoe. Tennis is a short stroll away.

In cold weather Bolton Valley's nearby ☛ new indoor sports center with swimming, exercise rooms, saunas, and tennis is the place to be when you're not skiing. There is so much to see and do in the area in all seasons, you'll find it a great place to bring your children.

There are a lot of bears up here (stuffed, of course) in many different poses. Some even are on skis. I have quite a few at home. One wears his foul-weather gear all year.

How to get there: Coming west on I–89, take Exit 10 at Stowe-Waterbury. Turn left, then turn right onto Route 2 and follow it 7 miles. Turn right onto Bolton Valley Road in Bolton where I–89 passes over Route 2. The inn is in 4 miles.

olive Metcalf

The Brandon Inn
Brandon, Vermont
05733

Innkeepers: Sarah and Louis Pattis
Address/Telephone: 20 Parker Street; (802) 247–5766
Rooms: 24, plus 4 suites; all with private bath.
Rates: $60 to $75, per person, double occupancy, MAP; $45 to $60, per person, double occupancy, EPB.
Open: All year.
Facilities and activities: Lunch Tuesday through Saturday. Bar, lounge, meeting facilities, swimming pool, trout fishing, summer theater and orchestra.

Facing the village green in lovely Brandon is this Queen Anne–style brick inn that is listed on the National Register of Historic Places. The inn has been here since 1786.

The rooms at the inn all come with private bath. There are king, queen, double, and twin beds. The choice is yours. Each room is different and has a charm of its own, perhaps created by a 🐾 cozy easy chair for curling up in with a book or an intimate corner desk perfect for letter writing.

Your room is not the only place to relax. There are cheery, comfortable sitting rooms on each floor, just right for watching television on a rainy day. The main floor also offers various spots where you can unwind: the main foyer, for example, where you can enjoy a roaring fire in the winter and gentle breezes in the summer. There are puzzles and chess and books.

The inn has excellent facilities for weddings, meetings, and conferences. The mirrored ballroom is perfect for an elegant reception.

The five acres of inn grounds provide outdoor recreation. The swimming pool is great, and the Neshobe River on the inn's grounds is perfect for ☛ trout fishing.

Luncheon has a goodie. Seafood spaetzle is seafood in a creamy sauce on homemade Austrian noodles. At dinner, try tortellini Alfredo. Doesn't it sound great? Go on to the special house salad with black pepper dressing. It's excellent. Breast of chicken is prepared with a spicy peanut sauce at one meal. It is surely different. A nice selection of desserts is also offered.

How to get there: The inn is on Route 7 in Brandon.

✳

E: *The lower barn is the home of Brandon's well-known summer theater and symphony orchestra.*

> *A country inn piled high with snow*
> *is a cheery fortress against the cold.*

The October Country Inn
Bridgewater Corners, Vermont
05035

Innkeepers: Richard Sims and Patrick Runkel
Address/Telephone: Route 4 (mailing address: P.O. Box 66); (802) 672–3412
Rooms: 10; 8 with private bath.
Rates: $100 to $130, double occupancy, MAP. Higher rate on weekends. No credit cards.
Open: All year except April and two weeks in November.
Facilities and activities: Pool. Nearby: downhill and cross-country skiing, antiquing, horse shows.

There are a lot of comfortable things about this inn. It has a very cozy living room with overstuffed furniture and a fireplace at one end and an old, old wood stove at the other. The fire is usually blazing, and the library offers an extensive supply of books as well as a great selection of games and puzzles. The innkeepers are always buying new books and games for you to enjoy. This room is a nice place for guests to relax and meet each other.

The rooms also are comfortable with good beds and mattresses. Some rooms have skylights, which I always like.

On a summer day you can sit by the pool, and a glass of lemonade will be brought out to you. The pool is in a peaceful meadow, and the view is great. If you want to stay out of the sun, relax under an apple tree or on the secluded deck. Of course, if you can tear yourself away from all the comfort and relaxation, there are lots of things to do in this area. ☛ The Queechee Hot Air Balloon Festival is in June and the Scottish Festival is in August; there are horse shows, antiquing, and Calvin Coolidge's Birthplace. Winter brings a winter carnival, and downhill and cross-country skiing are nearby.

Dinner is a real experience. The French menu has onion soup, French baguette, sole au gratin, vegetable strudel, oven-roasted potatoes, salad, and apple-cheese torte. The Italian menu offers summer-garden minestrone soup (the inn has its own vegetable and herb gardens), Italian bread, garlic-baked chicken, eggplant parmigiana, homemade pasta with garlic and olive oil, salad, and chocolate cake with raspberry-cassis sauce. They also have African, Greek, Scandinavian, and other menus. I'm impressed that they are so inventive. Breakfast includes fresh fruit, homemade granola, freshly baked small muffins, breads, and something hot like pancakes with Vermont maple syrup.

There are lots of reasons why I like it here, but two more are the beautiful inn cats.

How to get there: From I–91 North, take Exit 9 to Route 12, then go west on Route 4. From I–89 North, take Vermont Exit 1 to Route 4. The inn is at the junction of Routes 4 and 100A.

Olive Metcalf

Shire Inn
Chelsea, Vermont
05038

Innkeepers: James and Mary Lee Papa
Address/Telephone: Box 37; (802) 685–3031
Rooms: 6; all with private bath, 4 with working fireplace.
Rates: $130 to $165, double occupancy, MAP. $70 to $88, double
  occupancy, EPB.
Open: All year except one week in April and November.
Facilities and activities: Bicycles and cross-country skis available. Meeting
  facilities, fishing, biking, snowmobiling. Nearby: downhill and cross-
  country skiing, swimming, boating, theaters.

Constructed in 1832 of Vermont brick, this inn was truly built
to last. It is situated in a lovely part of the state. The White River
is close by—actually, it's in the back yard. It's a paradise for
fishermen. Cross-country skiing is in Chelsea, and downhill skiing
is good at the Sonnenberg Ski Area near Woodstock. Lake Fairlee
is the place to be for swimming and boating in the summer and ice
skating in the winter. Hanover, New Hampshire, the home of
Dartmouth College, isn't far and offers theaters, art, and more.
  The living room–library with its neat fireplace beckons all
who pass through the door. Lots of books and a good collection of
☛ *National Geographic* magazines make this room very enticing

on a cold or rainy day. A circular stairway goes up to some of the rooms, and they are lovely. Four rooms have working fireplaces. They are furnished with period antiques. A canopy bed is in one room; a king-sized bed is in another. Good feather or foam pillows assure you of a good night's sleep.

Mary Lee is the chef and wow, is she good. I hope you like to start your day with a stupendous breakfast, because you can do that here. ☞ Set your sights on freshly squeezed orange or grapefruit juice, fresh fruit, eggs any style, omelets, pancakes—banana or walnut—bacon, and sausage.

Dinner means such goodies as pasta pesto with sun-dried tomatoes; bouillon-sherry soup with ginger ravioli; sorbet (creme de menthe is exquisite); lemon–poppy seed veal (veal cutlets in a sauce of brandy, lemon juice, poppy seeds, garlic, and cream). You had some other wishes? No problem, the list goes on. If you can manage to find room for dessert, brandy-apricot cheesecake and chocolate truffle are outstanding, or you can request a special cake to be made for a special occasion.

Morrison is a huge Scottish deerhound. Say hello to him for me.

How to get there: From I–89 take the Sharon exit via Route 14 to South Royalton, then Route 110 north to Chelsea.

❄

E: *This inn is a neat place for weddings or any social event you have in mind.*

> *Were it not for a night's rest in a*
> *country inn*
> *tomorrow would be but another day.*

The Inn at Long Last
Chester, Vermont
05143

Innkeeper: Jack Coleman
Address/Telephone: Main Street; (802) 875–2444
Rooms: 30; all with private bath.
Rates: $90, single; $160 double occupancy; MAP.
Open: All year except April and second and third weeks of November.
Facilities and activities: Sunday brunch. Bar, lounge, gift shop, pool, tennis
    courts. Nearby: fishing in the stream, skiing.

Jack is a very different kind of innkeeper. There really is very
little that the man hasn't done in his former life. Talk to him and
you will see what I mean.

The library lounge is lined with books. Many are about things
Jack has done, such as being an inmate in prisons or working in
the New York sanitation department so he could write about them.
The topper is that he was president of Haverford College and most
recently was head of the Edna McConnell Clark Foundation, a
$340-million charitable fund in New York City.

This inn was the Chester Inn. It still sits on the village green,
but it has been 🖝 beautifully restored. Take the rooms, for
example. No two are alike, and each one is named for someone or
something in Jack's past life, or for people he has admired. The

Fair Winds Farm Room has a wood shovel and pick on the wall. The Connecticut River Room has a photo of Steamboat Dock. They really are nice rooms. The ☞ porch on the second floor runs the width of the inn. A 110-year-old sleigh is out here.

Napery in the dining room changes with the seasons. This is a nice touch. A magnificent ☞ back bar with mirrors, which is 12 feet long and 10 feet high, graces the dining room. It is a rare beauty. The food is exciting and the menu changes every night. Soups are unusual, such as curried apple and white wine soup and chilled strawberry soup. Or perhaps you'd like to order country lamb pâté with lingonberry sauce? You won't be sorry. One night you may find on the menu Norwegian salmon fillet, broiled and served with a creamy sorrel sauce. Another night might be bluefin tuna steaks, marinated and grilled, served with avocado butter. These are just a sample of what they have. Desserts like blueberry pandowdy or black raspberry sherbet are sure to get me back.

How to get there: From I–91 take Exit 6. Watch for Chester signs; the inn is on the green.

E: *I'm fascinated by this interesting innkeeper. The brochure in itself is worth sending for.*

olive Metcalf

Mountain Top Inn
Chittenden, Vermont
05737

Innkeeper: Bill Wolfe
Address/Telephone: Mountain Top Road; (802) 483–2311, (800) 445–2100
from out of state
Rooms: 33, and 22 cottage and chalet units; all with private bath, chalets
with kitchenette.
Rates: $88 to $125, per person, double occupancy, MAP.
Open: All year.
Facilities and activities: Lunch, bar, lounge. Heated pool, tennis, lawn
games, pitch and putt with full-size greens, game room, horseback
riding, sauna, whirlpool, exercise room, cross-country skiing, horse-
drawn sleigh rides. Nearby: downhill skiing.

In the 1870s the Mountain Top property was part of the Long
family's turnip farm. In 1940 William Barstow, an engineer and
philanthropist from New York, bought the farm and converted the
barn into a wayside tavern as a hobby for his wife. The year 1945
brought William Wolfe to Chittenden. He fell in love with the
place and Mountain Top Inn was born. His son, Bill, is now the
innkeeper.

The inn is just beautiful, with views that no money can buy.
At a 2,000-foot elevation, the inn overlooks Mountain Top Lake,

which is surrounded by fantastic mountains. When you enter the inn, you are in a very inviting living area with a large fireplace. Ahead of you are the view and a spectacular ☛ two-story glass-enclosed staircase that leads to the "Charlie James" cocktail lounge, presided over by a regal fox, and the dining room. The food served here is superb, beginning with appetizers like scallops sautéed with chutney and Dijon mustard, and seviche. One entree that I love here is New England seafood and biscuits—lobster, salmon, and scallops simmered in a hearty, creamy stew and served over homemade biscuits. The broiler provides a few interesting items as well.

The rooms, most overlooking the lake and mountains, are large and luxuriously furnished. All have spacious baths. A nice touch is your bed turned down at night with a maple sugar candy on the pillow.

The inn has an excellent ski touring program. With more than a thousand acres to ski on, the ☛ views are awesome. The sugar house, a wooden structure, is well located near several of the inn's ski touring trails. It has been turned into a ski-warming hut where skiers in the spring have the added bonus of watching the ☛ sap boiling-down process firsthand. There are two other warming huts on the property. The inn has a ski shop with instructors and all the latest equipment. Ice skating and toboggans also are fun, and downhill skiing is nearby at Pico and Killington.

Summer brings walking or hiking through the lovely countryside, and in fall the color show of the trees is breathtaking. And in winter, riding in sleighs drawn by draft horses is a wonderful yesteryear experience.

How to get there: From Rutland, head north on Route 7. Pass the power station, turn right on Chittenden Road, and follow it into Chittenden. Follow the signs up to the inn.

Olive Metcalf

Tulip Tree Inn
Chittenden, Vermont
05737

Innkeepers: Ed and Rosemary McDowell
Address/Telephone: Chittenden Dam Road; (802) 483–6213
Rooms: 8; all with private bath, 5 with Jacuzzi.
Rates: $144 to $200, double occupancy, MAP.
Open: All year except April and most of May.
Facilities and activities: Full license. Fishing. Nearby: swimming, hiking, golf, tennis, canoeing, bicycling, skiing.

In 1989 this inn was selected as one of the top ten country inns in the nation. You can't beat that! You arrive and a lovely front porch with wicker chairs beckons you at once. Beautiful woods surround you. You hear a brook babbling and a feeling of sheer peace comes over you. Inside you find a nice living room with a fireplace, a small bar and library, a den with a fireplace, and a great assortment of chairs, love seats, and couches throughout.

The rooms are the sort you never want to leave. Puffy comforters on the beds are inviting to curl up under, and the Jacuzzi tubs in five of the rooms feel so great after a long day. There are nice antiques, including a huge pine bed with a pineapple on top.

Dining is very special here at the inn. Pretty, too, with yellow

300

and white napery in the summer and red, white, and blue in the winter. Rosemary's breakfasts are full Vermont style. That means you'll find cold cereals; yogurt; juices; sweet breads; and apple, cheese, or blueberry pancakes or French toast, all with pure maple syrup.

If you think that's good, come back at dinnertime and Rosemary really shines. There are homemade breads and soups like zucchini and curried carrot. Salads are interesting, especially with Rosemary's dressings. A sorbet is brought to you to cleanse your palate, and then it might be ☞ medallions of pork with apricot-orange sauce or poached chicken breasts stuffed with mushrooms. Oh my, and her desserts. . . . Well, just save some room, because they are so good.

The inn is only a mile from the Chittenden Reservoir, where the fishing and swimming are superb. ☞ East Brook runs right by the house. Trout anyone?

How to get there: From Rutland, drive north on Route 7. Just outside Chittenden, you will see a red-brick power station on the left. Just beyond it is a Y in the road with a red country store in the middle. Keep right of the store and follow the road approximately 6 miles. Just past the fire station, go straight ahead ½ mile to the inn, which will be on your left.

The Craftsbury Inn
Craftsbury, Vermont
05826

Innkeepers: Blake and Rebecca Gleason
Address/Telephone: Route 14; (802) 586–2848
Rooms: 10; 6 with private bath.
Rates: $95 to $130, double occupancy, MAP. EP rates available.
Open: All year except April and November.
Facilities and activities: Bar, cross-country skiing. Nearby: canoeing, swimming, fishing, horseback riding, tennis, golfing.

The inn is a lovingly restored Greek Revival house that was built circa 1850. The little town of Craftsbury, said by *The Boston Globe* to be Vermont's most remarkable hill-town, was founded in 1788 by Colonel Ebenezer Crafts and lies in what is called the Northeast Kingdom. The population today is something less than 700, and that includes Craftsbury, East Craftsbury, and Craftsbury Common.

One year I arrived here on a chilly day in the middle of June and was greeted by a lovely 🐾 fire in the television room. Boy, did it feel good! Speaking of fireplaces, the one in the living room is the original fireplace that warmed the first post office in Montpelier, Vermont's capital.

The rooms here are filled with antique wicker, and the beds

have handsome ☛ heirloom quilts. Fresh paint and paper have made this lovely old inn even nicer.

All ice creams, breads, and pastries are prepared here. They also make their own stocks, and this does make a difference in the taste of food.

The food is very good and inventive here. You'll find appetizers like wild game soup, cream of mushroom soup, and duck en croûte. And for your entree, consider sautéed pheasant with a Frangelica sauce or poached salmon with a cucumber-dill sauce. Baked partridge is served with a sage stuffing and a white wine–fresh rosemary sauce. The desserts are yummy—Black Forest cake, apple flan, wild berry pie, and more.

There is much to do in this area. A cross-country ski trail is connected to the Craftsbury Sports Center. In the summer, you can rent a canoe, swim in nearby lakes, fish, ride horseback, play tennis, or play golf at Vermont's oldest course in Greensboro where the greens are fenced to prevent intrusion of the grazing cattle. Throughout July and August the Craftsbury Chamber Players perform every Thursday evening. Come and enjoy.

How to get there: Take I–91 to St. Johnsbury, pick up Route 2 west, and at West Danville take Route 15 to Hardwick. Follow Route 14 north to Craftsbury. The inn is on the right, across from the general store.

The Inn on the Common
Craftsbury Common, Vermont
05827

Innkeepers: Penny and Michael Schmitt
Address/Telephone: Route 14; (802) 586–9619; (802) 521–2233
Rooms: 17, in 3 buildings; all with private bath, 5 with fireplace or wood stove.
Rates: $95 to $115, per person, double occupancy, MAP. Ski touring and ski packages available.
Open: All year.
Facilities and activities: Food and drinks for house guests only. Heated swimming pool, clay tennis court, English croquet, boating, cross-country skiing.

It is a long way up here, but it's worth every mile you travel to be a guest of the Schmitts.

There are three buildings that make up the inn. The north annex is on the common with a lovely picket fence around it. All of its rooms are beautifully appointed. The wallpapers are 🖝 Scalamandre reproduction from a South Carolina historic collection. The sheets throughout the inn are brand new and Marimekko. There's a very unusual sofa, an English knoll; try and figure how the arms go down. Two of the bedrooms in the north annex have a fireplace. One of the bathrooms has such a cute, tiny bathtub. There's a lovely canopy bed in one room. In the main house are three new luxurious rooms that Penny loves to show off.

Across the street is the south annex. The guest lounge has a fireplace, comfy sofas, a large television, and ☛ Betamax. The north annex also has a Betamax. There's a library of over 200 films on tape so that even in bad weather there is something to do. You can fix lunch, make tea, or whatever you wish in the guest kitchen. Two Jøtul wood-burning stoves keep the rooms warm and cozy.

In the main house is the dining room with a ☛ glass wall overlooking the rose gardens. All the gardens are lovely. Penny has green hands and is a faithful gardener. The dining room has the perfect atmosphere to savor the sumptuous food. Roast native lamb with sorrel sauce is one entree; veal stew in an orange-lemon sauce is another. Salads are so good. I never had a red pepper mousse before and it is delicious. There is a superb wine cellar with many wines to complement your meal. Cocktail hour in the library is a fun, social time. Michael is bartender.

A staff of naturalists runs a sports complex near the inn. One hundred and forty acres include lake swimming, sculling, canoeing, cross-country skiing, nature walks, and bird watching. There is a summer walking map of Craftsbury, with walks along the appropriate ski trails, logging roads, and back roads. Come on up. There is something for everyone.

How to get there: Follow I–91 to St. Johnsbury, take Route 2 west, and at West Danville take Route 15 to Hardwick. Take Route 14 north to Craftsbury, and continue north into the common. The inn is on the left as you enter the village.

∽

E: *The solar-heated swimming pool has a little waterfall to let the water in. It disturbs nothing in its peaceful location behind the south annex. Sam, the inn dog, enjoys watching it.*

Silas Griffith Inn
Danby, Vermont
05739

Innkeepers: Paul and Lois Dansereau
Address/Telephone: South Main Street; (802) 293–5567
Rooms: 17, in 2 buildings; 11 with private bath.
Rates: $70 to $86, double occupancy, EPB.
Open: All year.
Facilities and activities: Dinner. Bar, swimming pool. Nearby: six ski areas, biking, horseback riding, golf, tennis, hiking, fishing, hunting, factory outlets.

In 1891 lumber baron Silas Griffith built this large stately mansion on a bluff overlooking the town of Danby as a gift for his wife. The workmanship is grand. I was really taken with the round, cherry pocket door that leads into the music room. Oak, cherry, maple, and other woods have been used throughout the inn.

When you are past the foyer of the inn, you are in a huge living room–library full of books, chairs, couches, and a welcoming fireplace. A small antique shop is off this room. There is another smaller living room with a television, which is a good spot to meet the other guests.

Eight of the rooms are in the carriage house, and nine are in the inn itself. Most of them have 🖘 queen-sized beds with fluffy quilts. Lois says she had a lot of fun—but I bet it was also hard work—visiting auctions and antique shops to find the lovely old beds and Victorian furniture for the rooms. Then she had the double beds extended to fit queen-sized mattresses. Apples in the rooms add a nice, welcoming touch.

The restaurant is in the carriage house. You'll find a good-sized bar, a fireplace, and attractively set tables. Every night there is a new dinner menu. The night I visited the inn, guests were able to start their dinner with brie baked with peach chutney or Vermont cheddar cheese soup. A choice of marinated pork tenderloin served with a delicate cherry wine sauce, boneless breast of chicken stuffed with crabmeat, steak, shrimp, and salmon was offered. There are assorted homemade desserts.

This is a nice area of Vermont with many activities to enjoy. Hikers like the 🖘 inn's proximity to the Appalachian Trail; shoppers enjoy the factory outlets for bargain shopping; skiers think it's super to have six ski areas to try; and historians like the nearby marble museum. The world's largest underground marble quarry is inside Dorset Mountain; marble from here was used to build the Jefferson Memorial and most of the other marble buildings in Washington, D.C. Even if you're not a historian, you will find the museum worth a visit.

How to get there: On Route 7 about 12 miles north of Manchester, look for the inn's sign on the right. It's a left turn into the inn.

Olive Metcalf

Barrows House
Dorset, Vermont
05251

Innkeepers: Sally and Tim Brown
Address/Telephone: Route 30; (802) 867–4455
Rooms: 22, plus 6 suites; all with private bath, some with air conditioning and TV.
Rates: $155 to $200, double occupancy, MAP.
Open: All year.
Facilities and activities: Brown-bag lunch available. Meeting facilities, cross-country ski shop rentals, swimming pool, tennis courts, bicycles. Nearby: golf, skiing, shopping.

The innkeepers say it very well. "Welcome to the Barrows House. Our door is always open to anyone seeking the relaxed life of rural, colonial New England." I could not have said it better. This is a lovely inn in a lovely part of the country.

There are eight houses that make up this inn. Each one is different. Truffle House has a living room with a fireplace. The Schubert has two rooms plus one suite, fireplace, and kitchen to use. Some are air-conditioned, and there is a 🖝 fire-control system in all buildings. Most of the beds are queens or kings.

Lunch is fun. Have it by the pool or 🖝 brown bag it anywhere. The brown bag I had contained diet cola, a sandwich and chips, a salad, a peach, and cookies. Quite a nice picnic. Would you like a ☞ special-event dinner for someone? Well, they honor the person in a unique way with a wow of a menu.

The regular menu changes nightly. If you stay a week or so, you will have many choices like chilled basil and sun-dried tomato soup, curry onion ginger soup, wild boar pâté with mustard mayonnaise, grilled boned quail on wild rice, rack of lamb with honey-thyme sauce, prime calf's liver on smoked bacon and leeks . . . the list goes on and on. The desserts are wonderful, as you can imagine. Try it once. I'm sure you will come back.

There's so much to do in this area. The skiing is superb, antique shopping is near, and the Dorset Playhouse is here. Horseback riding and hiking or golf are available in nearby Manchester. And when you're tired of all the activity, come back to the inn to enjoy the cozy tavern or the glowing fire in the main living room.

How to get there: The inn is 6 miles northwest of Manchester, Vermont, on Route 30.

❋

> *Innkeeping takes twenty-five hours*
> *of every twenty-four, but done right*
> *it makes a wonderful life.*

olive Metcalf

Dorset Inn
Dorset, Vermont
05251

Innkeepers: Sissy Hicks and Gretchen Schmidt
Address/Telephone: Route 30; (802) 867–5500
Rooms: 34; all with private bath.
Rates: $90 single; $160, double occupancy; MAP.
Open: All year except first three weeks in April.
Facilities and activities: Breakfast, lunch, dinner, bar. Wheelchair access to
    dining room. Nearby: golf, theater.

Built in 1796, this is the oldest inn in Vermont, and it has
been continuously operated as an inn. Today, the inn has been 🖝
completely restored and is listed in the National Register of Historic
Places. There are wide-board floors, and beautiful Vermont pine is
around the fireplace in the living room.

While the inn has retained the feeling of the eighteenth
century, it is modern in its conveniences. It has been completely
insulated. The bathrooms have been redone, some of the rooms
have been air-conditioned, and firm mattresses have been purchased. The whole inn is clean and neat.

The breakfast and luncheon room has a lovely old 🖝 lion
fountain. I love the sound of the water. The bar-lounge is spacious.
There is no crowding in this large and rambling inn.

310

☛ Sissy Hicks presides over the kitchen and is a very well-known lady. Some of the luncheon items are curried mussels and noodles on spinach, beef, and scallions with rice, and biscuit-crust apple and turkey pie. Sounds great! At dinner the appetizers are numerous. One is New England cheese chowder. Sissy's entrees are really different. Breast of chicken with pear and cider cream. Or veal medallions with a lime-ginger sauce. The breakfast menu is pure ambrosia. I like it here. I think you can tell.

The recently restored taproom has its own menu from Sunday through Thursday in the summer and every night in the winter. It's lovely in here.

A fine golf course is nearby for anyone who likes to play. Swimming is a lot of fun in a huge marble quarry up the road. If culture turns you on, the Southern Vermont Arts Center and the Dorset Playhouse will provide the comedy and drama of good theater. There are two inn dogs, both Labs. They are yellow and chocolate and named Chivas and Chloe.

How to get there: Leave I–91 at Brattleboro and go left on Route 30 to Dorset. Or take Route 7 to Manchester Center, and go north on Route 30.

olive Metcalf

Inn at West View Farm
Dorset, Vermont
05251

Innkeepers: Helmut and Dorothy Stein
Address/Telephone: Route 30; (802) 867–5715
Rooms: 10; all with private bath, 1 with wheelchair access.
Rates: $80 to $98, double occupancy, EPB; $155 to $170, double occupancy, MAP.
Open: May through October and mid-November through March.
Facilities and activities: Breakfast, dinner, tavern. Dining room closed on Mondays. Nearby: tennis, golf, swimming, skiing.

This is an authentic Vermont country inn. Informal and relaxed is the style of the innkeepers, who have thought of everything to make your stay here comfortable.

The living rooms with their glowing fireplaces and good couches and chairs are restful after a day of skiing or shopping. The guest rooms are warmly furnished with four-poster beds and antique dressers. One room has facilities for handicapped guests.

The dining room, which is done in shades of warm green, is just beautiful. It is highlighted by a tin ceiling and a broad bay window. The room seats forty-five people. The stunning place plates are a floral pattern from Villeroy and Boch, and Botanica made in Luxembourg. Needless to say with such magnificent surroundings, the food served here is extravagant, with hors d'oeuvres and soups such as terrine of pheasant, a fish pâté, or hot or cold ☛ cream of mustard soup. This was a first for me and very good. There are entrees like quenelles of scallops, fillet of salmon, or rack of lamb for two. A real favorite is ☛ chateaubriand flambé au cognac et poivres verts, also for two. Ready for dessert? A pastry tray has an enticing variety of tarts, tortes, and pastries. Or you can order creme caramel, homemade sorbet, or homemade ice cream. What a way to go.

A lovely stained-glass window separates the dining room from the bar. The bar is done in rich, warm wood and is a real beauty. The tavern has its own menu, with salad niçoise, cold poached salmon, soups, and other interesting foods.

The inn is only 5 miles north of Manchester, where there are shops for your every wish. Three downhill ski areas and cross-country skiing are all nearby, and the Dorset Playhouse is less than a walk around the block from the inn. Clancy, an Irish setter, is the inn dog.

How to get there: Take I–91 north to Brattleboro, then take Route 30 to Manchester. At the blinking lights take a right and an immediate left, which brings you back on Route 30 North. Go about 5½ miles north of Manchester. Look for the inn on your right.

❀

E: *To see this beautiful inn in the snow is a picture to remember. And in the warm weather the porch with its wicker furniture beckons me. What a great view from here!*

Olive Metcalf

Vermont Marble Inn
Fair Haven, Vermont
05743

Innkeepers: Shirley Stein; Bea and Richard Taube
Address/Telephone: Fair Haven Green; (802) 265–8383
Rooms: 13; all with private bath.
Rates: $145 to $175, double occupancy, MAP.
Open: All year except two weeks in November.
Facilities and activities: Full liquor license. Nearby: skiing.

The inn was built of locally quarried golden marble by descendants of Ethan Allen's family in the 1860s. The original carriage house and well house are still here, too. The fireplaces in the inn are marble. The ceilings are 13 feet high, and the ☛ carved moldings are elaborate. Crystal chandeliers are suspended from rosette medallions. The Victorian parlors are beautifully furnished. The library, which has a fireplace, has a chess set ready to play and a television available for watching. From one end of this Victorian beauty to the other, the inn is gorgeous, and there are three stories of it.

In 1926 an art deco wing was added. You really must see it to believe it. A two-faced Raggedy Ann doll, who is fifty or sixty years old, sleeps up here. There is a beauty of a bathroom on the third floor.

The rest of the rooms are named for English authors. There is a ☞ 120-year-old French brass bed in Lord Byron's room. The rooms reflect the style of the persons for whom they are named. Believe me, they are sumptuous. The beds are turned down at night, and a sweet is left for you.

The dining rooms are charming. The formal one has the original ceiling of papier-mâché and plaster. Tables are set with pink and white napery. The food is outstanding. Just consider: wine poached shrimp with a spicy cocktail sauce; loin lamb chop grilled with garlic and served with onion–bell pepper salsa; braised duck with port and raspberry sauce; and roast quail. These are only a few of the possibilities. Desserts are made by ☞ Bea, the dessert chef, who is great.

Shirley is the breakfast chef. Breakfast is served on the porch, which has lots of windows overlooking the grounds. Freshly squeezed orange juice is always a joy. The inn is a rare gem. Do try it.

How to get there: Take Route 4 from Rutland and watch for signs to Fair Haven. The inn is on the green.

*

E: A hundred-year-old stone wall separates the woods from the meadow. You can hike to the banks of the Castleton River from here.

olive Metcalf

Blueberry Hill
Goshen, Vermont
05733

Innkeeper: Tony Clark
Address/Telephone: Blueberry Hill; (802) 247–6735, (802) 247–6535, (800) 448–0707
Rooms: 12; all with private bath.
Rates: In summer, $76 to $100; in winter, $98; double occupancy, MAP.
Open: All year.
Facilities and activities: Packed lunch available, BYOB. Cross-country skiing, swimming, fishing.

The inn is a cross-country skier's dream come true. It is nestled at the foot of Romance Mountain in the Green Mountain National Forest and is surrounded by good clean air and well-groomed snowy trails. From the inn brochure I quote: "The Blueberry Hill Ski Touring Center, across from the inn, devotes itself to cross-country skiers of ☞ all ages and abilities. Inside the fully equipped Ski Center are retail and rental departments, a waxing area, repair shop, and an expert staff to see that you are skiing better with less effort. Upstairs you can relax, make friends, and share the day's events in our lounge with its large windows, comfortable seating, and old wood stove. Surrounding the Ski Center are 75 kilometers of both challenging and moderate terrain.

A loop around Hogback, a race to Silver Lake, or just making tracks in a snow world all your own . . . the activities never cease—from seminars, waxing clinics, night and guided tours, to the ☛ 60-kilometer American Ski Marathon.''

In the summer the ski trails are used for hiking, walking, or running. There are a pond for swimming and streams and lakes for fishing.

The inn is a restored 1813 farmhouse. Dinner is served family style in a lovely, candlelit dining room. There are four courses served in an unhurried, comfortable way. While I was here dinner included such delicious things as cold cantaloupe soup, scallion bread, broiled lamb chops with mint butter, stir-fried asparagus, lemon meringue tarts, and ☛ homemade ice creams. Tony's son made strawberry ice cream, and it was so good. Breakfasts are served in the greenhouse just off the kitchen. It is full of glorious plants. Three of the guest rooms and a new wing are out here, just beyond the greenhouse.

Their upside-down gardens hanging from the ceiling beams are a colorful and imaginative use of straw flowers, and the brick patio overlooking Dutton Brook is so restful and nice. There are plenty of books to read, and the rooms are comfortable with many antiques, quilts, and ☛ hot water bottles on the backs of the doors. Honest, they are there.

How to get there: From Rutland take Route 7 north to Brandon, then Route 73 east for 6 miles. Turn left at the inn's sign, and follow the signs up the mountain on a dirt road to the inn.

olive Metcalf

The Old Tavern
Grafton, Vermont
05146

Innkeeper: Richard Ernst
Address/Telephone: Route 121; (802) 843–2231
Rooms: 35, in 7 houses; all with private bath.
Rates: In main building and annex, $55 to $125, single or double occupancy, EP. Guest house, $65 to $335, per day, EP.
Open: All year except April and Christmas Eve and Christmas Day.
Facilities and activities: Breakfast for houseguest only, lunch, dinner, bar. Television in lounge, parking, elevator, swimming, tennis, nature walks.

If you're looking for perfection in a country inn, go to a charming Vermont village called Grafton where you'll find The Old Tavern. It has been operated as an inn since 1801. Since the inn was purchased by the Windham Foundation in 1965, it has been restored and is now one of those superb New England inns we are all seeking.

When you turn your car off pounding interstate highways to the tree-shaded route that winds to this quaint village, you step back in time. The loveliest of the old, combined with the comfort of the new, makes this an unbeatable inn. No grinding motors can disturb your slumber when you are in the best beds in all New

England. The sheets and towels are the finest money can buy, and there are extra pillows and blankets in each room. The spacious rooms are filled with antiques, all in mint condition. The guest houses across the street that are also part of the inn are enchanting.

There is no "organized activity" at The Old Tavern. ☛ The swimming pool is a natural pond, cool and refreshing. There are tennis courts nearby and marked trails in the woods for walkers. This is the place to calm your spirits and recharge your batteries.

The cocktail barn is charming, connected to the inn by a covered walk. There are flowers everywhere, hanging in baskets, in flower boxes, and on various tables in the gracious public rooms. The food is excellent, with unusual soups, varied entrees, all cooked well and served by pleasant waitresses.

☛ Up the street a bit there is a six box-stall stable that will accommodate guest horses, plus a four-bay carriage shed, if you care to bring your own carriage. All this for the exclusive use of Old Tavern guests.

How to get there: From I–91 take Exit 5 at Bellows Falls. As you come down the exit ramp, watch for Route 121, which you'll take to the inn.

❀

The snow could pile as deep as a mountain
with no worry for me, for I was in the tavern
of a friendly country inn.

Highland Lodge
Greensboro, Vermont
05841

Innkeepers: Willie and David Smith
Address/Telephone: RR 1, Box 1290; (802) 533–2647
Rooms: 11 rooms, plus 11 cottages; all with private bath.
Rates: $130 to $180, double occupancy, MAP.
Open: All year except April 1 to May 25 and after foliage season to
   mid-December.
Facilities and activities: Lunch, beer and wine license, setups available.
   Swimming, boating, fishing, cross-country ski touring center. Nearby:
   working dairy farm, golf.

When the snow starts falling up here, it has to be one of the
most beautiful places in the world. And you can bet that it's
popular with cross-country skiers. There is a complete ☞ ski
touring center with daily instruction, ski shop (sales, rentals, and
repairs), guided tours, marked trails, and skier's lunch. All this is
at an altitude of 1,500 feet, where there are miles of ski touring
through the wonderful scenery.

Winter isn't the only fun time of year to be here. Caspian
Lake, with the lodge's own beach house, is just across the road for
swimming, canoeing, and sailing. Fishing is good in June and
September until mid-October for salmon, lake trout, rainbow

trout, and perch. Tennis, golf, and riding are available for those so inclined.

Any inn that sends its chef to ☛ France to train for the kitchen surely gets my nod. The food has always been outstanding here and now it is even better. The menu is inventive and they have their great grilled black Angus sirloin steaks to prove it. They grow all their own herbs in a lovely herb garden. I love the dessert menu. They have great names, and taste equally great. Ishkabibble is a brownie topped with ice cream and homemade hot fudge. Forgotten Dessert is a meringue with ice cream and strawberries. It's nice to find these old favorites on a menu.

☛ Children are welcome here. Baby-sitters are available. In July and August a play lady comes in for the four-to-nine set when there are enough children. The playroom offers amusement for kids of all ages, and the playhouse has a supervised play program for youngsters. With the children happily occupied, the lounges and library remain free and quiet for you.

This is the place to get away from it all. The views and utter peace are so wonderful, they are hard to describe. Come and enjoy.

How to get there: Greensboro is 35 miles northeast of Montpelier. Take I–91 to St. Johnsbury and follow U.S. 2 west to West Danville. Continue west on Vermont 15, to intersection with Vermont 16 about 2 miles east of Hardwick. Turn north on 16 to East Hardwick and follow signs west to Greensboro, at the south end of Caspian Lake. Highland Lodge is at the north end of the lake on the road to East Craftsbury.

olive Metcalf

Three Mountain Inn
Jamaica, Vermont
05343

Innkeepers: Charles and Elaine Murray
Address/Telephone: Route 30; (802) 874–4140
Rooms: 16, in 2 buildings and a farmhouse across the street; all with private bath.
Rates: $65 to $90, per person, MAP. No credit cards.
Open All year except April to May 15 and November until Thanksgiving.
Facilities and activities: Pub, lounge, seminar room with fireplace, swimming pool, cross-country skiing. Nearby: downhill skiing, tennis, golfing, fishing, horseback riding.

The inn is well named, since it is within a few minutes of Stratton, Bromley, and Magic mountains. Mount Snow is also within easy range. Skiers should love this location. Cross-country buffs will find a multitude of trails beginning at the inn's doorstep, including a ☛ dramatic trail along the long defunct West River Railroad bed. Tennis is available both indoors and out at nearby Stratton. Horseback riding is superb on lovely trails in the area, or go swimming in the inn's own beautifully landscaped pool.

This small, authentic country inn was built in the 1780s. The living room has a large, roaring fireplace, complete with an original Dutch oven. The floors and walls are of wide, planked pine, and there are plenty of comfortable chairs. A picture window offers views of the Green Mountains to complete the scene.

A cozy lounge and bar area make you feel very comfortable for sitting back to enjoy good conversation and a before- or after-dinner drink. A good wine selection is at hand.

The rooms are tastefully decorated. One room has a four-poster, king-sized bed in it. Another has a private balcony overlooking the swimming pool and garden. A charming ☛ Hansel and Gretel cottage also is available. The beds have lovely sheets, and the bathrooms have color-coordinated towels.

The inn was featured several years ago in ☛ *Gourmet* magazine, so you can safely guess that the food served in the lovely dining rooms is good—served by candlelight, of course. Dinners are carefully prepared to order, and the menu changes frequently to bring you the most seasonal foods available. Cucumber soup is excellent. They have locally smoked fish, broiled trout, and yummy crisp hash brown potatoes. Strawberry shortcake is always in demand. Elaine also does wonders with berry pies. Be sure to order a piece.

How to get there: Follow I–91 to Brattleboro and take the second exit to Route 30, to Jamaica.

✳

E: *There are guided tours for fly fishermen on the West and Battenkill rivers. Write for these package deals, and remember you will eat what you catch. Angus, the inn dog, is a nice one.*

olive Metcalf

Jay Village Inn
Jay, Vermont
05859

Innkeepers: Bob and Jane Angliss
Address/Telephone: Route 242; (802) 988–2643, (800) 227-7452 (outside Vermont)
Rooms: 16, plus 1 chalet; 10 with private bath.
Rates: In winter, $30, per person, EPB. In summer and fall, $50, double occupancy, continental breakfast.
Open: All year except mid-April to mid-May.
Facilities and activities: Dinner, bar. TV in lounge, trout brook, swimming pool. Nearby: Golf, tennis, cross-country and downhill skiing.

When you get to Jay, you are nearly in Canada, so this makes the Jay Village Inn my most northern Vermont inn. Nestled at the foot of Jay Peak, this is a delightful country inn. Come any time of the year and enjoy the fireplace lounge and bar. It is especially noted for its après-ski, but it's equally pleasurable any season. Sip a hot buttered rum and enjoy the flaming fire. They have a player piano and some great old songs. Do any of you remember "The Teddy Bear's Picnic"? It is here.

They serve an ample breakfast up here in the hills. Pancakes, eggs any way you can imagine, French toast, and, of course, real Vermont maple syrup. Breads are freshly baked every day.

Gary Birchard, the chef, is known in these parts as Bear. He is an avid fisherman and outdoorsman. The lake trout, salmon, and other fish are as fresh as you can get them because he catches them and brings them in for dinner. He also does wonders with soups and bisques. Mussels Robert are wonderful, and so is the Jay Village Pâté, which is laced with brandy. ☛ Steak au poivre is the house special. Vermont baby lamb chops are two thick and lean ones. Roast duckling is very crisp, and the fish is the freshest anywhere. For dessert their warm apple crisp gets my nod. It is served with dollops of cream. It may be a long way up here, but boy, you'll eat well. As the menu says, "We are on the morning side of the mountain."

If you are a skier, you must know that Jay Peak has one of ☛ the longest, most dependable ski seasons in the East. The aerial tramway is a "trip," and there are exciting trails for every level of skiing, beginner to expert.

For other seasons there are two golf courses in the vicinity, and if you are a hiker you are close to the Long Trail. A relaxing summer day can be spent by the inn's pool that has a nice carpet-covered deck.

The dining room has been redecorated with crisp beige linens and nice curtains. The guest rooms all have good mattresses, so you will sleep well.

How to get there: Take I–91 to Exit 26. Take Route 5 north to Route 14 north to Route 100, a total of 8 miles. Go left here for 6 miles to Route 101, then right for 3 miles to Route 242. Go left on Route 242 for 1 mile to the inn.

Mountain Meadows Lodge
Killington, Vermont
05751

Innkeepers: The Stevens Family
Address/Telephone: RR 1, Box 4080; (802) 775–1010
Rooms: 15; 12 with private bath.
Rates: In summer, $45 to $50, per person, double occupancy, MAP. $35
to $40, per person, double occupancy, EPB. Higher rates in winter.
Open: All year except May.
Facilities and activities: BYOB. Television, game room, hiking, swimming,
boating, fishing. Nearby: cross-country and downhill skiing.

It was here that I met Bear, a mostly red setter, who had just
come off the Appalachian Trail carrying his own backpack. True,
I swear. If you are hiking inn-to-inn, this is the southernmost inn
and a good place to start.

The inn is very casual and relaxed and overlooks 110 acres of
lovely Kent Lake. The lake is stocked with ☛ rainbow trout and
largemouth bass. There are boats and canoes for your pleasure.
You can swim either in the lake or in the inn's pool.

Vermont home-style cooking at its very best is featured. The
inn has a BYOB bar and a game room.

326

The rooms are fully carpeted and comfortable as sin, but the place to really relax is the large living room, which has a big fireplace and lots of windows overlooking the lake. The view is lovely. This is a wonderful inn for family reunions.

The inn has ☛ the largest ski touring center in the area, and for you more daring types, Killington and Pico Peak alpine areas are but minutes away. When you return to the inn, say hello to Cori, the inn's golden retriever.

How to get there: The inn is 10 miles east of Rutland, just off Route 4. Follow Route 4 from Rutland for 12 miles, and at Thundering Brook Road you will come to the inn's sign. Turn left. The inn is ¼ mile beyond.

❈

*"Venite ad me ownes qui stomacho laboratoratis
et ego restaurabus vos."*
*"Come to me all whose stomachs cry out in anguish
and I shall restore you."*

The Vermont Inn
Killington, Vermont
05751

Innkeepers: Judd and Susan Levy
Address/Telephone: Route 4; (802) 773–9847, (800) 541–7795 (outside Vermont)
Rooms: 17; 13 with private bath, 1 with wheelchair accessibility.
Rates: In summer, $50 to $80; in winter, $55 to $90; per person, MAP.
Open: All year except mid-April to Memorial Day.
Facilities and activities: Dinner every day except Monday, bar. TV, game room, sauna, hot tub, pool, tennis, lawn games. Nearby: gondola ride, summer theater, Norman Rockwell Museum, farmers' market, skiing.

You may be greeted at the door of this friendly red house by a companionable dog named Harry. Judd and Susan are always here, and a nicer couple you'll have to travel a long way to find.

The Vermont Inn is well known locally for the fine food served in the lovely dining room. As a matter of fact, the restaurant was ☞ awarded the Silver Spoon Award two years in a row. Just a sample of the food is tenderloin of pork, so different, sautéed with fresh mushrooms and flavored in sherry wine with cream. Steak teriyaki is excellent, as is their good selection of fish dishes. They have cultivated ☞ a fine wine cellar to enhance the good food. There is also a children's menu, a true help for the traveling family.

The inn's guests are a mixed bag. You'll run into young professional people from Boston or New York, a grandparent or two, families, anyone from honeymooners to golden oldies.

This old house has sturdy underpinnings. Some of the original beams still have the bark on them, and how the rocks of the foundation were ever put in place I cannot imagine. Everything was changed around—the old dining room became a lounge to make the inn cozier—so take advantage of the glorious view of Killington, Pico, and Little Killington, straight ahead across the valley. The bar was handmade locally of Vermont cherry wood, and it's a beauty. Couches and a wood stove make this room a great spot for relaxing. There also is a room with a view that houses a hot tub, exercise machines, and lots of plants. It's a beauty and is ideal for anyone who wants to unwind after a day on the slopes or hiking.

I always love inn dogs, as you know, but Harry is really special to me because he's a bichon frise. I have one, too, so I know what wonderful pets they are. Mine is named Muffin. Harry's "Instructions to Guests" on how he is to be treated should be on the *must* list for every inn dog. They are tacked up at the desk. Drop in and read them, then stay awhile.

How to get there: The inn is 6 miles east of Rutland, via Route 4. It is also 4 miles west of the intersection of Route 4 and Route 100 North (Killington Access Road).

E: *The new room for handicapped guests has a ramp, a queen-sized bed, and a beautiful daybed.*

Nordic Inn
Landgrove, Vermont
05148

Innkeepers: Tom and Judy Acton
Address/Telephone: Route 11; (802) 824–6444
Rooms: 5; 3 with private bath.
Rates: $55 to $75, per person, MAP. Summer rates are EP.
Open: All year except weekdays from Memorial Day to third week of June.
Facilities and activities: Lunch in winter only, Sunday brunch, bar, lounge. Cross-country skiing, ski shop, hiking. Nearby: golf, tennis, horseback riding, downhill skiing.

I think it's nice to be able to go to an inn and have almost everything you want right there, so you do not have to go running around in your car.

This inn has ☛ 20 kilometers of groomed and marked trails through the Green Mountain National Forest. The varied terrain takes you through a winter wonderland, from stands of towering red pine, over beaver ponds, through meadows, and even past a very old cemetery on a hilltop. There are ☛ guided backpack tours from the inn, and, of course, downhill skiing is nearby at Bromley, Magic, and my personal favorite, Stratton. To make it even nicer for you, there is a ski shop right here with plenty of instructors, so come on up.

At other times of the year you can hike the trails or go fishing. Nearby are horseback riding, golf, and tennis. Summer theater is handy in Dorset and Weston.

The bar and lounge area has a large stone fireplace; very cozy on a snowy day. There are tables and chairs as well as a nice bar in here. The solarium is lovely. Imagine having some of their delicious food and watching the snow fall or the ski school in action. A very, very relaxing place to be. Murphy, a Welsh corgi, and Tinker, the inn cat, find lots of relaxing places in the inn.

The food is glorious, dinner or brunch. They serve dishes like a superb seafood salad, mussels Provençale, veal and chicken done in special ways, and ☛ broiled loin lamb chops served with a Dijon mustard, ginger, and rosemary sauce. There's a nice display of wines on a table, so it's easy to make a choice.

The bar has a special drink, hot glögg, containing vodka, cognac, red wine, slivered almonds, raisins, and cinnamon. Wow!

How to get there: The inn is between Bromley and Londonderry on Route 11, 14 miles east of Manchester.

The Village Inn
Landgrove, Vermont
05148

Innkeepers: Jay and Kathy Snyder; Elsie and Don Snyder
Address/Telephone: Weston Road (mailing address: P.O. Box 215); (802) 824–6673
Rooms: 18; 16 with private bath.
Rates: In winter, $75, per person, double occupancy, MAP; in summer, $45 to $75, per room, EPB.
Open: All year except April 1 to May 22 and October 20 to mid-December.
Facilities and activities: Dinner, except on Wednesdays in summer. Pool, tennis, pitch-and-putt, bumper pool, Ping-Pong, volleyball, cross-country skiing. Nearby: downhill skiing, alpine slide, summer theaters.

This is a family-run inn that welcomes families. ☛ Yes, that does mean you can bring your children. They will be well entertained, and so will you. Indoors is a fun game room, and outside are play things, a heated swimming pool, two Plexipave tennis courts, and a four-hole pitch-and-putt golf facility. A hike through the National Forest is unbelievably scenic, and summer theater is nearby.

Winter means snow, and there is plenty of it. It's only a short hop by car to Bromley, Stratton, Snow Valley, Magic Mountain, or

Okemo. Cross-country skiing begins at the inn's door, or try your skills at snowshoeing or ice skating. After a long day revive yourself in ☞ the whirlpool spa, and then enjoy the fireside warmth in the Rafter Room lounge. As the Snyders say, the lounge's ☞ provocatively supine couch is the ideal relaxation!

The architectural style of the inn is peculiar to Vermont, with one building added onto another building. It turns out to be charming. The first part was built in 1810. It has been an inn since 1939. The rooms are spick and span, spacious, and very comfortable. The common rooms, dining room, and just everything about this quiet spot are relaxing. And the Snyders, who are cordial and welcoming innkeepers, make you want to return year after year.

How to get there: Via I–91, use Exit 6 at Rockingham. Take Route 103 to Chester, then Route 11 to Londonderry. Continue past the shopping center for approximately a half mile, and turn right on Landgrove Road. Go 4 miles to the Village of Landgrove. Bear left after crossing the bridge and continue 1 mile to the inn, on your right.

From Manchester, take Route 11 past Bromley Ski Area, and turn left into Peru Village. At the fork in Peru bear left and continue 4 miles through the National Forest to the crossroads in Landgrove. Turn left toward Weston, and the inn will be on your right.

❀

E: *From horse-drawn sleigh rides in winter to the blueberry pancakes, this is a nice place to be*

Olive Metcalf

The Highland House
Londonderry, Vermont
05148

Innkeepers: Bill and Judy Raffaele
Address/Telephone: Route 100; (802) 824–3019
Rooms: 13, plus 4 suites, in 2 buildings; 15 with private bath.
Rates: $53 to $93, double occupancy, EPB.
Open: All year except last two weeks in April, first week in May, and Thanksgiving week.
Facilities and activities: Dinner Wednesday through Sunday, beer and wine license. Heated swimming pool, all-weather tennis court. Nearby: skiing, fishing, golf, horseback riding.

The Highland House has really grown. In the wonderful addition in the back of the inn, there is a living room with a fireplace that is just lovely. The suites are out here, but no matter where you put your head, you'll have a good night's sleep in this very quiet inn.

The ☛ heated swimming pool was built up on a hill. There are great views from here. The tennis court is also a nice addition to the property. The inn's grounds are just beautiful.

There is much to do here, no matter what season of the year you come. Trout fishing, golf, and horseback riding are nearby. Go picnicking and hiking in the Green Mountain National Forest.

Weston is close by, and its summer playhouse is fun. Fall foliage is spectacular throughout the area, or you can sit right here and watch the inn's 150-year-old maples turn colors. Winter brings cross-country skiing in the area, and downhill at Bromley, Magic, Stratton, or Okemo. All are ☛ within twenty minutes of the inn.

The dining room is charming and the food is glorious. Among the appetizers are escargots au beurre Breton, fettucine, smoked salmon, smoked trout, and chilled shrimp. Entrees include filet mignon, duck Shrewsbury, poached salmon with dill, shrimp Corsica, veal pecan, veal Marsala, and sundance chicken. Desserts are too good to list. Do give this inn a try.

How to get there: Take Exit 2 from I–91 at Brattleboro. Take Route 30 north to Route 100, and the inn is just north of town on Route 100.

Insomnia is almost a blessing if you are in an inn within easy earshot of a country church bell.

Rabbit Hill Inn
Lower Waterford, Vermont
05848

Innkeepers: John and Maureen Magee
Address/Telephone: Route 18, Box 55; (802) 748–5168
Rooms: 16, plus 2 suites; all with private bath, radio, cassette player. No
  smoking inn.
Rates: $90, single; 140 to $180, double occupancy; MAP. EPB rates
  available.
Open: All year except one week in November.
Facilities and activities: Bar, cross-country skiing, trout fishing.

In 1834 Rabbit Hill became an inn. It has had a few owners
over the years; however, this pair has really done justice to this
lovely old inn.

Each of the inn's rooms is done according to a theme. Some
are the Doll Chamber, the Toy Chamber, and Carolyn's Room,
which has a blue-and-white canopy bed. One has a cranky rabbit
sitting on a bed. I have never seen so many stuffed rabbits, dolls,
and such, all so tastefully arranged. I was in Victoria's Chamber,
which has a king-sized bed and wonderful Victorian touches. 🖝
The Magees have come up with a beauty of an idea. Each room
has a cassette player and a tape that explains what you would have
seen from your window more than a century ago. The 🖝 hats that

Maureen has had made are worth the trip alone. A diary is in each room for people to write in during their stay. They are fun to read. The suites are in the tavern building. There is a family of little bears on one of the beds.

The porch on the second floor faces the Presidential Range. It's a special place to just sit and rock with Hershey, the inn dog.

The Snooty Fox Pub has an old crane in the fireplace for doing hearth cooking. The dining room doors remain closed until six o'clock. They are then opened to reveal highly polished pine tables set with antique silver and lit by candlelight, 1850s Windsor chairs, and a fireplace. It takes ☞ two hours to dine here; it is all done right. The menu changes nightly. You are given a choice of appetizer or soup. How do you choose between chicken with smoked cheddar cheese in puff pastry or cream of green pepper soup? After a salad and a sorbet, the entree arrives. It might be rack of lamb, pheasant, swordfish or other seafood dishes, six different filet mignon dishes, five veal dishes, duck, or chicken. Save room for dessert. Whiskey toddy cake sounds divine. So does white chocolate tart. These are only a sampling of what you might find.

The inn is glorious. So is the whole area. You will not be disappointed with this one.

How to get there: Take Route 2 east from St. Johnsbury and turn right onto Route 18. Or coming from Route 5, take Route 135 east to Lower Waterford.

*

E: *In the evening while you're dining, your bed is turned down, your radio is turned on to soft music, your candle is lit, and a fabric heart is placed on your pillow. You are invited to use it as your do-not-disturb sign and then to take it home with you.*

The Andrie Rose Inn
Ludlow, Vermont
05149

Innkeepers: Rick and Carolyn Bentzinger
Address/Telephone: 13 Pleasant Street; (802) 228–4846
Rooms: 8; all with private bath, 5 with whirlpool tub. No smoking inn.
Rates: $95 to $105, double occupancy, EPB.
Open: All year.
Facilities and activities: Picnic lunches available, dinner, full liquor license. Meeting facilities, bicycles. Nearby: skiing.

Andrie Rose was the former owner of this lovely inn, built in 1829, and Rick and Carolyn have named it in her honor. She would be pleased to have her name connected with this very gracious inn.

☛ When you arrive, a personalized welcome card is in your room, highlighting area activities and events. If you are celebrating a special event, you may receive chilled champagne, balloons, flowers, or a Vermont specialty product. You can help yourself any time to the cookies and candies found throughout the inn. In the fall and winter, guests enjoy hot chocolate, cider, tea, or coffee; in the summer lemonade and iced tea are served. Complimentary hors d'oeuvres are served during cocktail hour. All of these are very nice, thoughtful touches.

The 👉 front porch is a great place to just relax, have a cocktail, or read a book. A fireplace is in the living room, and games are in the front room. Bombay paddle fans are in all of the common rooms and guest rooms. These are lovely any time of year. Carolyn and Rick are always thinking about what will make your stay memorable.

Carolyn has decorated the rooms beautifully. Some are done in Laura Ashley prints. Caswell Massey almond-scented bath accessories are in all the bathrooms. Soft pastel colors are used on the walls, towels, and linens. I found them very restful. There are five whirlpool tubs, so nice after a day of skiing.

A five-course dinner is served with a choice of two entrees. When I visited here in June, the appetizer was mushroom caps stuffed with crabmeat. The soup was chilled summer fruit medley. The third course was a good salad. The entrees were grilled New York strip steak or swordfish, accompanied by vegetables and bread. The desserts are homemade. The breakfast buffet is ample and always includes a special of the day.

Ludlow is a wonderful town. It is home to Okemo, a very popular downhill ski area. During the rest of the year, the inn has bicycles for your use, so go and have a Vermont adventure. Be sure to take along a picnic lunch.

How to get there: From I–91 or Route 131, follow Route 103 west to Ludlow.

❀

E: *The entire inn is available for a small business retreat or another function. What great surroundings you'd have!*

olive Metcalf

The Governor's Inn
Ludlow, Vermont
05149

Innkeepers: Charlie and Deedy Marble
Address/Telephone: 86 Main Street; (802) 228–8830
Rooms: 8; all with private bath. No smoking inn.
Rates: $180, double occupancy, MAP.
Open: All year except April.
Facilities and activities: Afternoon tea, picnic hampers available for lunch.
   Bar. Nearby: skiing, boating, fishing, historical attractions.

Deedy is the chef and she really does justice to the title. All the food is prepared each day for that day. She does not buy any prepackaged portion-control type foods and there is no microwave oven. Breakfast may feature the Governor's special breakfast puff or Charlie's nearly world-famous ☛ rum raisin French toast. In the picnic hamper for lunch, you may find the Governor's braised quail, or cucumber and dill butter sandwiches with Pacific smoked salmon. Sounds so nice and tastes so great by the side of a bubbling brook or any other spot in this marvelous countryside. On my last visit here, I had a great picnic, which included a sandwich of tenderloin of beef pâté.

Dinner is a grand six-course affair. I do not care for bluefish, but if I did, I'd surely have it here. It's flambéed with gin! Salads are different. One I like is ☛ strawberry chardonnay with champagne. The after-dinner coffees and Victorian tea are also special.

The inn's "Collection of Recipes" includes several that you may find in your picnic basket. "P.M. Magazine" and *Vermont Life* have discovered the inn. It's no wonder, because both Charlie and Deedy are graduates of the Roger Vergé Gourmet Cooking School, and Deedy recently came back from cooking school in northern Italy.

I think you get the message. The food is excellent.

The dining room where you enjoy this good food has restful blue tablecloths and a beautiful collection of ornate tea cups, added to quite often by contented guests. The parlor has a magnificent 1895 marbleized slate corner fireplace, a real work of art. The governor of Vermont who lived here surely had a beautiful home.

The bedrooms are so attractive, with lovely wallpapers. The beds have all new linen and a ☛ flannel top sheet to boot. There's one brass bed over one hundred years old. You will find miniature cordials in your room. Nice touch.

How to get there: Take Exit 6 north from I–91 and follow Route 103 west to Ludlow and the inn.

The Okemo Inn
Ludlow, Vermont
05149

Innkeepers: Rhinard and Toni Parry
Address/Telephone: RFD 1, Box 133; (802) 228–8834
Rooms: 12; 10 with private bath, some with brass beds.
Rates: $65 per person, double occupancy, MAP. Five-day ski and golf
  packages available.
Open: All year.
Facilities and activities: Liquor license, swimming pool, sauna, cross-
  country ski trails. Nearby: downhill skiing, golfing.

The Okemo Inn is the oldest established country inn in the
Ludlow area. Built in 1810, it has been lovingly restored into the
country inn it is today. It is practically at the foot of Okemo
Mountain, which it was named for.

Needless to say, skiing, both alpine and cross-country, is a
popular pastime for guests of the inn. In addition, golfers have
found the inn to be a nice home base for nearby Fox Run. The inn
has some interesting package plans for holidays, so do call and
inquire about them.

A good deal of care goes into this inn. There are flowers
everywhere and the grounds are lovely. Toni is a whiz with
stencils, as you will see when you visit. The rooms are decorated

with warmth, good beds, and antiques and are very clean. A collection of "necessary china" for bedroom use in times bygone is displayed on the bookshelf in the second floor hall. It's a wonder. They have installed a ☛ fully automatic state-approved fire detection system throughout the inn. This is a real plus.

☛ Meals are served family style. This is always a nice change. There are homemade soups and tasty tossed salads. Roast beef with oven-roasted potatoes and tender carrots in a delicate sauce is one example of a typical dinner. Do get there some special weekend for their old-fashioned barbecue. It contains everything you could desire.

The inn has a liquor license, and the lounge has a working fireplace and color television. There is a large ☛ sauna for tired muscles or just because. In warm weather the inn's own private pool is lovely. There is an abundance of things to do in this area, and the innkeepers are happy to help you plan your day.

A little dog named Chevas is here to greet you. K. C. is the black inn cat that guests here call the perfect host.

How to get there: Take Exit 6 north from I–91, and follow Route 103 to Ludlow. The inn is located 1 mile from Okemo Mountain public transportation, which includes Vermont Transit buses and Amtrak trains to Bellows Falls, and 25 miles from Springfield or Rutland airports.

❈

E: *A night at an inn adds a tinge to the coming day that cannot be described, only enjoyed.*

The Wildflower Inn
Lyndonville, Vermont
05851

Innkeepers: Mary and Jim O'Reilly
Address/Telephone: Darling Hill Road; (802) 626–8310, (800) 627–8310
Rooms: 15, plus 5 suites; 16 with private bath, 5 with kitchenette. No
   smoking inn.
Rates: $80 to $125, double occupancy, EPB.
Open: All year except the last week in October and the first three weeks in
   November.
Facilities and activities: Dinner. Gift Shop, meeting room, heated pool,
   sauna, spa, ice-skating pond, cross-country skiing.

Here's an inn that makes children feel more than welcome.
☞ It has a special children's playroom that comes complete with
dress-up clothes and toys for all ages.

The inn is situated on its own 500 acres on a ridge overlooking
the valley of Vermont's Northeast Kingdom. What a beatufiul view
it has! You're sure to enjoy roaming the inn's property, discovering
the pond, drinking in the fabulous view, petting the kittens, or
walking up the hill to see the Burkland Mansion. And in the
winter, of course, cross-country skiing and ice skating are right
here.

The main inn has four bedrooms with shared baths. The

dining rooms are located here. One overlooks the glorious valley. Help yourself at the appetizer buffet while having a cocktail, and then dig into the main entrees. Besides a daily special and fresh fish of the day, there are ribeye steak, veal chop Marsala, medallions of pork tenderloin sautéed with Grand Marnier and apples, and more. Chateaubriand for two is a onderful treat. Black Forest cake caught my eye for dessert, but there are many more choices.

The carriage house has suites with kitchenettes and lots of beds and is wonderful for families. An old schoolhouse is a bit removed from the inn. ☛ It's the honeymoon cottage. More suites are located near the pool—and what a pool it is! It is heated and has a spectacular view. There is also a children's pool out here. The all-purpose room (also with a view) is nice for conferences or meetings. After a day of work or play, relax in the sauna and spa.

How to get there: Take Exit 23 off I–91 in Lyndonville. Go north through town on Route 5 to Route 114. Follow Route 114 for a half-mile. Darling Hill Road is a left turn immediately after the second bridge you cross. The inn is in 2 miles.

Birch Hill Inn
Manchester, Vermont
05254

Innkeepers: Pat and Jim Lee
Address/Telephone: West Road; (802) 362-2761
Rooms: 5, plus 1 cottage for summer and fall; all with private bath.
Rates: $49 to $54, per person, double occupancy, EPB. No credit cards.
Open: All year except late October to December 26 and April 15 to
    Memorial Day.
Facilities and activities: Dinner every day except Wednesday, Thursday, and
    Sunday. Beer and wine license, BYOB other alcoholic beverages.
    Fishing, swimming, cross-country skiing, hiking. Nearby: golf, down-
    hill skiing.

At one time Birch Hill was a horse farm. Now it is a lovely inn
and about as perfect as a small country inn can be. Located on a
beautiful country road, it has a meadow with 🐄 beefalo roaming
and picture-perfect views. There are clumps of birch trees, which
were planted in 1917. Pat's family has lived here since then.

A 🐟 stocked trout pond is on the grounds, or you fishermen
can go cast your lines in the Mettawee and Battenkill rivers. The
inn also has a nice swimming pool, which is great for exercise or
relaxation on a warm summer day, and I have been told there is
a huge rock quarry nearby that is great for swimming. Downtown

Manchester has the Equinox Golf Club, which has a beauty of a course. There are all sorts of things to do in this area. Shopping is a must. Boy, I sure do have a good time while I'm here.

Alpine skiing is at two nearby courses, Bromley and Magic Mountain. Cross-country is right at the door of the inn, and the trails are uncrowded and suitable for all abilities. Nice for hiking in the summer, too.

The guest rooms are lovely and comfortable and afford views of either mountains or farm and pond. One has a fireplace. Books and flowers are in all of the rooms. This is a nice touch. Another thoughtful touch is ☛ a radio and tape deck in every room with extra tapes for you to choose from. The inn rooms are not well suited to children under six. There is a cottage for summer and fall use only, which is perfect for a family or honeymooners.

One entree is served at dinner. The beefalo, which is raised right here, is a real treat. It is tender and lower than beef in calories and cholesterol. Good soups and fresh vegetables are perfect accompaniments to the meal. This is all served at a lovely oval table. It's so nice when the innkeepers dine with their guests, as the Lees do here.

The living room has a library, fireplace, record player, piano, a lovely old spinning wheel, and an eighteenth-century grandfather clock. The screened porch in summer is wonderful. A guest refrigerator to keep your own mixers, soda, or whatever, and a pair of golden retrievers, Abby and Megan, add the perfect finishing touches. This is quite an inn.

How to get there: Go north on Route 7. Just past Equinox House is a fork in the road. Take the left side of the fork. This is West Road. In a few miles on the right is the inn. Or, from Route 30 going toward Dorset, turn left on West Road.

Olive Metcalf

The Inn at Manchester
Manchester, Vermont
05254

Innkeepers: Harriet and Stan Rosenberg
Address/Telephone: Route 7A; (802) 362–1793
Rooms: 20; 16 with private bath.
Rates: $65 to $105, double occupancy, EPB.
Open: All year.
Facilities and activities: Dinner, beer and wine license. Swimming pool.
   Nearby: skiing, golf, tennis, theater.

Lush greenery in the bay window of the living room is the sight that greets you when you walk in the front door of this inn. The many fireplaces surrounded by restful sitting areas, the numerous good antiques, and the dining room with ☛ Tiffany lamps add up to a warm country inn atmosphere. The antique Champion oak stove is the focal point in the game room, which is an ideal spot to unwind after a day on the ski slopes. Here you can watch television or play games or cards at a card table. A good library is also in here.

The guest rooms are spotless and so very nice. ☛ Sheets, comforters, dust ruffles, and towels are color coordinated, and the beds are perfect for a good night's sleep. The carriage house is luscious. Each room has its own private bath and is individually

348

decorated with coordinating sheets, comforters, towels, and antiques. There are Tiffany-style lamps, queen-sized beds, cast-iron and brass beds, and a beauty in cherry. Attractive artwork hangs throughout. All very nice indeed.

The food is homemade, even the breads. ☛ Apple pancakes with local maple syrup can start anyone's day right. Fragrant soups, creamy desserts, and vegetables from their organic gardens are just some of the many good things you can expect to find here. Meals are served family style. The menu changes daily and beer and wine are available.

The inn is conveniently located in the heart of just about everything, with skiing, downhill and cross-country, only minutes away. Summer brings great antiquing, summer theater, specialty craft shops, and boutiques. Golf and tennis are within walking distance of the front door, and the swimming pool is in a lovely meadow between the carriage house and the creek.

How to get there: The inn is approximately 22 miles north of Bennington, Vermont, on Route 7A. It is on the left.

✳

The style is the inn itself.

Olive Metcalf

The Reluctant Panther
Manchester Village, Vermont
05254

Innkeepers: Maye and Robert Bachofen
Address/Telephone: West Road and Route 7A (mailing address: P.O. Box
    678); (802) 362–2568
Rooms: 12, plus 4 suites; all with private bath and TV, some with air
    conditioning, fireplace, phone.
Rates: $95 to $140, double occupancy; $165 to $200, suites; continental
    breakfast.
Open: All year.
Facilities and activities: Lunch, dinner. Restaurant closed Wednesday,
    off-season on Tuesday and Wednesday, three weeks in spring and
    fall. Bar, lounge, elevator, conference room, florist, Jay Eade. Nearby:
    golf, tennis, hiking, skiing, American Museum of Fly Fishing, health
    club.

    The inn is mauve on the outside, and a good bit of lavender
and wine colors are inside. These are colors I love and, believe me,
the inn is hard to miss with its yellow shutters. There are marble
sidewalks and beautifully manicured gardens and lawns.

    Accommodations here are grand. The rooms are beautifully
decorated, and all have private baths. The suites have whirlpool
tubs. All of the beds, no matter the size, are comfortable. I saw a

wonderful king-sized brass bed. The goose-down quilts are heaven. Some of the rooms and all of the suites have a fireplace. There is nothing more restful than a crackling fire in your own fireplace. One suite in the Mary Porter house even has a fireplace in the bathroom. Wherever you say, you'll find a ☛ split of Robert Mondavi wine in your room for you to enjoy.

Robert is a Swiss-trained hotelier and former food and beverage director for the Plaza Hotel in New York. He was born and educated in Switzerland.

David Maggiani is the chef of Wildflowers, the inn's restaurant. His menu is a fine blend of country French and Vermont specialties. The greenhouse extension of the dining room is a spectacular setting for David's creations. A couple of the lunch choices are spinach and mushroom quiche and a tossed salad or chilled roast turkey salad with curry and pineapple. Dinner begins with appetizers such as ☛ cold poached salmon with dill sauce and lentil and vegetable soup. Some of the tempting entrees are tomato ravioli filled with broccoli and Vermont cheddar, broiled scrod, and boneless stuffed chicken with spinach and Gruyère, topped with a chardonnay and thyme sauce. The wine list is extensive and very good.

The tavern is cozy with a few bar stools, chairs, fireplace, and the sort of good company that is only found in a country inn.

Guests at The Reluctant Panther have spa privileges at the nearby spa and health club.

How to get there: As you approach Manchester Village from the south on Route 7A, keep an eye on the left and soon The Reluctant Panther will pop into view.

The Village Country Inn
Manchester Village, Vermont
05254

Innkeepers: Jay and Anne Degen
Address/Telephone: Route 7A; (802) 362–1792
Rooms: 30 rooms and suites; all with private bath.
Rates: $135 to $185, double occupancy, MAP.
Open: All year.
Facilities and activities: Bar, lounge, swimming pool, tennis, ice skating.
  Nearby: golf, skiing, shopping.

Manchester's favorite front porch beckons you as you arrive at the Village Country Inn, located in the heart of town. The porch is a hundred feet long with wicker furniture and rockers covered with rose chintz and full of pink flowers all summer long. It's the icing on this beautiful inn.

This is a French country inn done in shades of mauve, celery, and ecru, and stunning inside and out. Anne was a 🖙 professional interior decorator and the inn reflects her expertise. Mauve is a color I adore. The boutique is the French Rabbit, with well-dressed rabbits to greet you. Anne has wonderful taste, and the boutique is full of very nice things.

Tavern in the Green, the bar and lounge, has an upright piano and nice people who play and sing. One night I stayed here a playwright was in this room with a marvelous selection of music and songs. What an unexpected treat. A door from here leads out to the swimming pool and gardens. During the winter the large patio is flooded for ice skating. The inn has a large collection of skates for guests to use, and twinkling lights are hung in the trees all around the patio.

There is a large fieldstone fireplace dating back to 1889 in the living room with comfortable couches and chairs around it. Tables are provided for all sorts of games. Perhaps you'd just like to relax with Tiffany, a little Yorkie, or Cinnamon the cat.

The rooms are magnificent and each one is different. They are done in ☞ ice cream colors. One pair of twins has matching canopies. Lace, plush carpets, down pillows, and nice things on dressers and tables give the rooms an elegant atmosphere. Good towels are such an important feature to inn guests and, needless to say, they are here.

Dining is a joy in the lovely dining room. The bishop-sleeve lace curtains and trellis alcoves create a cozy and romantic atmosphere for the glorious food. Chilled tomato bisque with dill is excellent. Salads aren't run of the mill, and entrees are creative. Grilled loin of lamb with rosemary and juniper sauce, and medallions of veal with wild mushrooms, shallots, and Madeira in a natural veal sauce are just two of the selections. Vermont lambchops with black currant cassis and almonds are a house favorite. I chose creme brûlée for dessert. It was grand. Freshly made bread pudding with apples and hazelnuts captivated my dinner companion. Very good indeed. Breakfast is a full one, with many choices.

The Village Carriage Company comes to the inn with coach-men decked out in top hats and tails and horse and carriage. The inn has package plans for using the carriage, such as ☞ a champagne picnic in the carriage.

How to get there: Coming north on historic Route 7A, you will find the inn on your left in Manchester Village.

Olive Metcalf

Longwood Inn
Marlboro, Vermont
05344

Innkeepers: Andrea and Douglas Sauer
Address/Telephone: Route 9; (802) 257–1545
Rooms: 15; 13 with private bath, 4 with fireplace, 1 with Jacuzzi.
Rates: $95 to $145, double occupancy, EPB. $135 to $185, double occupancy, MAP. Off-season rates available.
Open: All year except Christmas Eve and Christmas Day.
Facilities and activities: Lunch during music festival and foliage season. Dinner daily in-season and Wednesday through Sunday in off-season. Sunday brunch in-season. Bar. Swimming, fishing, ice skating. Nearby: music, skiing.

The copper lanterns at the door of this over-200-year-old inn are magnificent. The inn has served many uses over its life: a dairy farm known as Five Maples when milk was eight cents a quart, a halfway house, a college dormitory, the site of a local theater, and now a lovely country inn watched over by Tasha, the inn cat. In nearby Marlboro is the 🐾 world-renowned music festival each summer.

Any time of year is a good time to come to the Longwood. In winter you can ski downhill or cross-country close by. The inn's pond is ideal for ice skating. Bring your bicycle in the other seasons, or rent a horse and see this pretty area from the ease of a saddle. Go fishing or swimming in the pond. In the fall there are crisp apples for you to munch on.

The rooms are lovely. Some have working fireplaces. On the nightstands and shelves you'll find plenty of reading material. There are five king-sized beds.

The most important ingredient to good living found at Longwood's restaurant is the restful ☛ luxury of dining at leisure. Try landing your own rainbow trout from the pond and then ask the chef to prepare it for your dinner. If the fish aren't biting, the menu offers Wisconsin duckling, ribeye steak, veal, curried lamb, pasta, and more. Champagne breast of chicken sounds good to me. Blackberry tartlet enticed me, but you can also order homemade ice cream and much more from the menu. Sound good? Come on up and try this inn.

How to get there: From I–91 take Exit 2 at Brattleboro. Take Route 9 west to Marlboro. The inn is on the right.

❧

*The groaning breakfast board
of a good inn always makes it difficult
to remember the word ''diet.''*

Olive Metcalf

Red Clover Inn
Mendon, Vermont
05701

Innkeepers: Ed and Judy Rup
Address/Telephone: Woodward Road; (802) 775–2290
Rooms: 13; all with private bath.
Rates: $130 to $150, per person, double occupancy, MAP.
Open: All year.
Facilities and activities: Bar, television, swimming pool. Nearby: downhill
   and cross-country skiing.

In the center of Vermont, just 5 miles east of Rutland, is a
flower of a country inn. The red clover is the state flower of
Vermont. The inn is the former summer home of General John
Woodward. It was built around 1840.

This is beautiful, peaceful country, and not far away there are
antique shops, outlet stores, and areas for cross-country and
downhill skiing. From June to October a ☛ farmers' market is
open every Wednesday and Saturday with produce and preserves,
local crafts, and musical talent. A bike ride on some of the back
roads around here is lots of fun.

The inn is very comfortable. The living room has cozy chairs
and couches. Curl up in front of a fire with a good book or a friend!
The pub is adjacent to the living room and will provide you with

your favorite drink. The rooms are beautifully appointed and restful, just what you expect in a good inn.

There are three dining rooms, and the food that comes out of the kitchen is divine. Some of the chef's creations are chilled curried Elberta peach and dill soup, warm tomato-and-mozzarella salad, smoked rainbow trout, and entrees such as coquilles St. Jacques, poached Norwegian salmon, and shrimp Arturo. There also are veal, tenderloin, and chicken entrees, and the sauces are good. Desserts are glorious. Try ☛ rhubarb crisp. Breakfasts are not ho-hum either. Do come up here and enjoy. Dinner is by candlelight, of course.

How to get there: Take Route 4 east from Rutland, and the inn is on the right, down narrow Woodward Road.

❁

E: *The converted carriage house is the Plum Tree House, surrounded by plum trees, so the chef serves his duckling with brandied plum sauce. Oh my.*

Middlebury Inn
Middlebury, Vermont
05753

Innkeepers: Frank and Jane Emanuel
Address/Telephone: Route 7; (802) 388–4961 or (800) 842–4660
Rooms: 73; 65 with private bath, air conditioning, cable TV, phone.
Rates: $90 to $150, EP.
Open: All year.
Facilities and activities: Breakfast, lunch, dinner, bar. Parking, elevator, gift
    shop. Nearby: skiing, swimming, golfing, fishing, boating, museums.

There has been an inn standing at this same location since 1788. There have been some changes, due to fire and the inroads of time, but the present brick building, known as the Addison House, was constructed in 1827. One hundred years later, when the Middlebury Hotel Company took over, extensive repairs were made, and in 1977 Frank and Jane Emanuel became the innkeepers. Their efforts to restore the inn to its former elegance have been aided by a grant from the Vermont Historic Preservation Division.

The inn has an excellent central location in the delightful town where Middlebury College is situated. There are many historic buildings, museums, and shops to visit in the town, and all around is an abundance of outdoor activities.

The Addison House has a delightful veranda and a really large lobby. ☛ The dining room is beautiful, and the food that is served here is delicious. The elegant candlelit buffets shouldn't be missed, from the served appetizer and sherbet courses to the finishing touch of a fingerbowl. The Morgan Room Tavern and Terrace offers excellent liquid refreshment, including the inn's own ☛ "Candied Apple." Upstairs the wide halls wander and dip, up one step and down three, wide enough for those ladies of long ago to have maneuvered their hoopskirts with grace.

Additional rooms are in adjacent buildings or wings off the original building. The Jonathan Carver Wing was constructed in 1897, and the Thomas Hagar House, which was built in 1816, is now attached to the Addison House. The Porter Mansion, built in 1825, has ☛ five handsome guest rooms, several fireplaces of rare black marble, and a lovely curving staircase in the front parlor. More contemporary-style rooms are found in the Governor Weeks House and the Emma Willard House. The East Wing has been completely and beautifully refurbished.

Whatever type of room you need, you'll find a wide variety of good choices here.

How to get there: Go up Route 7, and you run right into Middlebury. The inn is in the middle of town.

E: *I could stay forever, mooning over the jigsaw puzzle in the lobby or eating their nightly popovers.*

Swift House Inn
Middlebury, Vermont
05753

Innkeepers: Andrea and John Nelson
Address/Telephone: 25 Stewart Lane; (802) 388–2766
Rooms: 20; all with private bath, air conditioning, phone, and some with
    cable TV, working fireplace, wheelchair accessibility.
Rates: $85 to $150, double occupancy, EPB.
Open: All year.
Facilities and activities: Dinner. Sauna, steam room, downhill and cross-
    country skiing, hiking, fishing.

The Swift House Inn consists of three grand buildings. There
is the carriage house, where I stayed in a glorious room with its
own patio, cable television, and fireplace. It is so nice to find
terrycloth robes and hair dryers in your own bathroom. The steam
room and sauna are in the carriage house. The gate house is down
the hill, and the main house has lovely rooms, individually
decorated with handmade quilts and four-poster beds. The room
with ☞ facilities for a handicapped guest has a gas fireplace, a
king-sized bed, and a sleep sofa. There is an old elevator up to this
room that is home to a stuffed parrot.

The living rooms have fireplaces and very comfortable chairs
and couches. Many guests like to spend some time unwinding
here before going in to dinner.

The dining rooms have Queen Anne and Chippendale chairs. On the extensive menu, you might find chilled strawberry soup and various pâtés among the appetizers. Entrees include Green Mountains veal scallopine with mushrooms, prosciutto, and red pepper sauce; baked sea scallops; fresh homemade pizza; filet mignon; smoked and grilled salmon; grilled yellowfin tuna; and the list goes on. ☛ Everything is cooked to order. There are excellent wines by the glass. For dessert I had the white chocolate and raspberry velvet tart (superb), but I could have had vanilla cheesecake with a bing cherry and Courvoisier sauce. Oh, it's so hard to make choices! Wonderful coffees, even one called Fuzzy Navel, are served.

The grounds are glorious, with lovely flowers. They are nice to wander on after your marvelous dinner. This inn is on the must-go-and-visit list.

How to get there: Take Route 7 to Middlebury. The inn is 2 blocks north of the center of town on the corner of Route 7 and Stewart Lane.

Olive Metcalf

The Middletown Springs Inn
Middletown Springs, Vermont
05757

Innkeepers: Jane and Steve Sax
Address/Telephone: P.O. Box 1068; (802) 235–2198
Rooms: 9; all with private bath.
Rates: $70 to $80, double occupancy, EPB. $110 to $140, double
    occupancy, MAP.
Open: All year.
Facilities and activities: Full liquor license. Nearby: skiing, hiking, biking,
    golfing, fishing, swimming, canoeing.

The approach to this lovely old Victorian inn on the village
green is quiet and peaceful. The white wicker on the front porch
adds just the perfect accent to this stately building.

The windows throughout the inn are almost floor to ceiling. A
beautiful ☞ curved staircase takes you upstairs to the spacious
bedrooms, which are filled with antiques. I slept in a lovely sleigh
bed in the honeymoon suite. The inn provides ☞ robes for the
rooms that share baths. This is a nice touch if you have forgotten
to bring yours.

There are two high-ceilinged dining rooms. The rug in one of them is as old as the inn (1880) and really in great shape. Some of the furniture is massive and could be used only in a large home such as this. The library is unique, with a woodburning stove and a revolving fan hanging from the ceiling. The music room has an old grand piano. Please go and play—the innkeepers would love you to.

One entree is served each evening. Chicken cordon bleu, baked stuffed haddock, and beef Victorian (similar to stew, only it's better) are some of the dishes they make. Tomatoes with cognac is a vegetable dish I like. The carrot soup is excellent.

Behind the inn is the carriage house, built in 1840. It has three guest rooms with a shared bath. Nice for a large party of friends.

How to get there: From Manchester, Vermont, take Route 30 north to Pawlet to Route 133 north to Middletown Springs. The inn is at the junction of Routes 133 and 140.

∽

E: *The upstairs sitting area and small library are very quiet and cozy.*

> *Where else, in all good conscience,*
> *could I stay but at a country inn.*

Olive Metcalf

Zack's on the Rocks
Montgomery Center, Vermont
05471

Innkeepers: "Zack" and Gussie Zachadnyk
Address/Telephone: Route 58; (802) 326–4500
Rooms: 1 housekeeping cottage for two.
Rates: $90 per night, EP.
Open: All year except Mondays and Christmas Day.
Facilities and activities: Dinner by reservation only, bar.

After you finally find Zack's, you really will not believe what you see. His cottage home and restaurant are literally hanging on the rocks over an incredible valley.

This is my smallest inn. A cottage that sleeps two has a living room, dining ell, kitchen, two fireplaces, a bedroom, and a *wow* of a bathroom with a sunken tub. Even if you cannot stay here, stay in town and come up here to eat Zack's food. It is ☛ fantastic, and so are he and Gussie, his wife.

Zack's is so unique that it is almost impossible to describe. When you approach the door of his restaurant you will find it is locked. Ring the sleigh bells, and the door will be opened by Zack. He will be in a wondrous costume and the ☛ performance begins. I will tell you no more except about the food. The menu is printed on a brown paper bag, which is in beautiful contrast to his

364

restaurant and Gussie's bar. Zack does all of the cooking. He is the most 🖝 inventive chef and innkeeper I have had the pleasure to meet. The dining room has to be seen to be believed.

And Gussie's bar is something special. It has an organ with a full grand piano top built over it. This is my first organ bar. The room has a stone fireplace and is done pub style but with a flair. The bar has five stools, but to go with it is the best stocked back bar in Vermont. To top it all, the inn plays music from the forties. What a pleasant sound.

The inn dog is Gypsy, the largest German shepherd north of the Mason-Dixon line, and probably below as well. Pyewacket is a noisy Siamese cat who runs the inn and Zack.

Reservations here are an absolute must.

How to get there: Going north from Stowe on Route 100, turn left on Route 118 at Eden. When you reach Montgomery Center, turn right on Route 58. The inn is up the hill on the left, after the road becomes dirt.

✸

E: *Zack's cottage is called Fore-the-Rocks. The private home is called Off-the-Rocks, and the inn is called On-the-Rocks. Gussie's bar is After-the-Rocks. Lots of rocks up here. Some of them are even purple.*

Black Lantern Inn
Montgomery Village, Vermont
05470

Innkeepers: Rita and Allan Kalsmith
Address/Telephone: Route 118; (802) 326–4507
Rooms: 10, plus 6 suites; all with private bath, some with fireplace, Jacuzzi, TV.
Rates: $50 to $75, per person, double occupancy, MAP.
Open: All year.
Facilities and activities: Bar, cross-country skiing. Nearby: downhill skiing, fishing, swimming, golf, tennis.

When you get to Montgomery Village, you are nearly in Canada, perhaps 6 or 7 miles from the border. This is a quiet Vermont village, and the Black Lantern has been nicely restored by its hard-working owners. Whether you come in the snow for a skiing vacation, or on a green summer day, there is a warm welcome at this friendly inn. It is also surprising to encounter a rather ☛ sophisticated menu in this out-of-the-way corner of the world.

You can ski at Jay Peak, where there are 50 miles of trails for every kind of skier, outright novice to expert. Not too far away, over the border, there are four Canadian mountains, and ski-week tickets are available. Cross-country skiing starts at the inn door and is undoubtedly the best way to see beautiful Vermont in the winter.

Summer brings the joy of outdoor life. Fishing, swimming, golfing, tennis, and hiking are all very near. You've heard about those country auctions, haven't you? Or would you rather spend the day browsing through antique shops? Whatever you choose to do, there will be a superbly quiet night to catch up on your sleep. The inn's guest accommodations are very comfortable, and the three-room suite is a ☛ joy. It has a fireplace and a Jacuzzi. This is heaven. The Burdett House next door has more suites, all of which have a fireplace, a Jacuzzi, and a television with videocassette recorder. Some of these suites have a balcony. There is also a nice and bright lounge area.

The double-peaked roof on the old, 1803 farmhouse covers a typical north-country inn. Small, friendly, and just a little bit different, and well enjoyed by Blazer, the inn's golden retriever.

How to get there: Go north from Stowe on Route 100 and turn left on Route 118 at Eden. This will take you into Montgomery Center. Continue down the main street and out of town, and before too long you will reach Montgomery Village and the inn. From I–89 in Burlington, turn right at St. Albans onto Route 105, toward Enosburg Falls. Pick up Route 118 at East Berkshire and follow it to Montgomery Village and the inn.

olive Metcalf

The Four Columns Inn
Newfane, Vermont
05345

Innkeepers: Jacques and Pam Allembert
Address/Telephone: West Street; (802) 365–7713
Rooms: 13, plus 3 suites; all with private bath and air conditioning, 2 with fireplace.
Rates: $95 to $135, double occupancy, continental breakfast. MAP rates in fall. Ski packages available.
Open: All year except two weeks after Thanksgiving and two weeks in April.
Facilities and activities: Dinner, jacket requested. Restaurant closed Tuesdays. Bar, swimming pool. Nearby: hiking, ice skating, skiing.

The inn is located on the most photographed town common in Vermont. The area is just beautiful and so is the inn. Jacques and Pam are truly marvelous innkeepers with a friendly staff and a nice dog, a rottweiler named Jackson.

The rooms are full of antiques. One lovely room has a brass bed. Another room has a canopy bed with a lace top, and four-poster beds are in others. Handmade rag rugs are all over, and ➤ plants in your room are a wonderful touch. Big towels and good pillows and mattresses; all these things make up a fine inn. The third-floor suite has a lovely porch with wicker furniture facing the common. A nice place to sit and watch the world go by.

The inn has nice living rooms where you can gather to visit with other guests, read, watch television, or just relax. The dining room with a fireplace has blue and white napery. A beautiful armoire is used to display the superb wines served here.

The inn was given three well-deserved stars in the *Mobil Travel Guide* for its food and rooms. Jacques managed several restaurants in New York City before becoming an innkeeper. He always gave his diners the very best and he continues to do just that here in Newfane. Chef Gregory was a protégé of the former owner, who was a fine chef himself, and he stayed on with Jacques. He is inventive and loves to use local fare. He buys ☛ Vermont raised milk-fed veal and does his own butchering. I've had the veal here and it is heavenly. One of the chef's appetizers is ☛ quail marinated in olive oil, hot peppers, and lemon, then grilled and served with creamy polenta and mushrooms. There's a soup of leek and onion with herb biscuits, another made of wild mushrooms. Oh my. One dinner offering is shrimp, littlenecks, and calamari cooked in tomato sauce, jalapeño, and tequila. Another is boneless breast of chicken with ginger, fermented black beans, vermouth, and cream. And oh, the rest of the menu is glorious. The dessert cart is sinful. How do you choose between white or chocolate mousse?

The lounge has a pewter bar, which is very unusual. A piano is in here, plus plants and more country charm than you can shake a stick at. Do I like it here? Just wish I lived closer.

How to get there: The inn is 220 miles from New York and 100 miles from Boston. Take Exit 2 from I–91 at Brattleboro to Route 30 North. The inn is in Newfane, 100 yards off Route 30 on your left.

❧

E: *The inn has a lovely swimming pool. Down at the stream is a hammock waiting for you.*

olive Metcalf

Old Newfane Inn
Newfane, Vermont
05345

Innkeepers: Eric and Gundy Weindl
Address/Telephone: West Street; (802) 365–4427
Rooms: 10; 8 with private bath.
Rates: $75 to $95, double occupancy, continental breakfast. No credit
  cards.
Open: All year except April to mid-May, late October to mid-December,
  and Mondays.
Facilities and activities: Lunch in summer and fall, dinner, bar. Parking.
  Nearby: skiing.

The inn is well named, for old it is—1787 to be exact. It has
been carefully kept, however, and the weary traveler will find
great comfort and fabulous food.

Almost all the rooms have twin beds. The rooms are large and
tastefully furnished. Gundy is a very good decorator. There is an
informal bar and lounge, and the dining room has tables with pink
cloths over white ones. Very effective. There is a huge brick wall
with a fireplace in the dining room that gives a wonderful feeling
of warmth and good cheer. The ☛ floors here are polished to a
turn and beyond. And not just run-of-the-mill glassware for the
inn. ☛ The drinks I had before lunch were served in crystal.

Eric is a fine chef. His soups are a bit different and very good. I have tried both the cold strawberry and creamed watercress. Loved them both. By the way, I hate calf's liver, but Eric asked me to try his. What magic he performed I do not know, but I ate every bite. Veal is king here. Eric butchers his own, so he gets the exact cuts he wants. Of course, the menu also has seafood, lamb, fowl, and fine steaks. The dessert menu reads like poetry from the flaming suzette and jubilee to a fabulous omelette surprise. There are also some cream pies that demand that you do not even think of calories.

How to get there: Take Exit 2 from I–91 in Brattleboro, and follow Route 30 north. The inn is on Route 30, on the left in Newfane.

❋

"Come away, O human child!
To the waters and the wild
With a faery hand in hand . . ."
—William Butler Yeats

Olive Metcalf

The Inn at Norwich
Norwich, Vermont
05055

Innkeeper: Zeke Church
Address/Telephone: 225 Main Street; (802) 649–1143
Rooms: 22; all with private bath, cable TV, phone.
Rates: $60 to $136, double occupancy, EP.
Open: All year.
Facilities and activities: Breakfast, lunch, dinner, Sunday brunch, bar.
    Nearby: swimming, canoeing, golfing, skiing.

Right on the sign for the inn it says, "Since 1797," and it is truly said, because travelers up the beautiful Connecticut River Valley have been finding a warm welcome at this grand old house ever since. It is just a mile away from Dartmouth College, and alumni, skiers, tourists, and commercial travelers find a special homelike atmosphere here that is dignified but a lot of fun.

The friendly bar and lounge area is named 🖝 the Jasper Murdock Tavern, after the inn's first owner. The dining rooms are lovely, with good napery and comfortable Thomasville chairs. The big bow window in the main dining room is a delight, but I still love to eat on the flower-filled porch. It's a nice place to watch the snow in winter.

The food is glorious. The Sunday champagne brunch offers

you a glass of bubbly or a mimosa, along with eggs Benedict, a crepe or quiche of the day, or Kevin's crab cakes. A jazz group plays during brunch. Dinner is always good here. Shrimp pancetta is an appetizer done with cognac. For entrees there are poached Northern Atlantic salmon, ☛ crisp roasted boneless duckling with raspberry glaze, and roast New Zealand rack of lamb, among others. The desserts are wonderful. The wine list is one of the most extensive I have seen.

The rooms have very good beds and mattresses. There are canopied beds and some iron and brass beds. All rooms are beautiful, and each one has its own telephone.

How to get there: Take Exit 13 from Route I–91. Go west a bit less than a mile to the center of town. The inn is on your left.

E: *You can come to Norwich by air, car, bus, or rail, or walk if you must, but do come.*

Choose your inn, and enter in the world of relaxation.

olive Metcalf

The Four Chimneys
Old Bennington, Vermont
05201

Innkeepers: Alex Koks and Andra Erickson
Address/Telephone: 21 West Road; (802) 447–3500
Rooms: 6; all with private bath; 2 with Jacuzzi, 1 with fireplace.
Rates: $75, single; $100 to $125, double occupancy; continental breakfast.
Open: All year except January 2 to February 14.
Facilities and activities: Lunch, dinner every day but Monday, Sunday
   brunch, bar and lounge. Full license. Nearby: facilities at Mount
   Anthony Country Club.

The inn is a magnificent Georgian Revival built in 1912. As
you approach it, you can see its spectacular four chimneys. The
grounds surrounding the inn are glorious.

   Master chef ☛ Alex Koks was the former owner of the
Village Auberge, and his reputation follows him. Educated at the
prestigious Hotel Management School in the ☛ Hague, Nether-
lands, Alex brings a distinct European touch to the inn. His
cooking is basically French. Roast stuffed quail, a turnover with
hearty cheese, and a galantine of goose liver mousse are just a few
starters. These are followed by good soups and salads. There are
entrees like sautéed monkfish and grilled shrimp, supreme of
Cornish hen Normande flambée au calvados, rack of lamb, and

breast of duck with cherries. Save room for desserts like ☛ creme caramel (my husband's favorite), fresh sorbet, and ice creams. Or you can just enjoy fresh fruit in season. All this superb food is served on tables covered with pink and white napery in a lovely dining room with three fireplaces. In summer the porch overlooking the gardens is ambrosia.

There are six guest rooms, and they are beauties. They have queen- or king-sized beds, quilts, and color-coordinated sheets and towels. They provide a wonderful setting for your continental breakfast, which is always served in your room.

The upstairs living room has an American square piano circa 1850. ☛ Ask Andra to play for you, or try it yourself.

How to get there: From Boston take I–90 to Lee. Go up Route 7 to the center of Bennington, and then take Route 9 west to the inn.

≈

E: *Cut-glass lamps in the bedrooms are pretty and functional. They give good light for reading.*

olive Metcalf

Johnny Seesaw's
Peru, Vermont
05152

Innkeepers: Gary and Nancy Okun
Address/Telephone: Route 11; (802) 824–5533
Rooms: 30; all with private bath, some with fireplace.
Rates: In summer, $32 to $40, per person, EPB; in winter, $45 to $75, per person, MAP.
Open: All year except end of skiing to Memorial Day, and end of foliage until Thanksgiving.
Facilities and activities: Dinner, liquor license. Television, game room, swimming, tennis. Nearby: skiing, hunting, golfing, horseback riding, fishing.

Skiing Magazine says this inn has the best Yankee cuisine in New England. The food is good, ☞ tasty country food prepared with imagination, featuring home-baked bread and homemade soup. Val is the fine lady chef who turns out all this fine fare.

The inn has a unique character, mostly because of the guests who keep coming back. It is set 2,000 feet up, on Bromley Mountain. The 65-by-25-foot pool, marble-rimmed, is a great summer gathering place, and the tennis court is always ready. There are six nearby golf courses, and riding is offered at the Ox Bow Ranch near Weston.

For the many skiers who come to Vermont, Bromley's five chairlifts and GLM Ski School are right next door. Stratton and Magic mountains, the Viking Ski Touring Center, and Wild Wings X-C are but a few minutes away.

For fishermen and hunters, or those who wish to take up the sport, the Orvis Fly-Fishing and Wing Shooting schools in nearby Manchester have classes. The sportsman classes are held twice weekly, in three-day sessions through October, and participants may stay at the inn. The nearby towns boast many attractive and interesting shops.

The circular fireplace in the lounge really attracts me at the end of a long day, to say nothing of the cushioned platform along one side of the room. Argus, the inn dog, will keep you company here.

How to get there: The inn is 220 miles from New York, 150 from Boston. From Route 7 take Route 30 right at Manchester Depot. The inn is 10 miles east, on Vermont Route 11. From I–91, follow Exit 6 to Route 103 to Chester. The inn is 20 miles west, on Vermont Route 11.

❀

Cats, birds, flowers, and dogs
in companionate confusion are to be found
where hospitality has bested the world of commerce.

olive Metcalf

Wiley Inn
Peru, Vermont
05152

Innkeepers: Manfred and Helga Sobek
Address/Telephone: Route 11 (mailing address: P.O. Box 37); (802) 824–6600
Rooms: 17; 9 with private bath.
Rates: In winter, $125 to $145, double occupancy, MAP. Rest of year, $70 to $90, double occupancy, EPB.
Open: All year except two weeks in November and April.
Facilities and activities: Game room, heated swimming pool. Nearby: hiking, horseback riding, fishing, skiing, alpine slide.

The Wiley Inn is an attractive inn in a nice area of Vermont. The main house was built in 1835. Over the years it has served as a farmhouse, stagecoach stop, and tea room. It has changed a lot since it was built, having had at least ten additions.

Manfred and Helga are friendly and pleasant innkeepers who do a good job of making their guests feel right at home. The lower living room—actually it's a game room—has a fireplace, bar, a huge couch, and many fun things to do. The ☛ player piano has tons of rolls to play. The library has an old-fashioned phone booth from a Philadelphia drug store. The phone still works. There are lots of books in here.

Two of the guest rooms have fireplaces. There is another fireplace in the dining room. This surely feels good on a cold night. The food is very good, and wine, beer, and other drinks are available to dinner guests.

No matter what season, there are things to do at the Wiley Inn. In the summer, swim in the inn's heated pool. The Long and Appalachian trails are nearby; so are horseback riding, fishing in the Battenkill River, and the alpine slide at Bromley. In spring, watch the maple sugaring to see how the syrup is made. Fall, the foliage is king, and in winter there are Bromley, Stratton, and Magic mountains for you downhill skiers. Cross-country ski-touring centers are within minutes. Go and enjoy.

How to get there: From I–91, take Exit 6 to Route 103 to Chester, Vermont. Go left onto Route 11 and the inn is 20 miles west in Peru.

olive Metcalf

The Pittsfield Inn
Pittsfield, Vermont
05762

Innkeepers: Barbara Morris and Vikki Budasi
Address/Telephone: Pittsfield Green; (802) 746–8943
Rooms: 9; all with private bath.
Rates: $95 to $130, double occupancy, MAP.
Open: All year.
Facilities and activities: Bar, lounge. Nearby: tennis, racquetball, swimming, golf, horseback riding, skiing, theater.

The Pittsfield Inn has been here since 1835. The town is small with a one-room post office and a bandstand on the village green, but within minutes there are tennis, racquetball, swimming, golfing, horseback riding, rivers for fishing, and summer theater. In winter there is downhill skiing at Killington or Pico ski areas as well as ski touring and cross-country skiing. ☛ This inn is a pleasant home base for anything you care to do.

The inn's combination living room, bar and lounge has a woodburning stove, an upright piano—just waiting for you to play—and lots of games. The bar is of ☛ antique marble.

Guest rooms are warmly decorated with bright wallpapers, interesting antiques, and quilts on the comfortable beds. Some rooms are small and some are large. One is in my colors, lavender and white. They are all very clean.

The dining room is bright and airy. The food is good. Start your day right with the three-course country breakfast. The tart lemon muffins alone are worth the trip. Vikki's four-course dinner might begin with New England fish chowder, followed by garden salad with raspberry vinaigrette dressing and good rolls. A favorite entree is Cornish Caper, a game hen topped with a tomato-caper sauce, accompanied by parsleyed new potatoes. Desserts, as you can imagine, are wonderful.

The Tweed and White rivers are close by, so come on up all you fishermen. They are full of trout and salmon. Ski touring is close by, and so are downhill and cross-country skiing. The inn is part of an inn-to-inn hiking system. You also can bike or ski from inn to inn. This is fun to do.

How to get there: The inn is 20 miles northeast of Rutland. Take Route 4 east and Route 100 north to the village of Pittsfield. The inn is right on the green.

E: *A flower-arranging seminar is something you won't find everywhere. It's offered once a month, from May through August.*

The Golden Stage Inn
Proctorsville, Vermont
05153

Innkeepers: Kirsten Murphy and Marcel Perret
Address/Telephone: Route 131; (802) 226–7744
Rooms: 10; 6 with private bath.
Rates: $145 to $155, double occupancy, MAP.
Open: All year except April and November.
Facilities and activities: Full liquor license. Swimming pool, bike tours.
  Nearby: hiking, skiing, alpine slide, gondola rides.

The Golden Stage Inn still is known locally as the Skinner place, for Otis, the actor, and his daughter Cornelia Otis Skinner, the author. The house was built more than 200 years ago, shortly after Vermont's founding. It was once a stagecoach stop and is reputed to have been a stop on the Underground Railway.

When you drive in, you immediately notice the rockers on the porch and the abundance of flowers that surround the inn. It's very pretty in the summertime. Sit and rock on the porch and enjoy the breathtaking views of the Black River Valley and Okemo Mountain.

One of the rooms has its own little porch. There are lovely quilts, some antiques, and lots of books. The living room with its cozy fireplace is very comfortable after a day of doing your own thing. There are all sorts of games and puzzles. Maybe all you want to do is sit and knit or read or play with Mischa and Natasha, the inn cats. This inn is a nice place to do it.

Marcel is Swiss, and the delicious food he cooks reflects his Swiss background. Veal and mushrooms with a wine sauce and pork tenderloin in a mustard cream sauce are just two of his good entrees. Kirsten is the baker. She makes a ☛ chocolate walnut torte that would make a chocolate lover swoon. Croissants on Sunday morning are a heavenly way to start the day. The inn also has a huge vegetable and herb garden, so necessary to their good cooking.

Four acres of rolling lawns, beautiful gardens, and trees are just what you need for a picnic, a long walk, or for being alone. Surrounding this haven of loveliness are thousands of acres of forests to hike in and four mountains noted for their good skiing. They are Okemo Mountain, Mount Ascutney, Bromley (fun in summer, too, with its exciting alpine slide down the mountain), and Killington Peak, which has year-round gondola rides, the longest in the United States. Killington often has the longest ski season in the East.

☛ Biking from inn to inn is another way to see this wonderful country. While you bike to the next inn, a support van transfers your luggage. This is my idea of neat.

How to get there: Take Route 103 north out of Chester and just before you get to Ludlow you will see the Golden Stage Inn. From I—91 take Exit 8 onto Route 131 west to Proctorsville.

❧

E: *A cookie jar that is never empty. Nice.*

olive Metcalf

Okemo Lantern Lodge
Proctorsville, Vermont
05153

Innkeepers: Pete and Dody Button
Address/Telephone: P.O. Box 247; (802) 226–7770
Rooms: 10; all with private bath.
Rates: $130, double occupancy, MAP.
Open: All year except April and November.
Facilities and activities: Beer and wine license. Swimming pool. Nearby:
   golf, tennis, bicycling, skiing, skating.

The inn was built in the early 1800s. It is a lovely Victorian with natural butternut woodwork and original stained glass windows.

In the living room is an exquisite old pump organ. This room is all comfort, with armchairs, couches, a crackling fire to warm your toes, and an ☞ enticing chaise lounge in front of a sunny window.

Bedrooms are cheerful, clean, and neat. Furnishings include a bit of wicker, antiques, and canopy beds. Would you like a ☞ champagne breakfast in bed? Just ask.

Heavenly aromas are always coming from the kitchen, whether they are from the freshly baked bread, freshly perked coffee, or bacon sizzling on the grill. And I hear Dody is getting ☞

384

rave reviews for her butterflied leg of lamb cooked to perfection on the grill. Dinner begins by the fire with Vermont cheddar cheese and a relish tray. Then there's a compote of fresh melon with sherbet, followed by salad with a different entree each evening. Tenderloin of beef is another good choice here. All the desserts are made here and are so good. Light fruit desserts are featured, and a lot of raspberries are used. Yum.

There are lovely cut flowers inside the inn from the flowers that grow all over the beautiful property. You just know that a lot of care goes into this inn.

There is so much to do in this area all year. Spring is the time to watch the maple sugaring or just go fishing in one of the well-stocked lakes or streams. In summer golf, tennis, hiking, and bicycling are close at hand. Fall is foliage and cider. Box lunches are available if you wish. Winter brings skiing and skating, or you could also curl up with a good book by the fire.

How to get there: Take I–91 to Exit 6 in Bellows Falls. Go north on Route 103 to its junction with Route 131 and turn right. The inn is a quarter of a mile on the left.

❋

Spring flowers add the final brush strokes
at the edges of the granite walk
to the inn's front stoop.

Olive Metcalf

Parker House Inn
Quechee, Vermont
05059

Innkeeper: Ken Smith; Roger Nicolas, owner
Address/Telephone: 16 Main Street; (802) 295–6077
Rooms: 7; all with private bath.
Rates: $85 to $120, double occupancy, continental breakfast.
Open: All year.
Facilities and activities: Dinner, full license. Restaurant open daily in summer, closed Monday rest of year. Nearby: downhill and cross-country skiing, hot air ballooning.

The Parker House Inn and Isabelle's Restaurant are owned by Roger Nicolas, who also owns the Home Hill Inn and French Restaurant in Plainfield, New Hampshire. They are both superb.

In 1857 Joseph C. Parker, state senator, businessman, and mill owner, built the Parker House for his family and personal lavish entertaining. Today the rooms are named after the original Parkers. They all are grand. They are furnished with beautiful antiques, wonderful beds, and comfortable upholstered chairs and couches. The white and brass beds are so beautiful.

In remodeling the inn, walls were uncovered in the foyer, and the ☛ original stenciling on the plaster was still there. The stencil was restored by a local artisan, Tony DeGeorge, and is truly lovely. It is so nice to find such treasures in these old houses.

There are three lovely dining rooms. One overlooks the Ottauquechee River. The napery is very warm and rich. The porch, which also ☛ overlooks the river, is used for summer dining. Wherever you dine, you'll love the wonderful food that is served here. Want some ideas? ☛ For starters, goat cheese tartlet, fresh Maine crabmeat salad, and pasta. Scallopine of turkey breast, fresh yellowfin tuna, roast Vermont rabbit, and rack of lamb are just some of the entrees. Save some room for Isabelle's homemade desserts. There is a separate bistro menu. Breakfasts feature croissants, blueberry muffins, homemade jams and jellies, and fresh-squeezed juice.

This is a lovely inn. Wonderful food, great innkeeper, and an unbeatable location. Simon Pearce, an Irish glassblower, is next door. In summer there are hot air balloon rides, and winter brings skiing, alpine and cross-country.

How to get there: Take Exit 1 off I–89 north. Turn left on Route 4 for 4 miles, crossing the Quechee Gorge. Turn right at the flashing traffic light. Cross over the covered bridge and turn left. The inn is on the left.

olive Metcalf

The Quechee Inn
at Marshland Farm
Quechee, Vermont
05059

Innkeeper: Hal Lothrop
Address/Telephone: Club House Road; (802) 295–3133
Rooms: 24; all with private bath and TV.
Rates: $148 to $198, double occupancy, MAP.
Open: All year.
Facilities and activities: Lounge, full license. Cross-country-ski learning center, fly-fishing school, bicycles and canoes to rent, fishing, hiking. Nearby: downhill skiing, golf, tennis, squash, swimming, boating.

The first time I saw and heard Quechee Gorge I was standing on the bridge that spans it. Now I know another way to see this remarkable quirk of nature. The inn is but a half mile from it, and the innkeeper will show you how to see it from an unusual angle.

The inn was a private home from 1793 until 1976. Beautifully converted to an inn, it reflects the care the innkeepers give it. Some of the rooms have the largest 🖝 four-poster, king-sized beds I have ever seen, and others have comfortable doubles. Seven more guest rooms, in the wing off the original building, have windows overlooking the meadow and lake. All rooms are equipped with color cable television, and the whole inn is air-conditioned.

There are lovely stencils in the dining room and a beautiful awning over the porch. Adjoining the dining room is a small library and conference room wired for audio-visual equipment. It's a real treat to be able to have a business meeting at a place like this. The living room has an abundance of comfortable chairs and couches, a piano, color television, books, and a fireplace. One feels at home here any season of the year.

Breakfast is a sumptuous buffet. Everything is delicious. Dinner is equally good. Among their appetizers they include scallop seviche—fresh bay scallops, bell pepper, tomato, and avocado served chilled in a lemon-lime marinade—and a different chef's pâté of the evening. Just a few ideas of the entrees are Isle au Haut Pie, which is Maine lobster, bay scallops and fresh vegetable and champagne cream baked in a pie shell; duckling, seared, roasted, sliced, and served over a shiitake mushroom sauce with a counterpoint of fresh strawberries; and baby back pork ribs slowly braised with maple syrup, grilled, and served with fresh maple-apple puree.

The inn guests have ☛ full club privileges at the nearby private Quechee Club. The two championship golf courses are breathtakingly scenic and are great tests of golf. You may also play tennis and squash here. Guest fees are charged for most of these activities.

How to get there: From I–91 take Route 89 north to Exit 1. Go west on Route 4 for 1.2 miles, then right on Club House Road for 1 mile to the inn.

❧

E: *Old-fashioned New England dining with homemade breads,* ☛ *sticky buns, and regional specials such as trout and venison make a visit here a must.*

Clive Metcalf

Rowell's Inn
Simonsville, Vermont
05143

Innkeepers: Lee and Beth Davis
Address/Telephone: Route 11; (802) 875–3658
Rooms: 5; all with private bath.
Rates: $120 to $140, double occupancy, MAP. No credit cards.
Open: All year except three weeks in April and first two weeks of November.
Facilities and activities: Beer and wine license. Summer antique shop. Nearby: skiing, fishing, hiking, summer theater, and more.

Built in 1820 as a stagecoach stop, this inn has served many purposes over the years. It was a post office and general store, and then in 1900 F. A. Rowell came along, purchased it, and it became Rowell's Inn. He put in the ☛ elegant tin ceilings, ☛ cherry and maple planked dining room floors, central heating, and indoor plumbing. The brochure says during the mid-1900s the inn was a preferred luncheon stop on the "Ideal Tour" between Manchester, Vermont, and the White Mountains for a hearty fare of trout and chicken. Today the inn is on the National Register of Historic Places.

In Rowell's Tavern you will find an old checkers table, shoeshine chair, an icebox, an upright piano, and a wood-burning stove. Now where else but a country inn would you find a room such as this?

One entree is offered each night at the five-course dinner. Some examples are beef tenderloin, roast leg of lamb, veal Marsala, or chicken. ☛ Pan-fried trout is a house specialty. This course is preceded by appetizers like mushroom strudel, hot cream soups, and salad such as fresh greens with oranges and grapes and a delicious homemade dressing. Dessert may be apple pie or chocolate mousse or another dreamy thing. All this good eating is served in a nice dining room or a sun porch decorated with plants. Breakfast is a good, full one.

Three of the lovely rooms have sinks and two have working fireplaces. Some brass beds, quilts, and hooked rugs add to the tasteful decor of the rooms.

Close at hand you'll find hiking, golf, tennis, biking, trail riding, and fishing in trout streams. The area provides summer theater, great shopping, and antiquing. An antique shop connected to the inn is open from June through October. All this plus—as you'd expect in a good Vermont country inn—alpine and cross-country skiing.

How to get there: The inn is on Route 11, 7 miles west of Chester.

Olive Metcalf

The Londonderry Inn
South Londonderry, Vermont
05155

Innkeepers: Jim and Jean Cavanagh
Address/Telephone: Box 301-20; (802) 824–5226
Rooms: 25; 20 with private bath.
Rates: $31 to $75, double occupancy, EPB. No credit cards.
Open: All year.
Facilities and activities: Dinner, bar. Restaurant closed late October to mid-December, and April to mid-June. Pool tables, Ping-Pong, swimming. Nearby: skiing, horseback riding, hiking.

The inn sits high on a hill overlooking the village of South Londonderry. It is central to three big ski areas, Bromley, Magic Mountain, and Stratton.

In summer there is a large swimming pool to relax in. Nearby they have horseback riding, hiking, and bicycle trails. Any time of the year there is pool to be played on the inn's two ☛ vintage pool tables. In addition, there are many comfortable places to relax, read a book, do needlepoint, or just enjoy a blazing fire on the hearth.

The inn dates back to 1826 when it was a farmhouse. The rooms have twin, double, and king-sized beds with ☛ down comforters, down pillows, and large thirsty towels. Jean also puts fresh flowers in the rooms. These little touches are far too often overlooked by innkeepers.

The inn has a nice lounge and a service bar off the living room, so you can be comfortable by the fire before dinner with your favorite cocktail in hand. The menu changes nightly but always includes four to eight entrees served with fresh vegetables, four or five appetizers, at least one homemade soup, and great desserts.

Honey is the inn dog you will love.

How to get there: Take Exit 2 from I–91 at Brattleboro, and follow Route 30 north to Rawsonville. Then take Route 100 to South Londonderry. The inn is on your left.

✱

E: *The dessert names are really creative—FBI Cake, Orient Express Torte, and Hungarian Rhapsody.*

> *If you have never been drawn shivering*
> *from the warmth of a good bed*
> *by the sizzling lure of bacon on the grill,*
> *you have never been in a country inn.*

Olive Metcalf

The Inn at
South Newfane
South Newfane, Vermont
05351

Innkeepers: Connie, Herb, and Lisa Borst
Address/Telephone: Dover Road; (802) 348–7191
Rooms: 6; all with private bath.
Rates: $85 to $95, per person, double occupancy, MAP. No credit cards.
Open: All year except April.
Facilities and activities: Full liquor license, swimming and skating pond.
Nearby: skiing.

The entrance to the inn is the Great Room. It is a huge square room done in several shades of gold—very impressive. The living room is elegant comfort, with a fireplace and a table for cards or games. It is a nice room for quiet conversation. Off this room is a ☛ porch overlooking the lawns and pond, with rockers and chairs and utter peace. The pond is wonderful in all seasons, providing ice skating in the winter and swimming in the summer. The lounge, called the Map Room by guests, has a fireplace. This room also leads out to the porch and yard.

The bedrooms here are individually decorated in period-appointed comfort. They have extra pillows, fluffy comforters, and patchwork quilts. There are four rooms with queen-sized beds and two rooms with twins.

The dining room is lovely. White napery, gleaming crystal, candles, and soft lighting set the stage for daughter ☛ Lisa, the inn's chef and a graduate of the Culinary Institute of America. Lisa's menus are varied and imaginative and change with the season. Everything is made from scratch, including the breads, pastries, and desserts. (Her father's hand is in this department.) All the soups, salad dressings, and mayonnaise are made daily. Lisa established an ☛ airmail-order system that supplies her with red-tailed venison from New Zealand, Arctic pheasant from Sweden, and exotic mushrooms from the West Coast. Then she prepares such entrees as escargots in pastry cases with garlic, cream, and mushrooms; and curried lamb, garnished with peanuts, raisins, and coconut. Besides these you'll find fresh fish and a special of the day. Oh my, then one has to pick from the dessert tray.

How to get there: Take Exit 2 off I–91 into Brattleboro. From Brattleboro center, proceed north on Route 30 for 9 miles. You will see the inn's sign on the right. Turn left (west) and continue for 2 miles through Williamsville. Go over the covered bridge, and drive another 1¼ miles to the inn.

꧁

E: *This is a beautiful part of the world, topped off with good food, nice innkeepers, an inventive chef, and two marvelous cats, Gumby and Mocha.*

Kendron Valley Inn
South Woodstock, Vermont
05071

Innkeepers: Max and Merrily Comins
Address/Telephone: P.O. Box 145; (802) 457–1473
Rooms: 28, in 3 buildings; all with private bath, some with fireplace.
Rates: $106 to $220, double occupancy, MAP. $66 to $180, double occupancy, EPB.
Open: All year except April and a few days before Thanksgiving.
Facilities and activities: Bar, lounge, meeting facilities, private beach on pond, ice skating. Nearby: golf, horseback riding, tennis, skiing.

The inn's quilt collection alone is worth the trip here. There are thirty-four of them, some of which came from Merrily's family. Two of them were made by her great-grandmother more than 100 years ago. I was fascinated to find on display stories and pictures of the women who made these beautiful quilts.

There's wonderful history thoughout the inn. Two of the inn's buildings date from the 1820s. A secret attic passageway is rumored to have been used by runaway slaves during the Civil War. Another room has a walk-in safe with an iron door. The main building was once a post office, dance hall, tavern, and country store. More recently, the inn has been used in the Christmas Budweiser commercial with the Clydesdale horses pulling a sleigh.

Some of the rooms have fireplaces and some have wood stoves. I slept in a very comfortable ☛ queen-sized canopy bed. There are twins and doubles in the log house. Some of the rooms have a television. One of the largest rooms has a three-sided fireplace and lounge chairs on its private porch. This is real comfort, folks.

There is musical entertainment on weekends, holidays, and during fall foliage season. ☛ Max sings. He really has a very good voice. The bar and lounge area is a fun spot.

Dining at Kendron Valley is wonderful. The menu changes quite often and the chef is inventive. My spies tell me great stories about his food, and, of course, I've checked up on them and they're right. I thought the escargots in puff pastry were very different and good. The cool spinach and watercress soup is very tasty. I had the shrimp, scallops, and lobster with wild mushrooms, sautéed in shallots and white wine and served with Frangelica cream sauce. Another entree that looked tempting was the ☛ salmon stuffed with a herbed seafood mousse, wrapped in puff pastry, baked, and served with a different sauce each night. Desserts are grand. This is truly excellent food.

How to get there: Take Route 4 to Woodstock. Turn south on Route 106 and go 5 miles to South Woodstock and the inn.

❧

E: *The inn dogs are a yellow Lab and a golden retriever. The inn allows well-behaved pets to stay here.*

397

Clive Metcalf

The Hartness House
Springfield, Vermont
05156

Innkeeper: Robert Staudter
Address/Telephone: 30 Orchard Street; (802) 885–2115
Rooms: 44; all with private bath, air conditioning, TV, phone.
Rates: $65 to $78, double occupancy; $71 to $89, suite; EP.
Open: All year.
Facilities and activities: Breakfast, lunch Monday through Friday, dinner
Monday through Saturday. Bar and lounge, swimming pool, tennis.
Nearby: cross-country and downhill skiing.

Because the inn had its start as the home of James Hartness,
a one-time governor of Vermont, it has much to offer: ☛ a private
forest for walking, a clay tennis court, and most important, a 600x
turret telescope that has to be seen to be believed. It stands on top
of five underground rooms, which are connected to the inn by a
240-foot tunnel built in 1910. There are a library, workshop,
study, lounging room, and lavatory. It is soundproof, cool in
summer, warm in winter, and all under the front lawn of the inn.
Do go and see; it is truly amazing. (Do remember that it was built
a long time ago, so there is some decay.)
You can relax with a good book on the deck overlooking the
☛ heated swimming pool. For more strenuous exercise there is a

☛ lighted clay tennis court. The surrounding area offers skiing and pleasant roads for driving through the countryside. There is everything here for an overnight or an extended stay.

The guest rooms are cozy. They are tastefully done with period wallpapers and charm. Some are furnished with antiques. There is a grand staircase to the second floor. It does not take much imagination to envision a bride making a descent on a staircase such as this.

Dining is as elegant for breakfast as it is for lunch or dinner. Lunch selections include good salads, sandwiches, and hot entrees. Choose from dinner entrees like rack of lamb, veal piccata, or veal Marsala. There is much more, followed by a daily selection of sweets. A very good wine cellar helps add the finishing touch to the meal.

How to get there: From the police booth in downtown Springfield, go up Summer Hill, starting at the light. Keep going up the hill as it curves around to the left until it levels off (a cemetery is on the right) at the five-street intersection. Bear left on Orchard Street. The inn is 300 yards ahead of you.

❋

E: *Although James Hartness was something of a recluse and needed absolute quiet, he married a lovely butterfly of a lady. Do visit the house they created together.*

Butternut Inn
Stowe, Vermont
05672

Innkeepers: Jim and Deborah Wimberly
Address/Telephone: The Mountain Road (mailing address: RFD 1, Box
    950); (802) 253–4277, (800) 3BUTTER
Rooms: 18; all with private bath. No smoking inn.
Rates: $45 to $65, fall and summer, per person, double occupancy, EPB.
    In winter, $60 to $75, per person, double occupancy, MAP.
Open: All year except mid-April to mid-May and November to mid-
    December.
Facilities and activities: Afternoon tea, BYOB. Heated swimming pool.
    Nearby: skiing.

Through the red door and into a charming country inn, this is
Butternut, located partway up a mountain road ☛ with a
wonderful view of Mount Mansfield. It really does not matter
what season you arrive, as they are all spectacular. Stowe is the ski
capital of the East for downhill skiing, and there is excellent
cross-country skiing as well. In the fall the mountains look as if
they have been painted. In the summer the inn has a ☛
solar-heated swimming pool, and there's a lovely mountain
stream babbling along nearby.

The inn has a billiard room with a good library, a beautiful old pool table, and board games. It is well decorated with folk art and antiques. Next to it is an unlicensed bar—so bring what you want—and a beautifully carved piano. There is usually one in every crowd who can play. The dining room is beyond, cozily warmed by a huge fieldstone fireplace. Lovely stained glass Tiffany lamps hang over the tables. The most recent addition is a year-round, stained-glass sunroom with wicker furniture and antiques. French doors open onto the flower garden. All in all, this is an inn with almost everything.

Food is served family style, with one entree each evening. Everything is ☛ homemade and so good. Jim is the chef. There is a fine salad bar, something I really do like. In the wintertime, soups and finger foods are served as dinner. Afternoon tea is served with Deborah's yummy double-triple-x chocolate-chip cookies. Breakfast is served poolside in the summer and by the fireside in the dining room in the winter.

The rooms are delightful. Many are very large, and some have balconies. Everywhere the inn is very clean. Some rooms have king-sized beds. There also are handmade and carved sleigh beds and bear heads. You'll find many carved things in the inn, all done right here by a very handy man.

How to get there: From Stowe take Route 108 to the inn on the left.

☙

If I ever find an inn that bakes fresh macaroons daily,
I shall rent a room for a hundred years.

Edson Hill Manor
Stowe, Vermont
05672

Innkeepers: Larry Heath, Jr., and Anita Heath
Address/Telephone: RR 1; (802) 253–7371, (802) 253–9797
Rooms: 11, 5 with private bath, in the manor; 6, with 2 baths, in the annex; 17, all with private bath and fireplace, in the carriage house.
Rates: $73 to $89, per person, MAP; higher on holidays. In summer, $59 to $99, double occupancy, EP. Package rates available.
Open: All year.
Facilities and activities: Breakfast, lunch in winter only, dinner, fully licensed bar, après-ski lounge. Pool, fishing, horseback riding and instruction, cross-country skiing with rentals and instruction. Nearby: ice skating and golf at Stowe Country Club.

Here you are, halfway between Stowe and Mount Mansfield, 1,500 feet above the hubble-bubble of that lively village of Stowe that is growing every year. Here is truly luxurious living, in a house that was built in 1939 for a family that loved to ski and ride.
🖙 The swimming pool here is beautiful. It won an award from Paddock Pools of California. The stocked trout pond is a must for anglers, and you can use the inn's boat. How nice to go catch a fish and have it for your breakfast. When the snow comes, 🖙 the stables turn into a cross-country ski center, so there you are, practically taking off from the inn door.

This attractive house has been run as an inn since 1953, and there are still homelike touches. The old delft tiles around many of the fireplaces are so appealing. The pine-paneled living room has an aura of quiet elegance that reflects the feeling of gracious living all too often missing from our busy lives. Look closely at the living room curtains. Somebody shopped hard for that material.

Downstairs are bar and lounge. ☞ A skier's lunch is served here. Hot soup of the day, chef's salad, hot chili, and good sandwiches. A special on cold days is hot mulled cider. Dinner, from the homemade soups to the desserts, is just dandy. The raw vegetable selection with a maple curry dip is a nice change. Veal is prepared differently every day; what a grand versatile meat this is. Their baked stuffed scrod has a delicate crabmeat stuffing and a lobster-based sauce. Yum.

The inn has very nice guest accommodations. The rooms in the carriage house have beamed ceilings, brick fireplaces, and private baths.

This is a beautiful inn. Many of the paintings were done by Effie Juraine Martin Heath, the grandmother of the family. The view is spectacular, and Mollie, the black cocker spaniel, agrees.

A note of particular interest to all you moviegoers is that Edson Hill Manor was the winter filming location for Alan Alda's *The Four Seasons.*

How to get there: Take Route 108 north from Stowe 4.9 miles, turn right on Edson Hill Road, and follow the signs uphill to the Manor.

Foxfire Inn
Stowe, Vermont
05672

Innkeepers: Irene and Art Segreto
Address/Telephone: RR 2; (802) 253–4887
Rooms: 5; all with private bath.
Rates: $75, double occupancy, EPB.
Open: All year.
Facilities and activities: Dinner, bar. Parking. Nearby: downhill and cross-country skiing, fishing, skating, hiking.

The Segretos want to welcome old and new friends, and there are myriads of them, to their inn. The house is more than 150 years old and has been restored to easy comfort by these enthusiastic innkeepers. And there is so much to do here, from the finest skiing in the East to great lounging in this comfortable inn.

Irene has created a 🐾 garden room that is a great spot for breakfast and dinner. It is all white lattice with loads of hanging plants. This is a gazebo to end them all.

The best Italian kitchen in New England may seem a bit misplaced so far north in Vermont, but it is here. Taste, and you will agree. The 🐾 tomato sauce is an old family recipe brought over from Naples. And do try things like baked broccoli, which is a combination of tomato sauce, ricotta cheese, and broccoli. There are seven different and delicious veal dishes. Boneless breast of chicken is prepared five ways, and the eggplant parmigiana has a special place in my heart. Shrimp marinara I can still taste. On my last stay here, I had superb veal parmigiana and excellent clams casino. Art chose a wonderful red wine to complement the dinner. As the front of the menu says, here you discover ''The Italian Art of Eating.''

And when you can push yourself away from the table, you have Stowe at your door, with antiques, shops, skiing, skating, walking, hiking, fishing, and more.

How to get there: Take I–89 to Route 100 north into Stowe. The inn is on the right, 1½ miles north of town.

E: *Pass me another tortoni, please. I am settled in for the season.*

A cricket on the hearth of a country inn
is music beyond the angels.

Olive Metcalf

Green Mountain Inn
Stowe, Vermont
05672

Innkeeper: Patti Clark

Address/Telephone: Main Street (mailing address: P.O. Box 60); (802) 253–7301, (800) 445–6629

Rooms: 54, plus 4 suites; all with private bath, air conditioning, TV, phone, clock radio, and some with Jacuzzi.

Rates: $60 to $100, single; $70 to $110, double occupancy; $120 to $130, suites; EP. Higher rates in fall and during Christmas week.

Open: All year.

Facilities and activities: Breakfast, lunch, dinner. Lounge; beauty shop; gift shop; health club with sauna, whirlpool, massage, exercise machines, and aerobics; racquetball; squash; heated swimming pool; skiing.

This lovely inn turned 150 years old in 1983, and to properly celebrate the event, ☞ it was completely restored. There are period wallpapers, paints, and stencils, smoke alarms and sprinkler systems, and a handcrafted reproduction furniture line, named after the inn by the manufacturer.

The Health Club is fantastic. What a place! It has everything you could want in it. Massage, sauna, whirlpool—such luxury. Inquire about the inn's complete health package, which includes diet. If the Health Club isn't for you, there's a ☞ heated outdoor swimming pool with a sun terrace, a glorious spot on a summer day.

The Whip is the lounge area, which provides a casual setting for the food that is served all day. A beautiful, huge fireplace is along one wall, and the beer tap is the most unusual I've seen. It is colorful ceramic and serves three different beers.

The dining room is charming. At lunch the chicken salad plate was beautifully served and delicious. Dinner was even better. Everyone who works here makes you feel right at home.

After you've had an active day on the ski slopes, the public rooms are a great place to relax. The library has a chess set at the ready. The connecting parlor with a roaring fire in the fireplace has the daily newspapers, including the *New York Times*.

The guest rooms have twin beds or canopy-covered queen-sized beds, with comfortable mattresses. All are well appointed, with lots of towels and extra pillows. Six are nonsmoking rooms. Four suites have a Jacuzzi, and one has a fireplace.

This inn really has everything.

How to get there: Take I–89 to Route 100 north into Stowe. The inn is at the intersection of Routes 100 and 108.

Clive Metcalf

Ten Acres Lodge
Stowe, Vermont
05672

Innkeepers: Dave and Libby Helprin; Bob Howd, general manager
Address/Telephone: RR 3; (802) 253–7638, (800) 327–7357 outside Vermont
Rooms: 18 in 2 buildings, plus 2 guest cottages; all with private bath and phone. Pets welcome in cottages.
Rates: In summer, $60 to $150; in fall and winter, $70 to $150; double occupancy, EPB. Guest cottages higher.
Open: All year.
Facilities and activities: Dinner every night in-season, Friday through Monday off-season. Bar, swimming pool, hot tub, tennis court, cross-country skiing. Nearby: downhill skiing.

The living rooms at Ten Acres Lodge are the most inviting and comfortable these bones have enjoyed in many a mile. You find soft couches and chairs, large fireplaces, ☞ bookcases full of good reading, and windows that look out on sheer beauty year round. In summer, dairy cows graze in the rolling farm fields across the road; in winter, cross-country ski trails crisscross the hillside. Around the inn are maples more than one hundred years old that provide lazy New England shade.

The dining rooms are beautifully appointed from the poppy-

408

colored wallpapers to the napery. The food is thoughtfully prepared. The ☛ menu changes every night. There are things for
starters like fresh artichokes and scallops with saffron mayonnaise
or garlic sausage with roasted red peppers. And this I love, fried
brie with apples. The menu has a variety of fish, veal, steak, and
lamb entrees, all skillfully cooked by the chef. AAA has awarded
the inn a four-diamond rating.

The very comfortable guest rooms are carpeted and pine-
paneled or wallpapered with pine trim. The beds are queens and
doubles, covered with ☛ lovely homemade spreads. The newest
rooms have a beautiful black-and-brass king-sized bed, a nice
couch, and air conditioning. Another room has a canopy bed and
a lovely armoire painted white with birds and flowers. Hill House,
a recent addition to the inn, has eight deluxe rooms with cable
television, telephone, fireplace, and deck or patio. It is really nice.
The guest cottages have their own kitchens, working fireplaces,
and terraces that look out at all the wonderful scenery that
surrounds Stowe.

The inn has a neat bar and a game room all set for a game of
backgammon, chess, or checkers. Outside, you are in the ski
capital of the East. The mountains are just beautiful. Go and enjoy.

How to get there: From Route 100 north in Stowe, turn left at the three-way
stop onto Route 108. Proceed approximately 3 miles, then bear left onto
Luce Hill Road. Ten Acres is located in approximately ½ mile, on the left.

Tucker Hill Lodge
Waitsfield, Vermont
05673

Innkeeper: Zeke Church

Address/Telephone: RFD 1; (802) 496–3983, (800) 451–4580 (outside Vermont)

Rooms: 20, plus 1 suite; 15 with private bath.

Rates: $55 to $98, per person, double occupancy, MAP.

Open: All year.

Facilities and activities: Dinner served in-season. Sunday brunch only through October, cross-country lunches, bar. Swimming pool, ski touring center. Nearby: fishing, tennis, golf.

You will find Tucker Hill Lodge nestled on a wooded ridge overlooking the road that winds up to the Mad River Glen Ski area. This is Route 17, and it is one of the most spectacular roads I have found in many a country mile.

Flowers are the first thing you see as you arrive at the inn. They are everywhere and are glorious.

Rooms here are not fancy, but they are clean and comfortable. You will find antiques and fresh flowers and handmade quilts on the beds. The living room is pine paneled with a fieldstone fireplace.

Food is the name of the game here. The inn won the coveted

1985 Vermont Restaurateur of the Year award and is one of a few that was given four diamonds by AAA. The innkeeper grows his own herbs and vegetables, smokes his own meats, and makes his own jams and jellies and vinegars.

Are you ready for this? ☛ Fresh homemade ravioli with a filling that is too good to try to put into words, and broiled Long Island oysters are two of the dinner appetizers. Soups—shrimp bisque, ☛ smoked Vermont duck soup, or sweet red pepper and goat cheese soup. Wow! Do you want to hear about the entrees? Baked red snapper in pastry. Sautéed pork medallions with raspberries. Sautéed black Angus tenderloin of beef. Grilled center-cut Vermont lamb chops. Believe me, the list of these tempting entrees goes on and on. This is some menu. Eight or more fancy coffees are offered along with mind-boggling desserts like black currant cheesecake with blueberries, ☛ fresh peach brandy tart, and fresh fruit tart.

Breakfast and lunch are served outside by the pool and so are cocktails in season. In cool weather a neat lounge is a fun spot, decorated with antique farm and kitchen tools.

There is a lot doing up here. A ski touring center is right here at the inn. In addition, there is a Robert Trent Jones golf course nearby, plus swimming, tennis, fishing, and more. Or you can just relax in this lovely inn.

How to get there: Turn west off Route 100 onto Route 17 in Waitsfield in the Mad River Valley. Go 1½ miles west; the sign for the lodge will be on your left.

E: *I cannot think of a nicer place to sit than on the deck, under the trees, sipping something long and cool.*

The Waitsfield Inn
Waitsfield, Vermont
05673

Innkeepers: Judy and Bill Knapp
Address/Telephone: P.O. Box 969; (802) 496–3979
Rooms: 14; all with private bath.
Rates: $55 to $75, per person, double occupancy, MAP.
Open: End of May through ski season.
Facilities and activities: Sunday brunch, bar, lounge. Tennis, ice skating.
Nearby: cross-country and downhill skiing, sleigh rides, golf, antiquing.

The inn sits in the beautiful Mad River Valley in the middle of the Green Mountains. Within ten minutes is a choice of 🖛 one hundred ski runs of all degrees of challenge. There are plenty of cross-country ski areas and sleigh rides as well. Skating under the lights in the inn's own backyard also is nice. In fall the leaves are like a painting on the mountain, and during spring and summer bicycling, golf, tennis, and more are all nearby. I can vouch for the antique shop next door. I bought a beautiful copper coffee warmer set there.

The dining rooms are small and very inviting. The cuisine is authentic, regionally inspired Italian. All food preparation, including the baking, goes on right in the inn's own kitchen. Minestrone and the chef's soup of the day are homemade. Eggplant patties are served with red sauce. Scallopine of Vermont veal comes with light lemon sauce or Marsala sauce. Loin of spring lamb, fresh seafood, and all the traditional pastas are offered. Vegetables are fresh and cooked to order. ☞ There is also a children's menu. And as they say, "Save room for one of the homemade desserts." You'll be glad you did. For the crowning touch, order their espresso or cappuccino (regular coffee, of course, is also available). Sunday brunch has some real winners, and the full everyday breakfast is glorious. I'll tell no more about the food, so come on up.

The lounge has a big fireplace, piano, plenty of games and books and wonderful sitting areas of good couches and chairs. There is also a very small lounge with a fireplace. You can really relax in this lovely inn. A cup of mulled cider in either lounge would be a nice way to end a day.

All of the guest rooms are beautifully furnished with antiques and quilts. Some of the rooms have ☞ lofts for children. This is a very nice feature for the traveling family.

How to get there: The inn is on Route 100, 15 minutes south of Exit 9 off I–89.

❋

*To find a good inn as darkness glowers on the horizon,
there is no treasure to match it.*

The Wallingford Inn
Wallingford, Vermont
05773

Innkeepers: Joseph and Kathleen Lombardo
Address/Telephone: 9 North Main Street (mailing address: P.O. Box 404);
   (802) 446–2849
Rooms: 10; 8 with private bath.
Rates: $110, double occupancy, MAP. $50, single; $70, double occupancy;
   EPB.
Open: All year except one week in April and November.
Facilities and activities: Full liquor license, game room. Nearby: Green
   Mountain National Forest, fishing, cross-country skiing.

The inn is a beautifully restored Victorian mansion built in
1876 in the small town of Wallingford. It's nice to find an 🖝
in-town inn in the foothills of Vermont, allowing you the opportunity to stroll down tree-lined streets and browse in the various
shops and antique stores in town.

The mansion was kept in the original family until 1969, when
it became an inn. It has arched marble fireplaces, oak woodwork,
and polished wood floors. The guest rooms are spacious and nicely
furnished with either twins or doubles. Up on the third floor are a
🖝 sitting room full of magazines and a game room equipped with
lots of games. Comfort abounds in this lovely inn.

The menu changes daily. Clams casino is a real favorite of mine, and I was glad to find it here. Chicken florentine, chicken Marvella, veal scallopine, and shrimp scampi are but a few of the entrees offered. The desserts are all made here.

There are nice things to do in this area. The Battenkill River has good fishing. There are covered bridges, antique shops, and the Green Mountain National Forest—a photographer's paradise in every season. Winter brings cross-country skiing as well as all the other winter sports.

The beautiful cat that lives here is Chessie, a silver tabby, and being the cat person that I am, I was overwhelmed. Do go see her and then revel in the peaceful tranquility of Victorian splendor at this inn.

How to get there: The inn is about 20 minutes south of Rutland on the western side of Route 7 in Wallingford.

The Inn at Thatcher Brook Falls
Waterbury, Vermont
05676

Innkeepers: Kelly and Peter Varty
Address/Telephone: Route 100 (mailing address: RD2, Box 62); (802) 244–5911
Rooms: 24; all with private bath, phone, clock radio, and 6 with whirlpool tub.
Rates: $75 to $155, double occupancy, continental breakfast.
Open: All year.
Facilities and activities: Dinner, bar and lounge. Canoeing, biking, hiking, cross-country skiing from door. Nearby: golf, tennis.

Thatcher Brook, named after Colonel Partridge Thatcher, was quite a powerful stream in the late 1800s. It had two sets of beautiful waterfalls, and during the nineteenth century two mills were constructed at these falls. In 1894 Stedman Wheeler purchased the upper sawmill and a small house. He became so prosperous in his business that he decided to construct a larger house on land directly across from the mill. Today that house is The Inn at Thatcher Brook Falls.

It is obvious from the fine attention to detail and workman-

416

ship in the inn that old Stedman spared no expense. The house took two years to construct. Several types of lumber were used in the inn, including oak, bird's-eye maple, spruce, cherry, and birch. The hand-carved fireplace and stairway are original to the house, as are the pocket doors between the two front dining rooms and the windowseat in the lobby. Especially attractive is the 🖝 gazebo-type front porch.

The rooms are colorful, neat, and clean. One has a canopy bed. The shower curtains are remarkably lovely. 🖝 The decorating has been done well. A sitting area, well equipped with books and games, is up by the rooms. Another building has been added to the inn. It alone is worth a trip.

There are three dining rooms and a lovely deck with umbrellas. The tables are lovely with restful pink napery and darker, complementary napkins. Dinner is memorable. One favorite appetizer is Mushrooms A la Thatcher (I won't explain them; come see for yourself). Broiled garlic sea scallops and bacon are splendid; we all know how I love garlic. 🖝 A great soup is country red potato and cheddar au gratin. These are followed by entrees like roast stuffed pork tenderloin, grilled lemon and rosemary duck breasts, seafood in parchment, and vegetarian pasta. The possibilities are truly wonderful. With all this good food, you can imagine that the desserts are delicious.

Be sure to wander across the street to look at the two sets of beautiful waterfalls.

How to get there: The inn is ¼ mile north of I–89 on Route 100, the road to Stowe.

❋

E: *Bailey's Tavern is named after the liqueur. It's lovely with a fireplace and library.*

> *"The righteous minds of innkeepers*
> *Induce them now and then,*
> *To crack a bottle with a friend*
> *Or treat unmoneyed men."*
> —G. K. Chesterton

The Inn at Weathersfield
Weathersfield, Vermont
05151

Innkeepers: Mary Louise and Ron Thorburn
Address/Telephone: Route 106, Box 165; (802) 263–9217, FAX (802) 263–9219
Rooms: 10, plus 3 suites; all with private bath.
Rates: $75 per person, double occupancy, MAP plus afternoon tea.
Open: All year.
Facilities and activities: Tavern, horse and carriage stalls, tennis, sauna, pool table, Ping-Pong, TV and VCR with movies, exercise equipment.

This beautiful old inn was built circa 1776 and has a wonderful history. At one point during the Civil War, it was an important stop on the Underground Railroad, hiding slaves en route to Canada. The inn is set well back from the road on twenty-one acres of property. Your rest is assured.

Everything that Mary Louise and Ron do to improve this lovely inn is done with class and lots of care. In the new wing are five redone rooms with sensational ☛ old bathtubs. These are real honest-to-goodness Victorian bathrooms. There are Rumford fireplaces in all of these rooms and in a lot of the other rooms as well. Each suite has two rooms and can hold four people, but if you want, reserve the newest suite for just two of you. It's known as the bridal suite. All the rooms are beautiful with 🖝 fresh flowers, fresh fruit, canopy beds, and feather pillows.

Over the years Ron has built an extensive and good wine cellar. The tavern is handsome and so is the greenhouse dining area. Mary Louise found some old stencils to use and her quilt collection is a beauty.

Excellent food is served here. Gazpacho, baked brie with Mrs. Fox's mustard, good salad, and sorbet are followed by entrees like fillet of beef, rack of lamb, or baked fresh trout or swordfish. A special feature is their own farm-raised partridge, roasted and served with sauce chasseur. The menu changes daily, taking advantage of what is in season. They grow their own herbs in a special space in the garden. Be sure to save room for desserts, as they are glorious. Mary Louise is an extraordinary chef.

Daughter Heather and husband, Jack, are potters. Their fine work is used in the inn, and certain pieces are for sale here.

There is a 🖝 horse and carriage that will take you to the old swimming hole. The area here is full of berries. In winter you may go for a sleigh ride. All of this and a beautiful country inn and, of course, a nice inn dog named Big Max.

How to get there: Exit 7 from I–91. Take Route 106 north to Perkinsville. About a half mile short of the village you will find the inn on your left, set well back from the road.

⤳

E: *A wassail cup is served from a cauldron in the keeping room fireplace. High tea is special.*

Olive Metcalf

Deerhill Inn
West Dover, Vermont
05356

Innkeepers: Joan and Robert Ritchie
Address/Telephone: Valley View Road; (802) 464–3100
Rooms: 16; all with private bath.
Rates: $76.50 to $90, per person, double occupancy, MAP.
Open: All year except Easter to Memorial Day.
Facilities and activities: Lounge, full license, swimming pool, tennis. Nearby: golfing, skiing.

The setting for the Deerhill Inn is perfect. Surrounded by lovely maple and fruit trees, it is perched on a hill with views of the countryside's beautiful mountains and lush meadows. It is nice and quiet up here. This is good country for hiking or cross-country skiing. Nearby are Mount Snow, Carinthia, and Haystack for downhill skiing. In summer you're sure to enjoy the inn's swimming pool and tennis court. The Mount Snow 18-hole golf course is close at hand.

There are several large living areas with ☞ fireplaces and comfortable furniture. There also is a small, well-stocked library. The "snug" bar is a two-seater with a wood couch. It's very intimate. The ☞ views of Mount Snow from any place in this lovely inn are beautiful and so tranquil.

420

The guest rooms are clean, bright, and handsomely furnished. There's a choice of twin, double, queen, and king beds, and there are four lovely canopy beds. All very restful. Laura Ashley is very evident here in wonderful prints that look so pretty. There are nice lace touches, and good towels are in the bathrooms. The inn is not well suited to small children.

I love romantic dining, and here at the Deerhill it is by candlelight with attractive pink and white napery. The food has a touch of Europe blended with the best of Vermont. A different veal dish is offered every day. Filet mignon comes in pastry, and chicken dijonnaise—sautéed chicken with shallots, cream, white wine, and Dijon mustard—is delicious. There's a different Pasta Deerhill every day, and, of course, ☛ rack of lamb for one is my idea of heaven.

How to get there: Take Route 9 to Wilmington; turn north onto Route 100 at the traffic light and continue to West Dover village. Pass the church and post office; at the antique store turn right onto Valley View Road. The inn is 300 yards up the road on the right-hand side.

৵৽

E: *Finnbar is a greyhound adopted from Adopt-a-Pet. This is a service for racing dogs who can no longer race and would be put to sleep if someone didn't give them a home. He's a gentle and loveable animal. What a nice thing the Ritchies have done.*

A glass of good whiskey
before an open fire in a good inn
is an unspoken toast to life
as it should be lived.

The Inn at Sawmill Farm
West Dover, Vermont
05356

Innkeepers: Rodney, Ione, and Brill Williams
Address/Telephone: Cross Town Road (mailing address: P.O. Box 367); (802) 464–8131
Rooms: 10, plus 11 in cottages; all with private bath, some with fireplace.
Rates: $260 to $320, double occupancy, MAP. During Christmas week, $10 higher. No credit cards.
Open: All year.
Facilities and activities: Bar, lounge, swimming pool, tennis court, trout and two bass fishing ponds.

The Williams have transformed an old Vermont barn into the gayest, warmest, most attractive inn that I have seen in many a country mile. Ione is a professional decorator and Rod is a noted architect, which makes for a wonderful marriage of talents for just a perfect inn. The Williams' son, Brill, runs the kitchen and he does a superb job of it.

The inn's copper collection is extensive. The 🖙 oversized fireplace in the living room is surrounded with it, and there's a huge copper-topped coffee table that's a beauty. They also have a handsome brass telescope on a tripod for your viewing of Mount Snow. A most incredible bar of solid copper also lives here. This is in the Pot Belly Lounge.

Accommodations are very different, with some Victorian rooms, some done in Chippendale, and all with the flavor of New England at its best. The cottage rooms have fireplaces. The accommodations upstairs in Spring House have a living room with fireplace, bedroom, and bath in the most glorious colors imaginable. I was in Farm House, and my room was done in the softest pastels, with a king-sized bed and a lovely dressing room and bath. They are all color coordinated with thick towels and extra pillows. ☛ Little boxes of Godiva chocolates are in each room. A very nice touch. The inn's facilities are not well suited to children under ten.

Dinner is beyond belief. Brill is a fine chef. There are twelve appetizers. ☛ Coquille of crabmeat imperial under glass was my choice. A friend of mine had thinly sliced raw sirloin of beef with shallot and mustard sauce. Of course I tasted some of hers. Outstanding. The soups are inventive and good. One entree is medallions of pork tenderloin with cognac, cream, and walnuts. There are many more. They are perfectly complemented by wines from Brill's impressive wine cellar. Desserts are all homemade. Breakfast also is special. Fresh orange juice and homemade tomato juice are just starters. The staff who serve all these goodies are very courteous.

The inn makes a specialty of special occasions. Do try to get up here for Christmas. It's something you will never forget.

How to get there: Take I–91 to Exit 2 in Brattleboro. Take Route 9 west to Wilmington, and then follow Route 100 north 6 miles to West Dover.

West Dover Inn
West Dover, Vermont
05356

Innkeepers: Donald and Madeline Mitchell
Address/Telephone: Route 100; (802) 464–5207
Rooms: 8, plus 2 suites; all with private bath, TV.
Rates: $75 to $110, double occupancy, EPB. Suite higher. MAP rates in fall.
Open: July through March.
Facilities and activities: Dinner every day but Wednesday, bar. Nearby: skiing, hiking, golfing, swimming, and more.

The Mitchells are to be complimented for restoring this fine old inn. An inn since 1846, it became the site of the town offices and had many changes before 1889, when the first addition was completed. It was known as the Green Mountain Inn until 1955.

The rooms have been redecorated and have hand-sewn quilts and antiques. The suites are lovely. They are identical. Each has a fireplace in the sitting room, a queen-sized bed, and a Jacuzzi in the spacious bathroom. The magnificent old organ in the parlor is a dream. The inn is not well suited to children under eight. Henry and Iodine are the inn cats. I love their names. Smoky is the inn dog.

The Capstone is the restaurant. I've known the chef for a

number of years and, believe me, he is good. He prepares appetizers like shrimp scampi, herring in mustard sauce, and soups such as Bavarian dumpling soup. It is super. One entree I really like and don't see often enough on menus is ☛ pot roast. Shrimp papillon en Cajun is shrimp broiled in a fine blend of Cajun spices. Frogs legs Provençale and braised lamb shanks are excellent. The tableside service is nice. Try the fettucine Alfredo or Caesar salad, both of which are prepared for two. The menu changes often, and specials are always featured. I could go on, but I believe you get the message. The food is memorable. And the dining room's fireplace is very warming.

The inn's location is a perfect base for whatever you care to do—swimming, sunning, leaf peeping, skiing, hiking, shopping, and much more. You could also come here to just relax and enjoy.

How to get there: Take Exit 2 for I–91 at Brattleboro, Vermont, then take Route 9 west to Route 100 north. In West Dover you will find the inn on your right in the village.

∾

Let us escape for a day, or better a week,
and hide away in a country inn.

Olive Metcalf

Willough Vale Inn
Westmore, Vermont
05680

Innkeeper: Gary Gitchel; owners, Frank and Joan Symcak
Address/Telephone: Route 5A; (802) 525–4123 or (800) 541–0588
Rooms: 9, plus 4 cottages; all with private bath.
Rates: $80 to $125, double occupancy, expanded continental breakfast.
    Cottages have a weekly rate.
Open: All year.
Facilities and activities: Lunch, summer and fall; box lunches available in
    winter for skiers. Dinner, bar and lounge. Fishing, swimming, and
    boating at the lake. Nearby: snowshoeing, snowmobile trails, hiking.

This is a scenic paradise with one of the most beautiful lakes
I've seen in many a country mile. Do you like to fish? There are
lake trout, ☛ landlocked salmon, perch, and rainbow trout just
waiting for your line. In the main dining room is a large lighted
display case of fishing rods, indicative of the fine fishing in the
lake.
A porch with a gazebo at one end overlooks the lake. Under
it are beautiful flowers. Lupine and wildflowers are all over the
place.
The inn is full of antique and Vermont-handcrafted furniture.
The guest rooms are all furnished differently. There are twin and

double beds, and one room has a four-poster bed. There's even a
☛ Jacuzzi for two in a lovely bathroom. Clock radios are in all the
rooms. I liked the nice parlor and library. It's a quiet spot for cards,
writing, reading, or just relaxing after an active day.

The taproom has an elegant bar and tables. It offers a special
menu all the hours it's open. Escargots, mushroom caps, French
onion soup, chili, and more are featured. At lunch my friends
Mary Ellen and Herb Sorenson went wild over the ☛ fried
calamari. The quiche was grand and so was the scrod with lobster
sauce.

Dinner can be enjoyed along with the lake view. The menu
features steak, delicious veal dishes, and pork a l'orange (sautéed
pork loin prepared with orange juice, white wine, and marmalade), which is so very good and different. Salmon fillet comes
poached or baked, and there is a nice vegetarian pasta dish.
Freshly baked desserts and good teas and coffee bring your meal to
a grand conclusion.

There are climbing trails on Mount Hoar and Mount Pisgah
and skiing at nearby Burke Mountain. Snowmobiling across the
frozen lake is invigorating. Or go visit the nearby llama farm.

How to get there: From the south, leave I–91 at Lyndonville (Exit 23) and
proceed north on Route 5 and 5A. From Canada, get off I–91 at Barton
and follow Route 16 to Route 5A.

Olive Metcalf

The Inn at Weston
Weston, Vermont
05161

Innkeepers: Jeanne and Bob Wilder
Address/Telephone: Route 100; (802) 824–5804
Rooms: 19; 12 with private bath, some with phone and TV, 1 with wheelchair accessibility.
Rates: $106 to $140, double occupancy, MAP. EPB rates available.
Open: All year except two weeks in April.
Facilities and activities: Dining room closed Wednesday except in foliage season. Sunday brunch, bar. Wheelchair access to dining room. Game room. Cross-country skiing. Nearby: downhill skiing, golf, tennis, horseback riding, hiking, summer theater, museums.

Weston is a small Vermont village that has a lot going for it. The Weston Playhouse is the ☛ oldest professional summer theater in Vermont, and the building is a landmark, too. At the Old Mill Museum, you can watch craftsmen at work in authentic period workshops. The Vermont Country Store and the Weston Bowl Mill also are here. These, plus the lovely village green, are all within a pleasant stroll from the inn.

Built in 1848 as a farmhouse and converted to an inn in 1951, this is a lovely full-service inn. Its pleasant tavern with a fireplace and a pub-style bar is very nice.

Rooms for the most part are small and comfortable. There are sinks in the rooms that do not have baths. ☞ Quilts are on the beds. In the back of the house are two rooms that share a living room. The living room has a wood-burning stove, nice chairs, and couches.

The Coleman House, named for the family who owned it for several generations, was built in 1830. It is across the street from the inn and has six guest rooms. They are larger than the rooms in the inn, and each one has a private bath. These rooms are lovely; most have queen-sized beds. There are sixteen acres of land around the house.

Pretty beige napery is used in the candlelit dining room. ☞ *Gourmet* magazine has written about the inn. That's a good indication of how memorable the food is. Pâté maison is made right here. Other appetizers are escargots and ravioli made with a different filling and sauce every day. Salmon is also treated differently every night. Duck is served two ways—the breast with a plum sauce, the leg potted and crisp. Roast loin of lamb, steak, veal, and pork chops are excellent. Oh, it's hard to make a choice when everything is so tempting. All breads and desserts are made here.

How to get there: Off I–91, on Exit 6, take Route 103 to Chester. Follow Route 11 to Londonderry, and turn right on Route 100 to Weston. The inn is in the village.

Olive Metcalf

The Silver Fox
West Rutland, Vermont
05777

Innkeepers: Pam and Gerry Bliss
Address/Telephone: Route 133; (802) 438–5555
Rooms: 6, plus 2 suites; all with private bath.
Rates: $60 to $75, per person, double occupancy, MAP.
Open: All year except April.
Facilities and activities: Bag lunch available, full liquor license. Bicycles, fishing, swimming, cross-country skiing, hiking. Nearby: downhill skiing.

The inn is part of what was a thousand-acre dairy farm in 1825. The living room of the inn dates back to 1768. Today this room has a woodburning stove, television, and lots of books. Cocktails are served in here. Nothing nicer on a cold snowy day in Vermont.

There are a few ☞ silver fox in the area, hence the name of the inn. There are a lot of other wild animals around—deer and raccoons, as well as many birds. The Clarendon River, fourteen hundred feet of it, runs along the property. It's stocked with ☞ trout, so fishing for supper could be fun. There also is a swimming hole. There are a thousand acres of cow trails, which are great for cross-country skiing or hiking. And Gerry tells me there are bridges, waterfalls, creeks, and a fresh spring along the way. The inn has bicycles for guests, plus maps, and a lot of state parks are nearby. In the winter, sleigh rides can be arranged. Maybe Joey and Sandy, the inn dogs, would like to come along.

The bedrooms and suites are lovely. They are spacious and decorated in nice colors, and some have four-poster beds. One suite has two bedrooms, living room, and bath. The other suite has one bedroom and sitting area with bath.

Breakfast is a two-course country one. What a great way to start your day. For dinner you can choose country pea soup with ham, or prime ribs of beef with creamed horseradish sauce, or Cornish hen with bacon and apple stuffing, or fillet of sole with sautéed shrimp Provençale and French onion rice. Nice choices! The vegetables are fresh, and their salads are different. There's warm spinach or Caesar salad; Pam says ☛ no iceberg lettuce at The Silver Fox. You're sure to enjoy their freshly baked breads and desserts like Bavarian chocolate layer cake and cheesecake with strawberries. You should try The Fox.

How to get there: From Rutland take Business Route 4 west for 4½ miles to Route 133 south. Turn left. Go 1½ miles to the inn, which is on the right.

Windham Hill Inn
West Townshend, Vermont
05359

Innkeepers: Linda and Ken Busteed
Address/Telephone: RR 1, Box 44; (802) 874–4080
Rooms: 15; all with private bath.
Rates: $115, single; $170, double; MAP.
Open: All year except April and first half of November.
Facilities and activities: Full liquor license. All the activities of all seasons.

At Windham Hill Inn you are sitting on the top of the world. It is beautiful up here. The West River Valley stretches as far as the eye can see. Built originally about 1825, it was a working dairy farm, and in 1962 it was converted into an inn, which it has remained.

The meals are memorable. Linda is the chef, and she makes all her own breads and desserts as well as her soups and appetizers. In season all the vegetables are fresh, for most of them come from the inn's gardens. Guests are given their choice of dining with others at one of two large tables, or at tables for two in the Frog Pond Room. The pond is ☞ spotlighted after dark. Ken is the breakfast chef, and together this pair make a great team.

Taffy Morgan, the inn's sous chef, has a reputation for creating sumptuous picnics. As the inn's brochure says, ☞ "A

432

vintage 1890 horse-drawn surrey squires you to a secluded spot in the countryside where an old-fashioned wicker hamper awaits. Crisp linen, crystal, and Limoges china complement such delectables as lobster pie, fresh fruit tarts, and chilled wine. You are left alone to enjoy a leisurely, romantic luncheon and to savor the serenity of the Vermont hills. An hour or so later, Taffy will return to escort you back to the inn."

The rooms are charming. Linda and Ken renovated the lovely old barn on the property to add five more guest rooms to the inn. They are very unusual, plus their views are spectacular. Two of the rooms in the house 🖝 have their own balconies.

The living room is full of Victorian wicker and has a good New England wood stove. Off of this is a lovely balcony that overlooks the world. The whole inn feels like home. There are plants everywhere. I found a large stack of old *Life* magazines, something I love. They also have a well-stocked library.

The inn has its own Cross-Country Learning Center. Under the personal supervision of a professional ski instructor, the program is targeted for beginning to intermediate skiers. If downhill skiing is your preference, the inn is close to Stratton Mountain, Big Bromley, Magic Mountain, Mount Snow, and Maple Valley. A schuss-boomer's dream come true. The inn also has its own floodlit ice-skating pond, tobogganing, sledding, and snowshoeing.

As the innkeepers say, the inn continues to be one of the best-kept secrets in Vermont.

How to get there: Take Exit 2 off I–91 in Brattleboro, then Route 30 for 21 miles to West Townshend. At the Country Store turn right, up the hill, onto Windham Road. Look for the inn's sign on the right in 1½ miles.

∽⅍∾

E: *The peonies were in bloom. They have some in two colors. Another garden sight I have never seen before was their magnificent Fringe tree. And let us not forget Tober the cat and Tucker and Peggy, the dogs.*

Brook Bound
Wilmington, Vermont
05363

Innkeepers: Jim and Lois McGovern
Address/Telephone: Coldbrook Road; (802) 464–5267
Rooms: 14; 10 with private bath.
Rates: $65 to $100, double occupancy, EPB. No credit cards.
Open: All year.
Facilities and activities: Breakfast only meal served. Dinner served at the
    Hermitage nearby. BYOB. Recreation room, pool table, Ping-Pong,
    swimming, tennis. Nearby: music, skiing.

In the beautiful Green Mountains of southern Vermont, off a
country road in a lovely quiet setting with commanding views of
Haystack and Mount Snow, there is this warm and friendly inn
waiting to welcome you.

The grounds are spacious, and the 🖝 pool is heated. It sits up
above the inn with the tennis courts beyond. There are glorious big
trees all over, and in the fall they are a sight to behold.

Breakfast is the only meal served at Brook Bound, but the
Hermitage, which is also owned by Jim and Lois, is nearby, and it
is a great spot to have some dinner. Setups are provided for your
drink at Brook Bound; and in the winter it all happens around a neat
fireplace. The inn has 🖝 a refrigerator especially for guests to keep
luncheon food and snacks or drinks. This is a nice thing to do.

The inn is close to several ski areas for both downhill and cross-country skiing. There is so much to do in this area any season of the year that it would take pages just to list everything.

You are only 12 miles from the Marlboro Music Festival or the Brattleboro Music Center's Bach program. A real turn-on for a music lover.

How to get there: From Wilmington take Route 100 north and turn left on Coldbrook Road. Go 2.2 miles to the inn.

E: *Cross-country ski trails connect the Brook Bound to The Hermitage, so you can go right out the front door.*

A warming fire, a strong drink, a genial innkeeper . . .
and winter is somewhere in the hills, but is not here.

Olive Metcalf

The Hermitage
Wilmington, Vermont
05363

Innkeepers: Jim and Lois McGovern
Address/Telephone: Coldbrook Road; (802) 464–3759
Rooms: 15; all with private bath and wheelchair accessibility, 11 with
   fireplace.
Rates: $90 to $100, per person, double occupancy, MAP.
Open: All year.
Facilities and activities: Lunch in winter. Sauna, wine cellar, game bird
   farm, trout pond, tennis, hiking, cross-country skiing from the door.

High on a windy hill facing Haystack Mountain, you will find
a unique and heartwarming country inn, The Hermitage. The
owner is a man for all seasons who knows what he is doing. He
also has a certain charm, maybe it is the quick smile or a fleeting
twinkle as he says, ☛ "No piped-in music in *my* inn." You might,
though, find a classical guitarist some night or someone at the
piano in the lounge.

Come in the very early spring, and you will find maple
sugaring going full blast. There are four sugarhouses on the
property, and Jim McGovern makes about 700 gallons of maple
syrup a year. In summer the big kettles are kept simmering,
making homemade jams and jellies. Along with this talent for

making the most of nature's bounty, Jim is an oenophile (wine lover) and has a ☛ wine cellar with a stock of 30,000 bottles. You are never at a loss for the perfect wine to enjoy with this inn's first-rate food.

Dining at The Hermitage is truly gourmet and includes homegrown game and fresh vegetables. The dining rooms are lovely. The Delacroix Room was named for Michael Delacroix, whose paintings are featured throughout the inn. There's a fireplace to warm you while you enjoy some of Jim's wines.

Jim raises as many as sixty different species of game birds. Most of them, such as pheasant, partridge, duck, quail, turkey, and goose, are raised for gourmet dining. Jim also has ☛ show birds, brilliantly colored species of ducks and peacocks and a pair of black swans. He has an incubator for the eggs and I watched the babies breaking out of the eggs. Cognac and Burgundy, two friendly English setters (Jim also raises them), may come by to say hello, but they are likely to be distracted by a passing gaggle of geese that will fly off in a flurry of wings. Jim also has a large collection of decoys of every description on display and for sale.

The comfortable rooms, eleven with their own working fireplaces, are furnished with antiques and, oh, those brass beds. In the carriage house you will even find a sauna.

How to get there: Take Route 9 to Wilmington, follow Route 100 north 2 miles to Coldbrook Road on the left. The Hermitage is 3 miles down Coldbrook Road.

୬

E: *The wine cellar, with its two crystal chandeliers and marvelous selection of wine and gifts, turned me on. What to do with your old claw-footed bathtub? Use it to store wine.*

Nutmeg Inn
Wilmington, Vermont
05363

Innkeepers: Del and Charlotte Lawrence
Address/Telephone: Route 9 West; (802) 464–3351
Rooms: 9, plus 4 suites; all with private bath, some with fireplace and TV.
Rates: $65 to $145; suites, $100 to $180; double occupancy, EPB.
Open: All year except two weeks in April.
Facilities and activities: Dinner for houseguests by reservation on weekends only. BYOB. Nearby: Marlboro Music Festival, downhill and cross-country skiing.

The Nutmeg Inn was originally an early American Vermont farmhouse with a connecting carriage house. In 1957 the house was remodeled and restored into a country inn. Sonny and Maggie, the Lawrences' golden retrievers, think it's a fine place to call home.

The rooms at Nutmeg are quaint, cozy, and creatively decorated. The old-fashioned ☞ quilts are real beauties and the warm color schemes used make the rooms very inviting. Two of the rooms have fireplaces and king-sized beds. One suite has a balcony, skylights, and a king-sized four-poster. It's a beauty. Another suite has two bedrooms with queen-sized beds and skylights.

The living room is rustic with a lovely fireplace made of stone. This is in the original carriage house. There are books and color cable television, or, as the Lawrences say, come and meet old or new friends around our "bring your own cocktail bar." It is well equipped with an icemaker.

The dining room has a bow window and a wood stove. It is very nice to sit here and look out at the snow falling on the lovely lawns. A full breakfast is served. Choice of eggs done any style, French toast, or pancakes are just a few possibilities of what you may find. At dinnertime it's fun to meet and dine with people from many different parts of the country. Dinner may be roast beef, or chicken in a tarragon cream wine sauce, or pork tenderloin with herb dressing. It is all beautifully served.

How to get there: The inn is on Route 9 in Wilmington, 1 mile west of the traffic light in town.

৵৵

E: *Wilmington is a lovely area in southern Vermont, offering much to see and do. Marlboro Music Festival in summer, colorful leaves in fall, and skiing in winter.*

> *"There is nothing which has*
> *been contrived by man by which*
> *so much happiness is produced*
> *as by a good tavern or inn."*
> —Dr. Samuel Johnson

Olive Metcalf

Red Shutters
Wilmington, Vermont
05363

Innkeepers: Carolyn and Max Hopkins
Address/Telephone: Route 9 West; (802) 464–3768
Rooms: 7, plus 2 suites; all with private bath, some with fireplace and TV.
Rates: $80 to $85, double occupancy; $135 to $150, suites; EPB.
Open: All year except April and three weeks in December.
Facilities and activities: Dinner, bar, lounge. Golf packages at Haystack.
    Nearby: music, skiing.

Nestled among many well-established maples, pin oaks, and evergreens on a lovely hillside is the Red Shutter Inn. There are five acres of property around the inn. The inn itself dates back to 1894.

The rooms and suites are individually decorated with fine taste. The suite in the carriage house has a fireplace and television and a wow of a bathroom. It has a two-person Jacuzzi with a skylight over it.

Max is the breakfast chef. He does wonders with eggs and pancakes and more. The dining room is spacious with a huge fireplace—so needed in winter up here and so pretty to see. The menu is written on a blackboard and lists luscious things. One appetizer I like is 🖝 mushroom caps stuffed with crabmeat. The

440

inn is known for its fresh fish. Broiled garlic shrimp is a winner, garlic lover that I am. Charbroiled tuna steak and poached salmon in dill butter are two great selections. If fish isn't your thing, try their Vermont spring chicken, lean loin lamb chops, or filet mignon. There is a lovely dining porch in summer, and it's a winner. The living room is comfortable and has a wood stove. The small bar is very nice.

The inn offers a golf package in conjunction with the Haystack Golf Club. It's a 6,700-yard champion course, located minutes from the inn. What a spectacular place to play golf. The views are incredible.

How to get there: The inn is located on Route 9, just past the intersection of Route 100.

❀

E: *Sam is the resident Labrador. Enjoy the pub and Sam.*

"Does the road wind uphill all the way?
Yes, to the very end.
Will the day's journey take the whole day long?
From morn to night, my friend."
—Christina Rossetti

Olive Metcalf

Trails End
Wilmington, Vermont
05363

Innkeepers: Bill and Mary Kilburn
Address/Telephone: Smith Road; (802) 464–2727
Rooms: 18, plus 2 suites; all with private bath.
Rates: $65 to $85, double occupancy, $125, suites; EPB. No credit cards.
Open: All year except last three weeks of April and first three weeks of November.
Facilities and activities: Dinner, BYOB. Guest refrigerator and glasses. Cross-country skiing from the door, ice skating, swimming pool, clay tennis court. Nearby: downhill skiing, Marlboro Music Festival.

Once you arrive at Trails End, you would never know Route 100 is just a stone's throw away. The elevation is 1,000 feet. There are miles and miles of untrampled nature walks and cross-country skiing trails right from the door. You'll find a manmade pond to skate on and open meadows to browse in. Utter peace surrounds you.

You enter the inn through a lounge area. Here are books, games, and ☞ bumper pool. Another lounge area has a ☞ 15-foot fieldstone fireplace and a cathedral ceiling. Floor-to-ceiling windows overlook the swimming pool and gardens. I can just see myself sitting up here on a cold winter night, snow outside and warm comfort inside.

The bedrooms range from small to large. All are cozy and clean. Two have fireplaces and refrigerators in them, and one also has a deck. The four rooms with queen-sized beds have been redecorated, and they are lovely. The two suites have been redone with skylights and whirlpool tubs, and wet bars with refrigerators and cable televisions have been added.

There are a few round tables in the dining area. This is a nice way to dine, because you can really get to know the other guests. Antique kerosene lamps provide the lighting. Dinner consists of four courses, served family style. A single entree is offered, such as veal Marsala, pork loin with Madeira sauce, or a variety of chicken dishes. ☛ Cookouts are held during the summer, with steaks, corn on the cob, and watermelon. The kitchen here is really the heart of the inn. Hard cider and cookies are always available during the winter and cookies and lemonade in the summer—you cannot beat this.

The innkeepers tell me this is a popular place to stay for the Marlboro Music Festival. I can see why. Of course, I also enjoy coming here to visit with Madison, the inn dog.

How to get there: From Wilmington go up Route 100. Across from Philip Davis's sign turn right. Then take the first right and go ²⁄₁₀ mile up the hill to the inn on your right.

Olive Metcalf

The White House
Wilmington, Vermont
05363

Innkeeper: Robert Grinold
Address/Telephone: Route 9; (802) 464–2135
Rooms: 12, plus 1 suite; all with private bath, 4 with fireplace.
Rates: $95 to $115, per person, MAP.
Open: All year.
Facilities and activities: Sunday brunch, skier's lunch in winter. Bar,
    lounge, swimming pool inside and out, health spa with sauna,
    steamroom, whirlpool. Nearby: cross-country and downhill skiing.

You would expect an inn named The White House to be
elegant and, believe me, this one is. Built in 1914, the mansion has
much to offer.

The gallery on the main floor has an extremely unusual
wallpaper that was printed in Paris in 1912. There are high ceilings
throughout the inn, and the living room is large with a fireplace
and beautifully covered (blue, of course) couches and chairs. The
Casablanca bar has wicker chairs, couches, pretty flowered pillows,
and Bob's collection of angels all around. So nice to come back to
after a day on the ski trails.

There are two dining rooms, both of which are very elegant,
and a small private dining room. The food served in this 🖝

three-star inn is superb, but would you expect anything else in The White House? Here's just a sampling of what they offer. There are nine appetizers, including brandied grapefruit and interesting soups. The one I liked best was shrimp-stuffed mushrooms. Entrees are numerous and varied with always a special one or two. All are oh, so good and served with excellent salad and breads. Of course, all the desserts are homemade. I get hungry just writing about Bob's inn.

The grounds are sumptuous, with a lovely rose garden and fountain, and below this is a ☛ 60-foot swimming pool. There's another small fountain outside the lounge, and from this delightful room you watch spectacular sunsets over the Green Mountains.

The guest rooms here are all sizes. Each one has a good view. There are some nice loft rooms, with queen-sized sofa beds downstairs and queen-sized beds upstairs.

The ☛ health spa is what you need after a day of fun; exercise and massage room, sauna, whirlpool, steamroom, and showers. There's also an inside pool to relax in. Ah, what an inn.

How to get there: From Route I–91 take Route 9 to Wilmington. The inn is on your right just before you reach the town.

∽

E: Intrigue! Why did the original owner of the house put in a secret staircase? You will have to ask where it is.

> *The warmth of a country inn*
> *can only be likened to*
> *a well-made down comforter.*

Olive Metcalf

Juniper Hill Inn
Windsor, Vermont
05089

Innkeepers: Jim and Krisha Pennino
Address/Telephone: Juniper Hill Road; (802) 674–5273
Rooms: 15; all with private bath, 9 with working fireplace.
Rates: $80 to $115, double occupancy, EPB.
Open: All year exccpt first weekend of November until about December 20, plus the last week of March and April.
Facilities and activities: Dinner. Nearby: downhill and cross-country skiing, golf.

This inn has been many things. Once it was known as a summer White House, because former presidents Rutherford Hayes, Benjamin Harrison, and Theodore Roosevelt were guests of the original owners. It has also been a school, an inn, and then a teaching and retreat facility for the Catholic Xaverian Brothers. In 1980 it started a long restoration trek back to its original stateliness. Four years later Jim and Krisha purchased it and did more restoration work. Today it is simply lovely.

Large white columns lead into a 30-by-40-foot oak-paneled entry hall that once displayed hunting trophies and was used as a ballroom. It now is the main parlor and called The Great Room. Two smaller parlors are provided for reading or quiet conversation. There is a ☛ beautiful grand staircase centered on a large Palladian window in a very private library wing.

Nearly all the rooms have been refurnished with the Penninos' personal collection of ☛ antiques acquired while they lived in Europe for four and a half years. (The inn is not well suited to children under twelve.) Some rooms have marble sinks and one has a summer porch. Beds include a sleigh bed, brass beds, and four-posters. They all afford you a very good night's sleep. As one guest put it, "Most comfortable bed I've slept in."

Jim and Krisha really care about furnishing the inn well. They have found the ☛ dining table that was originally in the house. It is a rare gem. The top alone weighs over a thousand pounds.

Jim is the breakfast chef, specializing in dishes like homemade apple pancakes or French toast. He also cooks eggs, of course. Dinner is Krisha's department. There are four courses, with one entree offered. She makes soups such as Vermont cheddar cheese or barley. Leg of lamb is prepared two different ways. Stuffed breast of veal and Rock Cornish hens with blackberry sauce are two other specialties. Krisha includes a variety of Greek foods on the menu. Now that's something not often found in New England inns! Homemade jams and desserts. Jim says Krisha makes a great pie crust. Come on up and see for yourself.

How to get there: From I–91 going south, take Exit 9. Go about 3 miles on Route 5 south to Juniper Hill Road, which is on the right. Go ½ mile up the hill to the driveway on the right.

Olive Metcalf

Lincoln Covered Bridge Inn
Woodstock, Vermont
05091

Innkeepers: Harry and Pat Francis
Address/Telephone: Route 4; (802) 457–3312
Rooms: 6; all with private bath.
Rates: $160 to $200, double occupancy, MAP.
Open: All year except two weeks in November and Mondays.
Facilities and activities: Dinner, Tuesday through Saturday, Sunday brunch. Bar, lounge, TV room, games, and VCR for movies. Nearby: golf, fishing, cross-country and downhill skiing.

The Lincoln Covered Bridge is the only known remaining wooden bridge of its kind and design left in America. Built in 1877 and renovated in 1947, it spans the Ottauquechee River. It is at one end of the inn's property.

Five acres of land and this beautiful river are right here at the inn. A nice spot to go wading or fishing, so you fishermen should bring your lines and catch some fish. There is an 🖝 old stone fireplace for cookouts and a picnic table with umbrellas and chairs, so do come and relax. The swing in the old maple tree beckons me. In the wintertime it's snowmobiles and skiing that will keep you busy.

The summer porch is the ski room in winter. There is a nice

living room with a television and 🖝 videocassette recorder with a library full of good movies. This is a great place to relax on a snowy winter night.

Accommodations are cozy in both the inn and the lovely carriage house. The queen- and king-sized beds are new and comfortable. The facilities are not well suited to children under eight.

The dining rooms are cool and comfortable. The riverside room is lovely. Chef Frank Duffina does well. He offers such appetizers as marinated artichoke hearts and honeydew and prosciutto. The salads are good. There are pastas plus entrees like chicken calvados, veal Marsala, and 🖝 lamb déjà-vu (boneless loin of lamb with a honey-Dijon mustard coating, served with a seasoned broiled tomato). Fish and steak dishes also are available. Sunday brunch is ample, beginning with a Mimosa or a Bloody Mary. Belgian waffles and omelettes are made to order. I had a delicious omelette. Other choices were prime rib, a chicken dish, a fish dish, and pasta, and the list goes on.

For a very special event, arrange to have your dinner in the gazebo on the knoll overlooking the river. On my most recent visit to the inn, a very private dinner for two was held here with a silver service, a waiter dressed in a tuxedo, and simply grand food.

There is so much to do in the area. Come and enjoy.

How to get there: From I–91, take Exit 9 and follow Route 12 north to Route 4. The inn is on Route 4, three miles west of the village green in Woodstock.

☙

E: Two tees on the grounds for golfers to practice is a nice extra.

Olive Metcalf

The Village Inn
Woodstock, Vermont
05091

Innkeepers: Kevin and Anita Clark
Address/Telephone: 421 Pleasant Street; (802) 457–1255
Rooms: 8; 6 with private bath, all with air conditioning.
Rates: $65 to $120, double occupancy, EPB.
Open: All year.
Facilities and activities: Dinner, bar, lounge. Nearby: golf, tennis, skiing, swimming, boating, shopping.

Woodstock is a beautiful area. The Village Inn is within walking distance of the lovely village green. Once this was a forty-acre estate on the Ottauquechee River. The Victorian mansion and carriage house, built in 1899, are all that remain of the estate.

Lots of charm and comfort are found in the bar. The very pretty ceilings are of carved tin, and there is a beautiful stained glass window. The room also has a nineteenth-century oak bar. Upstairs is a large common room with a porch, television, and games. And—this is a good thing to know—the inn has a fire alarm system.

Rooms are gracious, comfortable, and furnished nicely. Some have marble sinks in them. One has a 🖝 king-sized bed and a working fireplace.

I loved the romantic dining room, complete with a working fireplace, the original tin ceilings, and natural oak woodwork. A chef-owned inn is always a plus. The menus are enticing. Among the appetizers I saw chicken tempura, vegetable egg roll, and fettucine Anita. I chose the stuffed baked potato skins, which were very good. ☛ Roast Vermont turkey is an entree that is too often forgotten on menus. Roast duck with a cognac and orange sauce has people coming back again and again. Roast lamb, roast prime ribs of beef . . . and the menu goes on. Desserts, well, all I'll say is that they're homemade and delicious.

Covered bridges, elegant shops, skiing, sleigh rides, golf, or tennis anyone? Go swimming or boating in one of the many lakes. Come on up and enjoy yourself. This whole area and this lovely refurbished inn get my applause.

How to get there: From I–91 take Route 89 north to Exit 1. Turn left into Woodstock. The inn is on the left.

✹

*I love all good inns, but secretly I have
a rather special fondness if the boniface is fat.*

451

Indexes

Alphabetical Index to Inns

Romantic Inns

Inns Serving Lunch

Inns Serving Afternoon Tea

Riverside Inns

Lakeside Inns

Inns on or near Salt Water

(* Denotes on Beach)

Inns Owning Boats for Guests' Use

Inns with Swimming Pools

Inns with Golf Course or Tennis Court

Inns with Cross-Country Skiing on Property

Inns with Health Clubs or Exercise Rooms

(* Denotes Health Club)

Inns with Meeting Rooms or Conference Facilities

Inns with Separate Cottages

No Smoking Inns

About the Author

The "inn creeper" is the nickname Elizabeth Squier has earned in her almost seventeen years of researching this guide to the inns of New England. And a deserved name it is, for she tours well over 200 inns every year from top to bottom, inside and out, before recommending the best ones to you.

A recognized author on fine food and lodging, Elizabeth is a gourmet cook and has written travel and food columns for many periodicals. Like you, she recognizes readily the special ingredients that make a good inn exceptional.